Behavior Modification

APPLICATIONS to EDUCATION

Contributors

M. Delith Balabán

Don Bushell, Jr.

Roxanne Evison

Salvador A. Galesso

James G. Holland

Fred S. Keller

John Kidder

Florente Lopez R.

Tom Lovitt

M. Luisa Mendonqa

Jack L. Michael

David Phillips

Emilio Ribes-Inesta

J. Gilmour Sherman

Debby Smith

Roger E. Ulrich

Nelson Zanata

Behavior Modification

APPLICATIONS to EDUCATION

Edited by

FRED S. KELLER
Department of Psychology
Western Michigan University
Kalamazoo, Michigan

EMILIO RIBES-INESTA
Faculty in Psychology
National Autonomous University of Mexico
Mexico City, Mexico

ACADEMIC PRESS   New York San Francisco London   1974

A Subsidiary of Harcourt Brace Jovanovich, Publishers

ACADEMIC PRESS, INC.
111 Fifth Avenue, New York, New York 10003

United Kingdom Edition published by
ACADEMIC PRESS, INC. (LONDON) LTD.
24/28 Oval Road, London NW1

Library of Congress Cataloging in Publication Data

Keller, Fred Simmons, Date
    Behavior modification: applications to education.

    Includes bibliographies.
       1.   Educational psychology—Addresses, essays,
lectures.   2.   Behaviorism (Psychology)   I.   Ribes-
Inesta, Emilio, joint author.   II.   Title.
[DNLM: 1.   Behavior therapy.   2.   Reinforcement.
(Psychology)   WM420 K31b 1974]
LB1051.K359   370.15   73-20469
ISBN 0-12-403950-2

Contents

List of Contributors   ix

Preface   xi
    Emilio Ribes-Inesta

Introduction   xiii
    Fred S. Keller

Contents of the Previous Volume   xv

**RESEARCH ON SOME BASIC MECHANISMS IN THE
DEVELOPMENT OF SOCIAL BEHAVIOR**   **1**
    Florente Lopez R., M. Delith Balabán, Salvador A.
    Galesso, M. Luisa Mendonqa, and Nelson Zanata

Cooperation and Competition   2
Imitation   12
References   24

**USING ARRANGED AND PROGRAMMED EVENTS TO ALTER
SUBTRACTION PERFORMANCE OF CHILDREN WITH
LEARNING DISABILITIES**   **27**
    Tom Lovitt, Debby Smith, John Kidder, and
    Roxanne Evison

Experiment I   30
Experiment II   44
General Discussion   59
References   62

CASE HISTORY OF A BEHAVIOR-MODIFICATION PROJECT IN A PUBLIC SCHOOL   63

David Phillips

Special Education   64
Appendix: Application of Behavioral Principles to Classroom Settings   73

MEASUREMENT AND ANALYSIS OF CLASSROOM BEHAVIOR   107

Emilio Ribes-Inesta

Evaluation of Relevant Behaviors   108
Functional Analysis of Classroom Behavior   112
Preliminary Data On a Descriptive Pilot Study   115
Final Considerations   123
References   124

THE DESIGN OF CLASSROOM CONTINGENCIES   127

Don Bushell, Jr.

The Question of Usefulness   128
Behavior Analysis in Project Follow Through   129
Signs of Progress   134
A Closing Comment   141
References   142

AN INTERNATIONAL VENTURE IN BEHAVIOR MODIFICATION   143

Fred S. Keller

A PERMUTATION ON AN INNOVATION   157

J. Gilmour Sherman

THE ESSENTIAL COMPONENTS OF EFFECTIVE INSTRUCTION AND WHY MOST COLLEGE TEACHING IS NOT   163

Jack L. Michael

BEHAVIOR MODIFICATION AND THE ROLE OF THE UNIVERSITY IN EFFECTING SOCIAL CHANGE

177

Roger E. Ulrich

Effecting Change in the University   179
Behavioral Instruction   181
Effecting Change in Community Institutions   183
Establishing a New Institution   187
References   191

ARE BEHAVIORAL PRINCIPLES FOR REVOLUTIONARIES?

195

James G. Holland

Index   209

List of Contributors

Numbers in parentheses indicate the pages on which the authors' contributions begin.

M. DELITH BALABÁN (1), Department of Psychology, University of Veracruz, Veracruz, Mexico

DON BUSHELL, JR. (127), Follow Through, The University of Kansas, Lawrence, Kansas

ROXANNE EVISON (27), Experimental Education Unit WJ-10, University of Washington, Seattle, Washington

SALVADOR A. GALESSO (1), Department of Psychology, University of Veracruz, Veracruz, Mexico

JAMES G. HOLLAND (195), Learning Research and Developmental Center, University of Pittsburgh, Pittsburgh, Pennsylvania

FRED S. KELLER[1] (143), Department of Psychology, Western Michigan University, Kalamazoo, Michigan

JOHN KIDDER (27), Rainier School, White River School District, Buckley, Washington

FLORENTE LOPEZ R. (1), Department of Psychology, University of Veracruz, Veracruz, Mexico

TOM LOVITT (27), Experimental Education Unit WJ-10, University of Washington, Seattle, Washington

M. LUISA MENDONQA (1), Department of Psychology, University of Veracruz, Veracruz, Mexico

[1]Present address: Center for Personalized Instruction, Georgetown University, Washington, D.C.

JACK L. MICHAEL (163), Department of Psychology, Western Michigan University, Kalamazoo, Michigan

DAVID PHILLIPS (63), The Child Development Program, Winston-Salem, North Carolina

EMILIO RIBES-INESTA (107), Faculty in Psychology, National Autonomous University of Mexico, Mexico City, Mexico

J. GILMOUR SHERMAN (157), Psychology Department, Georgetown University, Washington, D.C.

DEBBY SMITH (27), Experimental Education Unit WJ-10, University of Washington, Seattle, Washington

ROGER E. ULRICH (177), Department of Psychology, Western Michigan University, Kalamazoo, Michigan

NELSON ZANATA (1), Department of Psychology, University of Veracruz, Veracruz, Mexico

Preface

Most of the studies appearing in this book were reported at the Second Symposium on Behavior Modification held at the National Autonomous University of Mexico, in Mexico City, January 24–25, 1972. The Symposium was dedicated to Professor Fred S. Keller, in recognition of his brilliant career in the field of behavior analysis and education.

The purpose of the Symposium was to set forth and examine a series of problems related to the use of behavior analysis in education. The significance of radical change in education as a fundamental feature of social development was a matter of constant concern in each of the contributions. The studies reported here range from those in which specific variables were employed in experimentation at the preschool level (Lopez *et al.*) to a consideration of behavior analysis in relation to revolutionary change in societal control (Holland).

The bulk of these contributions focus on grade-school and university education. Lovitt *et al.* treat the generalization process in problems of subtraction, and its bearing upon the teaching of arithmetic skill at the grade-school level. Ribes presents an account of the methodological problems met in the measurement and analysis of behavior in the classroom. Phillips reports a study in the use of behavior modification methods by minimally trained teachers within a traditional primary school. Also on the grade-school level, Bushell reports encouraging results of a behavior-analytic attempt to overcome the educational deficiencies of underprivileged children.

With respect to higher education, Keller describes the international origin of personalized instruction, and Sherman offers a new suggestion as to source of proctors for this system. The papers by Professors J. G. Sherman and J. L. Michael were not presented at the Symposium, but were included here in order to take account of the growing importance of personalized instruction in modern education. Michael examines the essential factors in effective teaching and Ulrich considers the university's possible rôle as an agent of social change.

I cannot conclude this preface without an expression of gratitude to Dr. Luis Lara Tapia, Head of the Department of Experimental Psychology and Methodology of the UNAM, without whose support this Symposium could not have taken place, and to all those others who in one way or another, efficiently and unselfishly, helped make possible the meeting.

Emilio Ribes-Inesta

Introduction

The power of a psychological system can be seen in two important spheres: first, in the realm of basic science—in the initiation of new research, the discovery of new techniques, and in the subsumption of facts that previously belonged within a different context. Secondly, it can be seen in practical use—in the elimination of some of man's discomforts or in the satisfaction of his needs.

The strength of *reinforcement theory* (or the *experimental analysis of behavior*) is reflected in each of these domains. Its basic-science fruitfulness has been without parallel in the systems of the past. The infant born in 1938 is now a lively, healthy child, of growing promise. An enormous bulk of integrated and supportive data have been gathered, new experimental methods and devices have been fashioned, and a viewpoint in psychology has been developed in which context laboratory findings since the days of Wilhelm Wundt can be meaningfully brought together.

In its application to the practical affairs of daily living, reinforcement theory has also been successful, far more so than any previous point of view. From simple beginnings in the field of human skill, its principles and procedures have found their use in many other settings. In the areas of psychopharmacology, mental health, child care, and rehabilitation, progress has been and continues to be steady. Advances in the field of formal education are exemplified within the covers of this book, as are the even wider uses of the basic system. In terms of human welfare, the experimental analysis of behavior has more than earned its keep.

Within this book the reader will find several reports of classroom research, introducing novel methods of investigation. He will discover an analysis of instruction based upon a laboratory model; learn about a student-centered teaching plan—its origins and extensions; read of a means of apprenticing psychology students to their teachers, and of efforts to carry reinforcement theory to the public schools. Also, the reader will find interpretation of the larger scene, including a great deal more than formal education.

The strength of a system is represented also in the rate at which its basic science and technology break down the language barrier and spread to other lands. Here, too, reinforcement theory has had phenomenal success. In 40 years, it has extended to many countries of the world. There are operant laboratories, for example, in such far-off places as India, Israel, and Japan. But the major effect has so far been to the north and south. In Canada, the system flourishes both in basic and applied sciences; and the Latin American movement is growing every day, especially in Mexico and Brazil. The British and the Europeans, with notable exceptions, have been slower to adopt the viewpoint, but now seem to be more interested.

The present volume is a symbol of this movement and should be a source of satisfaction not only to Emilio Ribes and the other contributors to the 1972 Symposium on Behavior Modification, but to anyone engaged in furthering an individual psychology and the technology of education that must be based upon it. It is also a step, however small, toward international understanding.

There is fancy in this book as well as fact—dreams as well as data. Some readers may dwell upon the one, some upon the other. Each is needed if this volume is to represent the current impact of reinforcement theory upon the educational problems of our time. And each is needed if the movement is to prosper.

Fred S. Keller

Contents of the Previous Volume

SOME RELATIONS BETWEEN BEHAVIOR MODIFICATION
AND BASIC RESEARCH
    B. F. Skinner

SOME ECOLOGICAL PROBLEMS IN CHILD BEHAVIOR
MODIFICATION
    Robert G. Wahler

DISCUSSION: THE ROLE OF PARENTS AND PEERS IN
CONTROLLING CHILDREN'S BEHAVIOR
    Jorge Peralta

THE TECHNOLOGY OF TEACHING YOUNG HANDICAPPED
CHILDREN
    Sidney W. Bijou

DISCUSSION: IMPLEMENTATION OF OPERANT
PROCEDURES FOR THE TREATMENT OF HANDICAPPED
CHILDREN
    Florente Lopez R.

THE TEACHING FAMILY: A NEW MODEL FOR THE
TREATMENT OF DEVIANT CHILD BEHAVIOR IN
THE COMMUNITY
Montrose M. Wolf, Elery L. Phillips, and Dean L. Fixsen

PROGRAMMING ALTERNATIVES TO PUNISHMENT: THE
DESIGN OF COMPETENCE THROUGH CONSEQUENCES
Harold L. Cohen

DISCUSSION: METHODOLOGICAL REMARKS ON A
DELINQUENCY PREVENTION AND REHABILITATION
PROGRAM
Emilio Ribes-Inesta

THE ENTRÉE OF THE PARAPROFESSIONAL IN THE
CLASSROOM
K. Daniel O'Leary

DISCUSSION: THE ROLE OF TEACHERS AND
PARAPROFESSIONALS IN THE CLASSROOM
Rodolpho Carbonari Sant' Anna

NEW ROLES FOR THE PARAPROFESSIONAL
Teodoro Ayllon and Patricia Wright

DISCUSSION: A NEW PERSPECTIVE: CHRONIC PATIENTS AS
ASSISTANTS IN A BEHAVIOR REHABILITATION PROGRAM
IN A PSYCHIATRIC INSTITUTION
Benjamin Dominguez T., Felipe Acosta N., and Dementrio Carmona

AN EXPERIMENTAL ANALYSIS OF CLINICAL PHENOMENA
C. B. Ferster

Author Index

Subject Index

Research on Some Basic Mechanisms in the Development of Social Behavior

FLORENTE LOPEZ R., M. DELITH BALABÁN, SALVADOR A. GALESSO, M. LUISA MENDONQA, and NELSON ZANATA

The experiments described here are not directly related to the development of procedures to deal with specific educational problems. Instead, they represent our attempts to initiate an experimental analysis of several important mechanisms—imitation, cooperation, and competition—basic to the development of infant behavior in both school and nonschool environments.

Some comments are necessary with regard to the experiments on cooperation and competition. Our main purpose was to analyze the effect of cooperative and competitive conditions on behavior. However, we were also interested in developing a situation that would provide an occasion for verbal interaction, since this would allow the participants to develop procedures dealing with deficits in verbal behavior in a social context. We considered this development to be important because we were observing some retarded children who, although able to speak, would not talk to other children or adults unless required. To create the conditions we wanted, the experiments were conducted in a relatively unstructured situation.

The experiments on imitation were made to analyze the contribution of social and nonsocial stimuli to generalized imitation. We felt that both sets of experiments, along with those dealing with social behavior, would contribute to a technique for developing social and academic repertoires. From our point of view, the development of behavior modification techniques depends basically upon applied research in the natural environment as well as upon experimental analysis of human and animal behavior. Integrating both kinds of research may result in benefits for the planning of education.

COOPERATION AND COMPETITION

Such behaviors as cooperation and competition, as well as most of the so-called social behaviors, are usually considered the result of "social motives" or "personality traits" (Deutsch, 1949; Rotter, 1954). However, behavior in itself has nothing to make us call it cooperative or competitive. These terms are more evaluative than descriptive—a fact that frequently leads to their erroneous identification.

In the present analysis of cooperation and competition, these are not identified as specific behaviors but as different ways of programming contingencies of reinforcement in a way similar to that proposed by Lindsley (1966). Cooperation is defined as the case in which reinforcement is given for two or more subjects responding whenever all of them meet a specified requirement, whereas competition is the case in which reinforcement is given to the first subject completing a requirement.

Several variables have been investigated in analyzing cooperation and competition. Lindsley (1966) investigated the effects of such variables as the schedule and nature of reinforcement, the nature of discriminative stimuli, and the kind of leadership. Lindsley and Cohen (1964) studied the catalyzing effects of human stimulation upon leadership development differentially reinforced in a cooperative situation. Schmitt and Marwell (1968) analyzed specific details of the procedures used in the above studies, as well as such variables as sex and interpersonal risk (Marwell, Schmitt, & Shotola, 1971) and risk avoidance (Schmitt & Marwell, 1971).

Since most of the experiments on cooperation and competition are conducted in a face-to-face situation, it is obvious that a great amount of social interaction occurs. Thus it may be that not only the behaviors under study are affected by the specified contingencies, but also other behaviors, which may be altered by them or by unspecified contingencies resulting from the social interaction itself.

In these experiments, the possible collateral effects of the cooperative and competitive contingencies were studied under different conditions. In the first study, cooperative contingencies were kept constant throughout the experiment, but the type of reinforcement was varied. In the second study, cooperative and competitive contingencies were compared while the type of reinforcement was kept constant. The dependent variables under study were the time required to complete the requirement and the amount of verbalization.

Experiment I

Subjects

Six children attending a local primary school served as subjects. Except for sex (masculine) and age (from 5 to 7 years), they were chosen on a random basis. Three groups were formed: Group I (S1, 5 years, 8 months; and S2, 6 years, 4 months), Group II (S1, 5 years, 1 month; S2, 5 years, 3 months), and Group III (S1, 5 years, 1 month; S2, 5 years, 10 months).

Experimental Setting

Two chairs and a table were placed in the experimental room (5 × 3 meters), and two subjects were seated facing each other. Three objects were placed on the table in front of each child.

1. A wooden plate (22.5 centimeters long × 9.8 centimeters wide), blue for one of the subjects and red for the other. Each of these plates contained 30 holes 2 centimeters equidistant from each other, arranged in three rows.
2. At the right side of each subject there was a box with 30 sticks (10 centimeters long; 4 millimeters in diameter), 15 of which were blue and 15 red. These sticks could be inserted in the holes of the wooden plate.
3. A case with a 45° slope was placed between the box of sticks and the plate of each subject. Since the subject's task was to insert the sticks in the holes matching the color of the plate, the sloped cases were positioned so that the subjects could exchange the sticks of the wrong color. Sticks placed on the top of the sloped case would slide where the subject on the other side could reach them.

Procedure

Daily sessions were conducted, each session consisting of three trials. Each trial was terminated when both subjects inserted all the sticks in the plate matching the color. The time between trials was approximately 5 minutes.

Once the two children were seated, the experimenter gave the following instructions to one: "This is a game. You can play it by inserting the red sticks in here [the experimenter picked up a red stick and inserted it in one of the holes of the red plate]."

The other child was told: "You can play by inserting the red sticks in here [the experimenter picked up a blue stick and inserted it in one of the holes of the blue plate]."

Then, the experimenter turned back to the first subject and told him: "Since you are not going to use the blue sticks, you may pass them to him [pointing to the other subject] by delivering them on the top of this case [the experimenter delivered a blue stick on the top of the sloped case facing the subject]." Next, the second subject was told: "Since you are not going to use the red sticks, you may pass them to him by delivering them on the top of this other case" [the experimenter delivered a red stick on the top of the sloped case facing the second child]." Then both subjects were instructed to pass only one stick at a time.

Finally, both subjects were told: "You can play the game the way you want but without leaving your seats. As soon as I say 'go ahead,' you may start. Raise both of your arms when you are finished."

Experimental conditions were the same for the three groups, but were presented in a different order. Reinforcement contingencies all through the experiment were set up for cooperation (except, of course, during base-line conditions). Experimental conditions for each group were as follows:

Group I	Group II	Group III
Base line	Base line	Base line
Reinforcement II	Reinforcement I	Reinforcement I
Reinforcement I	Reinforcement II	Reinforcement I and II
Reinforcement I and II	Reinforcement I and II	Reinforcement II
Base line	Base line	Base line

Base Line. There were five pre-base-line sessions in which time to complete the task as well as frequency of verbalizations were recorded for each subject. An averged time to complete the task was computed for each group in these sessions, and it was used to specify the time requirement during the reinforcement conditions. No explicit consequences for specific behavior during these sessions were programmed. Base-line conditions were the same as above, except that a bell sounded at the end of a specified period (the average computed time for each group). The average times for the different groups were the following: Group I, 2 minutes, 12 seconds; Group II, 3 minutes; and Group III, 2 minutes, 30 seconds. First and second base-line determinations were identical.

Reinforcement I. The following instructions were added: "Each of you will receive 20 cents [Mexican currency] if both of you finish before the bell sounds." As specified, whenever both children finished before the specified requirement, each received 20 cents, permitting him to obtain a maximum of 60 cents per session.

Reinforcement II. The following instructions were added: "Each of you will receive some candy if both of you finish before the bell sounds." Otherwise the procedure was similar to the previous one. Several types of candy were used as reinforcers.

Reinforcements I and II. The following instructions were added: "Each of you will receive 20 cents and some candy if both of you finish before the bell sounds." As before, the reinforcement was given whenever both subjects satisfied the requirement.

Recording. Once the instructions were given, the experimenter went to a wall near the table and the observers were placed at opposite corners of the room. The observers were instructed not to interact with the children. Occurrence of or absence of children's verbalizations was recorded in 10-second intervals, as was the specific interval in which the children finished the task.

Observers' Reliability. Reliability was computed by dividing the number of agreements over the number of agreements plus disagreements, with the quotient multipied by 100. Reliability for frequency of verbalizations was from 84% to 100%. No systematic relationship between high or low reliability and any of the experimental conditions was observed. The time recorded by the experimenter was always within the 10-second interval recorded by the observers, so that reliability for recording the time to complete the task was considered 100%.

Results

Figure 1 shows the frequency of verbalization per session for each of the subjects in the three groups. Figure 2 shows the time it took each of the subjects in the three groups to complete the task.

No effect on the frequency of verbalization was observed in Groups II and III in any of the conditions. Frequency of verbalization was similar during the first base-line determination and Reinforcement I condition for Group I, but a considerable increase was observed during candy reinforce-

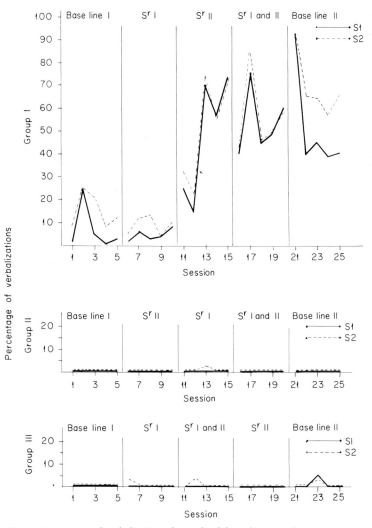

Fig. 1. *Percentage of verbalizations for each of the subjects in the three groups.*

ment (Reinforcement II). However, this did not return to its previous level in the following conditions (Reinforcement I and II and second base-line determination).

Regarding the time required to complete the task (Fig. 2), it was only for Group I that a clear effect for combined Reinforcements I and II was observed. For Group II, a similar effect was observed for the same conditions.

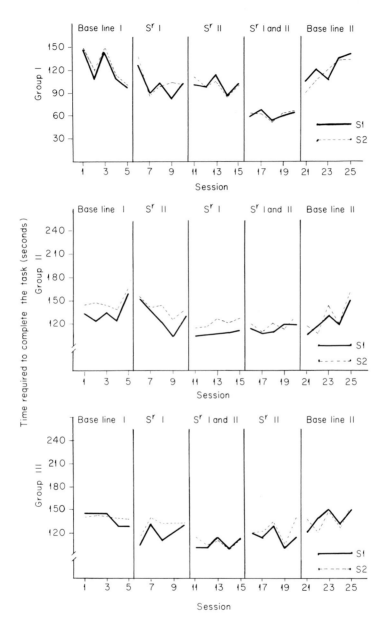

Fig. 2. *Time required for each of the subjects in the three groups to complete the task under three reinforcement conditions: money (Sʳl), candy (Sʳll), and candy plus money (Sʳl and Sʳll).*

7

However, the time required to complete the task did not return to its previous base-line level during the second base-line determination. Thus except for Group I, no systematic effect was observed.

Experiment II

Subjects

Four children from different primary schools were chosen randomly for this experiment. Group I consisted of a 7-year-old boy and an 8-year-old girl. Group II consisted of a 7-year-old and a 9-year-old boy.

Experimental Setting

The experimental setting was identical with that of the previous experiment.

Procedure

Daily sessions were conducted from Monday to Friday. There were three trials per session. A trial was terminated whenever both subjects finished the task, and the time between trials was approximately 5 minutes. After the children entered the experimental room and took their seats, instructions were given in a way similar to that of the previous experiment, except that for competitive conditions the following instructions were given: "The first one to complete the task will receive a reward. Remember, only the first one to complete the task." Several types of candy were given as reinforcement.

There were four phases to the experiment.

Group I	Group II
Base line I	Base line I
Cooperation	Competition
Base line II	Base line II
Competition	Cooperation

The base line for Group I did include the sound of the bell, and the mean required time to complete the task was determined directly from it. For Group II, the first five base-line sessions were used to compute the mean time to complete the task, and the bell was introduced by the sixth base-line session. During cooperative conditions, both subjects received reinforcement whenever both of them finished before the bell. During competition, reinforcement was given to the first subject who completed the task before the specified requirement. In effect, the reinforcement contingencies were indicated to the subjects through the instructions, as in the previous experiment.

Recording and Observers' Reliability. Recorded behaviors and recording systems were identical to the ones described in the previous experiment. Observers' reliability for recording verbalizations was between 81% and 94.5%, and no systematic relationship between any of the conditions and

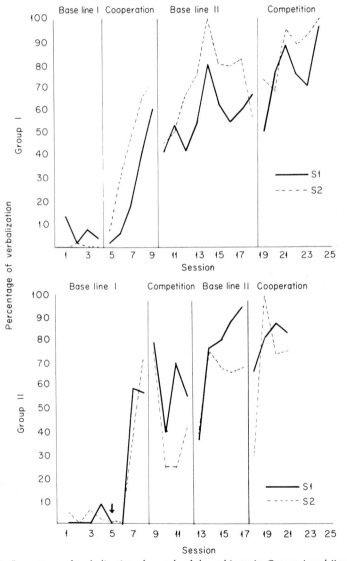

Fig. 3. *Percentage of verbalizations for each of the subjects in Groups I and II under co-operative and competitive conditions. The arrow in the second group indicates the session in which the ringing sound was introduced.*

high or low observers' reliability was observed. As in the previous case, the time recorded by the experimenter was always within the 10-second interval recorded by the observers. So, again, we considered reliability to be 10%.

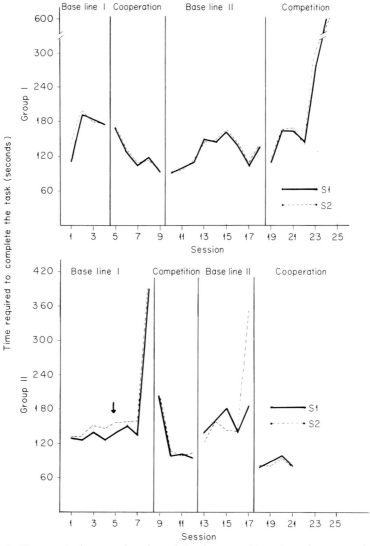

Fig. 4. Time required to complete the task for the two subjects in each group under co-operative and competitive conditions. The arrow in the second group indicates the session in which the ringing sound was introduced.

Results

Figure 3 shows the verbalization frequency for each of the subjects during the different phases of the experiment. Figure 4 shows the data for the time required to complete the task in both groups.

Verbalization frequency was observed to increase gradually as the sessions proceeded up to a more or less stable level. However, this seemed to be an irreversible effect.

Time required to complete the task was lower during cooperative conditions for both groups, even when a clearer effect for Group II was observed. In the last group it was also observed that competitive conditions decreased the time to complete the task as compared to the base-line conditions, but not to a level as low as the one produced by cooperative conditions. In Group I, the reverse effect was observed—that is, competitive conditions tended to produce an increase in time as compared to the previous base line.

General Conclusions

The time to complete the task was a variable that depended on cooperative and competitive conditions of the present experiments. However, informal observation suggests that the differences in time to complete the task under cooperative and competitive conditions may be the result of differences in the temporal distributions for exchanging the sticks. During cooperation, exchanging the sticks was made at a faster pace, whereas during competition children tended to retain the sticks so that the time to complete the task increased. It may be interesting to record these behaviors and observe the resulting changes.

Regarding the verbalization frequency, Groups II and III of the first experiment produced an initial level of almost zero (base line I) and the remaining phases did not alter this level. In the remaining cases, for both Experiments I and II, verbalization frequency during the first base-line determination was higher than zero. Once the verbalization frequency increased, it was maintained at a high level regardless of the change in experimental conditions. This seems to indicate that the experimental situation facilitates or sets the occasion for verbal interaction, but it may be that the variables controlling it are associated with the interaction itself and not with the experimental conditions. At any rate, it may be interesting to analyze the content of the verbalizations as well as the amount during both types of conditions. Another possibility might be to require an arbitrary response, such as pressing a button, before a subject is permitted to verbally interact with the other subject.

IMITATION

Imitation has been considered as a basic process in the study of social psychology for a long time and, in spite of an extensive literature in the area, a clear understanding of imitation as a behavioral phenomenon has not been achieved. However, operant research in the area has contributed to the identification of the variables potentially involved in the control of imitation.

The main point of interest has been research about generalized imitation, which has acquired special importance after the work by Baer and Sherman (1964), and studies by other authors (Baer, Peterson, & Sherman, 1967; Brigham & Sherman, 1968; Metz, 1965; Peterson, 1968; and Peterson & Whitehurst, 1971, among others).

Perhaps the best ways to analyze the generalized imitation phenomenon is to consider it as a complex discriminated operant. Burgess, Burgess, and Sveldt (1970) have pointed out that the original statement about generalized imitation was oversimplified since there are several sources of stimulus control: for example, similarity itself, instructional stimuli, noncontrolled concurrent stimuli presented by an experimenter, and conditional stimuli such as those in matching to sample. Peterson and Whitehurst (1971) conducted an experiment suggesting that the experimenter's presence could function as a setting event involved in evoking nonreinforced imitative responses, whereas Steinman (1970b), with a procedure similar to the one used by Peterson and Whitehurst (1971), analyzed the possible effects of three conditions: (a) whether an experimenter never paired with reinforcement will produce imitative responses; (b) whether reinforced imitative responses may or may not be attributed to the children's difficulty in discriminating the reinforced from the nonreinforced responses; and (c) the functional role of instructions. From his experiments, Steinman (1970a and 1970b) suggests that generalized imitation may be the result of more than one source of control, and that the role of instructions and other social variables along with the role of differential reinforcement should not be overlooked.

The experimenter's function and the function of the stimuli presented to the subject were studied in the following experiments. The first one was based upon a design similar to that used by Steinman (1970b). Discriminative functions of the experimenter (paired or not paired with reinforcement) and discriminative functions of the stimuli presented to the subject (Sd and SΔ) were analyzed. The second experiment attempted to eliminate the experimenter's influence by presenting stimuli through a tape recorder. Interaction between the experimenter and the subjects was avoided whenever possible.

Experiment I

Subjects

Two boys and one girl, ages 7 to 8, served as subjects. Two of them (a boy and a girl) came from a local primary school, the other one was attending a Center for Special Education of the University of Veracruz and was considered as mildly retarded but showing well-developed social and verbal behaviors.

Experimental Setting

Daily sessions were conducted in a small room (3.90 meters × 2.60 meters) in which there were two tables. Subjects were seated in front of the experimenter(s) with the larger table in between. Materials used during the experiment were placed on a small table at the side of the experimenter(s). Observers were placed in an adjacent room, where they could observe through a one-way mirror.

Procedure

Stimuli presented to the subject throughout the experiment were the following:

Sds	SΔs
1. Hands on the lap	A. Crossed hands on the table
2. Hands grasping the ears	B. Putting one match on a second one
3. Hands moving on the head	C. Rotating a foot
4. Applauding	D. Hands grasping the feet
5. Hands on the head	
6. Hands on the table	
7. Moving a pencil on the table	
8. Grasping a small paper bag	

There were six phases to the experiment:

Phase I. Individual presentation: Two experimenters were used throughout the experiment. In this phase, one of the experimenters (E+) always presented an Sd stimulus, and the other experimenter (E−) always presented an SΔ stimulus). The initial four to six stimuli of the first session were preceded by the instructions, "Do this." Afterwards, the stimuli were presented without previous instructions (cf. Baer & Sherman, 1964).

At the same time that the experimenter presented a stimulus, he activated a stopwatch to record the time the subject took to respond. A response was considered correct whenever the subject topographically matched the stimulus presented by the experimenter within a maximum of 10 seconds from the presentation of the stimulus. Only correct responses to Sd stimuli were reinforced. In such cases, the experimenter (E+) said, "Very good" to the subject. Under any other conditions, interaction or visual contact with the subject was avoided by both experimenters. When the 10 seconds were over, the experimenter left the room and, after 15 seconds, the other experimenter (or the same one depending on the pre-arranged order) came in.

At the end of a session, E+ would ask the subject to count the beads he had won. These could be exchanged for different trinkets or several kinds of candy according to the numbers of beads obtained.

Phase II. Individual presentation and choice: Three blocks were presented to the subject. The first block was identical to the ones described in the previous phase. The second and third blocks contained 16 stimuli. Each one was presented in eight pairs, and each pair included one Sd and one SΔ (SΔ models were repeated once each so that the number of Sds could be matched).

Procedure for the first block was identical to that of the previous phase. However, the following two blocks were presented in a different way. In this case, E+ and E− came into the room at the same time. One of the experimenters instructed the subject to "do this" while presenting a model at the same time. Immediately afterwards, the other experimenter said, "Or do this," and presented another model. (Instructions were used only during the first trials of the first session, and afterwards the models were presented in the same successive way but without instructions.)

These two later blocks were also different from the first in that each experimenter (E+ or E−) presented both kinds of stimuli (Sds and SΔs). For example, during the second block, E+ would present four Sds and four SΔs, and E− would present four Sds and four SΔs. Stimuli presented by one particular experimenter were not presented by the other. Regardless of the previous procedure, E+ was the only experimenter associated with reinforcement, since only the correct imitative responses to Sds presented by E+ were reinforced. In all other cases reinforcement was not delivered. In these two blocks, only the first response meeting the previously specified requirements was considered correct. (A few times one subject responded to both of the presented stimuli, but in most of the cases they imitated only one of the stimuli.)

Phase III. Same as Phase I.

Phase IV. Individual presentation, reversing the experimenters' roles. Procedure was the same as that for Phase I, but the experimenter E+ became E− (presenting only SΔs), and E− became E+ (presenting only Sds and delivering reinforcement for correct imitative responses).

Phase V. Same as Phase II, but maintaining the reversed experimenters' roles.

Phase VI. Same as Phase IV.

Results

Figure 5 includes the data for all three subjects, but only for the procedure of individual presentation. That means that the percentages plotted for

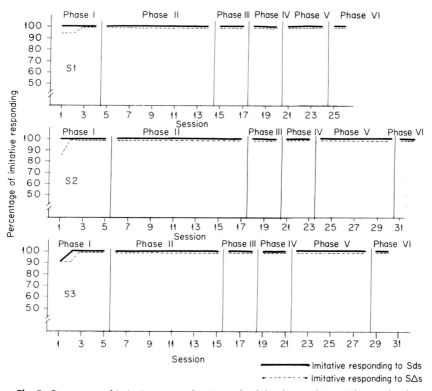

Fig. 5. *Percentage of imitative responding in each of the three subjects. The graphs show the data relating to individual presentation, so that Phases IV and V include data from only the first block. The continuous line indicates percentage of imitative responding to Sds presented by E+. The broken line indicates the percentage of imitative responding to SΔs presented by E−.*

Phases II and V were obtained by taking into account only the first of the three blocks. According to the data, all the subjects imitated the stimuli presented by the experimenters whether or not the stimuli were Sds (presented by E+) or SΔs (presented by E−). These data are comparable to the results obtained by Steinman (1970a), demonstrating the possibility of maintaining nonreinforced imitative responding under individual presentation conditions.

Data for the second and third blocks of Phases II and V (choice procedure) are plotted in Fig. 6. Remember that these phases are equivalent, except that the experimenters' roles were reversed in Phase V. The top graph of each subject shows percentage of imitative responses to Sds presented by E+ (filled circles) and E− (open circles). The bottom graph for each subject shows the percentage of imitative responding to SΔs presented by E+ (filled circles and E− (open circles).

In general it may be observed that when E+ presented Sd stimuli, imitative responding in the three subjects was about 100%. However, when E+ presented SΔ stimuli, imitative responding sensibly decreased (this effect was not as clearly observed in S1).

On the other hand, when E− presented SΔ stimuli, no imitative responding was observed. However, when E− presented Sd stimuli, imitation increased up to about 50% in S2 and S3. Again, a clear effect was not observed in S1.

Results were consistent for Phases II and V, even when the experimenters' roles were reversed.

The range of reliability for the observers' recordings of imitative behavior was from 97 to 100%. Reliability was obtained through the customary procedure.

Experiment II

Subjects

Three boys and one girl served as subjects for this experiment. All subjects were considered retarded and were attending the Center for Training and Special Education of the University of Veracruz. Their main deficits were in social and academic behaviors, but with an acceptable level of verbal behavior. The four children had already had some experience under token systems. Ages of the children were as follows: S1, 17 years; S2, 11 years; S3, 11 years; and S4, 9 years.

Experimental Setting

The experiment was conducted in a 3.9 meters × 2.6 meters room. In an adjacent observation room with a one-way mirror, observers recorded

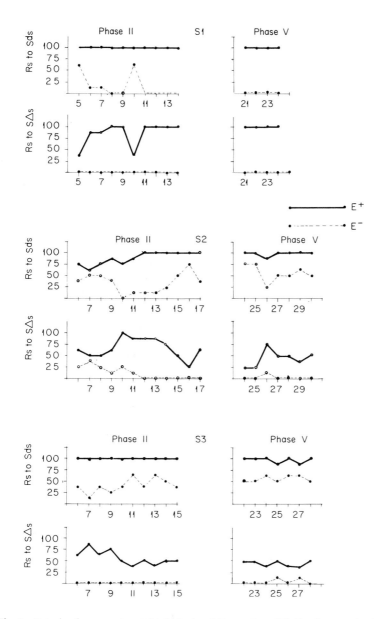

Fig. 6. Data for the second and third blocks of Phases II and V. The four graphs for each subject represent imitative responding to Sds presented by E+ (continuous line) and by E− (broken line). The bottom graph for each subject represents imitative responding to SΔs presented by E+ (continuous line) and by E− (broken line). In Phase V, the roles of the experimenters were reversed.

the children's behavior. A table stood in front of the mirror; on it were a cassette-type tape recorder and a case into which tokens (beads) were manually delivered through a tube from the observation room. Beads could be exchanged at the end of the session for several kinds of trinkets and candy.

Before starting the experiment, several tests were made in order to ensure that the stimuli presented through the tape recorder were audible and clear. Subjects' responses were perfectly audible in the observation room.

Procedure

The experimenter took the subject to the experimental room and seated him in front of the tape recorder. Then the experimenter went out of the room and the tape recorder was turned on.

Twenty different words were presented to the subject through the tape recorder, with each work presented twice in random order. Sixteen of these words were arbitrarily designated as Sd stimuli and the remaining four as SΔ stimuli. Every 20 seconds, a word was presented, so each session lasted 13 minutes. Daily sessions were conducted. The following is a list of the words presented:

Sds	SΔs
papa (papa)	*mesa* (table)
vaso (glass)	*hoja* (leaf)
coche (car)	*cama* (bed)
piso (floor)	*leche* (milk)
pelo (hair)	
pala (shovel)	
boca (mouth)	
mama (mama)	
gato (cat)	
aqui (here	
casa (house)	
lápiz (pencil)	
sala (living room)	
calle (street)	
mano (hand)	
taza (cup)	

There were four phases to the experiment:

Base Line I. During this phase none of the imitative responses was reinforced. If the subject did not respond to the stimuli for two sessions,

at the start of the third session the experimenter turned on the tape recorder and, in the subject's presence, imitated the first three stimuli presented through the tape recorder. After that, the experimenter turned back the tape recorder and went out of the room. This procedure was used only in in two cases (S2 and S4). No explicit instructions were given during the experiment.

Reinforcement I. During this phase, correct imitative responding to Sds was followed by the delivery of a bead to the subject's reinforcement case, whereas no consequences followed imitative responding to SΔs. Delivery of reinforcement was accompanied by the sound of a bell in the case of Subjects 1, 3, and 4.

Base Line II. Base-line conditions were reintroduced so that no consequences followed the subjects' responses.

Reinforcement II. Same as the Reinforcement I phase.

Base-line conditions were reintroduced for S1 for reasons to be explained. By the same token, another phase was introduced for S3 in order to test for the effect of the social stimuli presented.

Recording and Observers' Reliability. Two observers recorded from an adjacent room. One of these observers was in charge of delivering reinforcers through the tube. Imitative behavior was defined in terms of similarity of topography and temporal relation to the stimuli presented. A response had to occur within 10 seconds after stimulus presentation in order to be considered as imitative.

Average reliabilities for each subject's behavior were the following: S1, 98.5%; S2, 96.8%; S3, 100%; S4, 99%. The overall range of the reliabilities obtained was from 85 to 100%.

Results

Figures 7, 8, 9, and 10 show the data for each of the four subjects. Percentages of imitations to Sds (continuous line) and percentage of imitations to SΔs (broken line) are plotted.

Subject 1 (Fig. 7) imitated from the first session without instructions or prompting. No change in the frequency of imitative responding to Sds or SΔs was observed when the first reinforcement phase was introduced. Nor did the introduction of the bell sound associated with the delivery of reinforcement produce any change in the subject's response level. The same level of responding was observed when the base-line conditions were

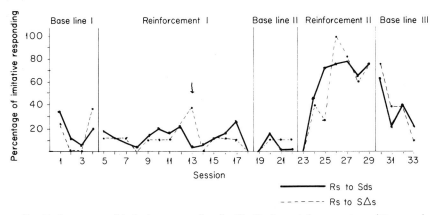

Fig. 7. *Percentage of imitative responding for S1. During reinforcement conditions, only correct imitative responses to Sds were reinforced. The arrow indicates the session in which the bell sound paired with the delivery of reinforcement was introduced.*

reintroduced (Base line II). However, the percentage of imitative responding to both Sds and SΔs did increase when the third phase was introduced (Reinforcement II). The increase in imitative responding for both reinforced and nonreinforced imitative responses was clearly over the level in the previous phases. In order to control for extraneous variables, an extinction phase was introduced again (Base line III), in which gradual decrease in both reinforced and nonreinforced imitative responses was observed.

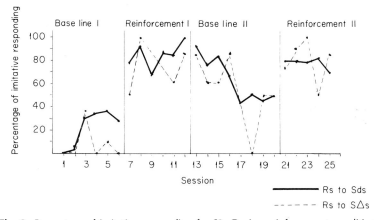

Fig. 8. *Percentage of imitative responding for S2. During reinforcement conditions, only correct imitative responses to Sds were reinforced. From Sessions 3 to 6, the experimenter imitated the first three stimuli presented through the tape recorder.*

Since the percentage of imitative responding for S2 (Fig. 8) was almost zero during the first two sessions, beginning with the third session the experimenter imitated the first three stimuli presented through the tape recorder while the subject was present, then went out of the room without any comment. The percentage of imitative responding showed a slight increase after this procedure, the increase being slightly higher for responses to Sds. During the next phase (Reinforcement I), a clear increase in the percentage of imitative responding, both reinforced and nonreinforced, was observed. Under the third phase (Base line II), both percentages decreased again and increased when reinforcement conditions were reintroduced (Reinforcement II).

The percentage of imitative response was noticeably higher during reinforcement conditions than during base-line periods.

Data for S3 (Fig. 9) initially showed a high level of imitative responding (about 90%), with imitative responding to Sds consistently higher. The percentage of imitative responding to both Sds and SΔs was stabilized at a high level during the first reinforcement phase. Except for the first three sessions during the rest of the phase, a level of imitative responding to Sds above 90% was observed. Except for Sessions 7 and 12, the values for imitative responding to SΔs were always 100%. Even when a slight decrease in imitative responding was observed during Base line II, the level did not increase when the last phase of the experiment was introduced (Reinforcment II).

Data for S4 show that the initial imitative responding of this subject was zero (Fig. 10). A new procedure was tested during Sessions 5, 6, and 7 of the second phase. Every time the subject repeated the stimulus in the presence of the experimenter, the experimenter said, "Very good" and placed his hand on the subject's shoulder. These consequences were

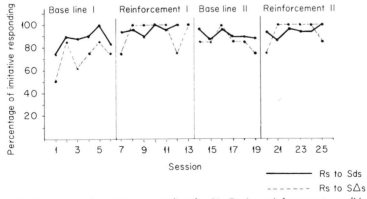

Fig. 9. *Percentage of imitative responding for S3. During reinforcement conditions, only correct imitative responses to Sds were reinforced.*

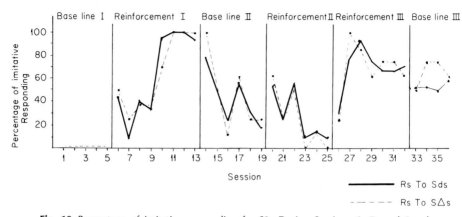

Fig. 10 *Percentage of imitative responding for S3. During Sessions 6, 7, and 8, whenever the child imitated Sds correctly, he was socially reinforced by the experimenter. This was done for only the first three stimuli presented through the tape recorder. During reinforcement conditions, only correct imitative responses to Sds were reinforced. The Reinforcement III condition was introduced to test for the effect of social reinforcement provided in Sessions 6, 7, and 8.*

effected only during the first three stimuli of the list whenever the subjects responded to an Sd; otherwise, no consequences occurred. After that, the normal procedure was used. From session 9 to the end of the phase, the above-mentioned special procedure was discontinued. Imitative responses to Sds were reinforced with beads, and responses to SΔs had no consequences. Under the previous conditions, an increase of about 30% was observed for both responses to both Sds and to SΔs during the first four sessions of this phase. Afterwards, an abrupt increase up to about 100% for both types of responding was observed. During Base line II (Sessions 14 to 19), clear decrease in imitative responding occurred. However, it never reached the zero level of Base line I. During the next phase (Reinforcement II), when imitative responses to Sds were reinforced again, no increase in the level of responding to Sds or SΔs was observed. On the contrary, both values decreased gradually to about zero.

Since the observed effects of the first reinforcement phase could be due to the social reinforcement delivered by the experimenter, two phases were added to test for the effects of that variable. In the fifth phase (Reinforcement III), the experimenter repeated the first three words presented through the tape recorder, followed by the subject's correct repetition of the same words (which he repeated without any instruction). Correct repetition to Sds was followed by the experimenter's saying, "Very good" to the subject and patting him. Then the experimenter left the room, after turning back the tape recorder. No consequences followed the subject's imitative responses once he was left alone in the experimental room. Under the previous conditions, imitative behaviors had increased remarkably to a stable value of about 70%.

Finally, in the last phase (Base line III) no consequences were programmed for imitative responses. Although the frequency of imitative responses was consistently lower, no dramatic reduction in responding was observed. The experiment was terminated by the 37th session, since the subject had stopped attending the Center.

General Discussion

Data provided in the first experiment seems to support Steinman's findings about children's imitative behavior depending upon the specific procedure of stimuli presentation. Thus in the present case, all stimuli presented to the children were imitated when the individual procedure was used, but when the choice method was presented children preferably imitated the experimenter associated to Sds (E+).

Some interesting data are observed in Fig. 6, which correspond to the last two blocks of Phases II and V. Except for S1 in the remaining subjects, E+control over imitative responding was higher when he presented only Sds than when he presented SΔs. By the same token, E−control over imitative responding was zero when he presented SΔs and increased when he presented Sds. These results seem to suggest that children's imitative behavior may be the result of two kinds of variables: (a) the experimenter's discriminative function—that is, his pairing or not pairing with the reinforcing event, and (b) the discriminative function of the stimuli to be imitated (Sds or SΔs). This would support an interpretation in terms of a compound Sd controlling imitative responding.

In the second experiment, when presentation of social stimuli (basically the experimenter's presence) was avoided, generalized imitation was observed in only two of the four cases (S1 and S2, Figs. 7 and 8). However, the first case constitutes only a partial demonstration of this effect, since no increase in imitative responding was observed during the first reinforcement phase. An increase in both types of imitative responding (Sd and SΔ) was observed only after the second base-line determination. In the second case (S2), generalized imitation was observed in Reinforcement I and II phases. However, both phases were preceded by a procedure implying social stimulation, since from the third session up to the end of Phase I the experimenter imitated the first three stimuli in the subject's presence (however, he never reinforced the subject).

No effect of the procedure used can be determined for S3, since imitative responding to Sds and SΔs was consistently high all through the experiment (Fig. 9).

Finally, for S4 (Fig. 10) the effect obtained during the first reinforcement phase, in which an increase in imitative responding to both Sds and SΔs was observed, could not be replicated in the second reinforcement phase. In general, all results might be attributed to the effects of the social reinforcement given by the experimenter before the session was initiated. An attempt to analyze the experimenter's influence was made in the third reinforcement phase. The effects of this procedure were persistent, since it could be observed in the last phase that a relatively high percentage of imitative responding was maintained.

In general terms, the results from both experiments suggest that:

1. A generalized imitation phenomenon is related to the way in which the stimuli to be imitated are presented. When the procedure of individual presentation was in effect, generalized imitation was observed, but when the choice procedure was in effect, the subjects preferably imitated the Sds presented by E+.
2. Besides the experimenter's discriminative function, it seems that the stimuli themselves acquire discriminative function, depending on their pairing or lack of pairing with some reinforcing event.
3. From Experiment II, it can be said that the presence of social stimuli plays an important role in generalized imitation, even when those stimuli are not contingent upon imitative behavior. Their function can be that of setting events.
4. In the same experiment, it was observed that once the child is behaving properly in an imitative situation, the presence of an adult or supervisor is not required. This may be of some practical importance for education or programmed teaching.

We believe that the data provided in the previous experiments strongly suggest the necessity of analyzing generalized imitation as resulting from the intervention of several sources of control, such as physical or social setting events, discriminative control from the experimenter as well as from the presented stimuli, similarity between the imitative response and the presented stimuli, and the like.

REFERENCES

Baer, D. M. & Sherman, J. A. Reinforcement control of generalized imitation in young children, *Journal of Experimental Child Psychology*, 1964, **1**, 37–49.

Baer, D. M., Peterson, R. F., & Sherman, J. A. The development of imitation by reinforcing behavioral similarity to a model. *Journal of Applied Behavior Analysis*, 1967, **10**, 405–416.

Brigham, T. A. & Sherman, J. A. An experimental analysis of verbal imitation in preschool children. *Journal of Applied Behavior Analysis,* 1968, **1**, 151–158.

Burgess, R. R., Burgess, J. M., & Sveldt, K. C. An analysis of generalized imitation. *Journal of Applied Behavior Analysis,* 1970, **3**, 39–46.

Deutsch, M. A. A theory of cooperation and competition. *Human Relations,* 1949, **2**, 129–152.

Lindsley, O. R. Experimental analysis of cooperation and competition. In Tom Verhave (Ed.), *The experimental analysis of behavior.* New York: Appleton-Century-Crofts, 1966.

Lindsley, O. R. & Cohen, D. J. Catalysis of controlled leadership in cooperation by human stimulation. *Journal of Child Psychology and Psychiatry,* 1964, **5**, 119–137.

Marwell, G., Schmitt, D. R., & Shotola, R. Cooperation and interpersonal risk. *Journal of Personality and Social Psychology,* 1971, **18**, 9–32.

Metz, J. R. Conditioning generalized imitation in autistic children. *Journal of Experimental Child Psychology,* 1965, **2**, 389–399.

Peterson, R. F. Some experiments on the organization of a class of imitative behavior. *Journal of Applied Behavior Analysis,* 1968, **1**, 225–235.

Peterson, R. F. & Whitehurst, G. J. A variable influencing the performance of nonreinforced imitative behaviors. *Journal of Applied Behavior Analysis,* 1971, **4**, 1–9.

Rotter, J. B. *Social Learning and Clinical Psychology.* Englewood Cliffs, New Jersey: Prentice-Hall, 1954.

Schmitt, D. R. & Marwell, G. Stimulus control in the experimental study of cooperation. *Journal of the Experimental Analysis of Behavior,* 1968, **11**, 571–574.

Schmitt, D. R. & Marwell, G. Avoidance of risk as a determinant of cooperation. *Journal of the Experimental Analysis of Behavior,* 1971, **16**, 367–374.

Steinman, W. M. The social control of generalized imitation. *Journal of Applied Behavior Analysis,* 1970a, **3**, 159–167.

Steinman, W. M. Generalized imitation and the discrimination hypothesis. *Journal of Experimental Child Psychology,* 1970b, **10**, 79–99.

Using Arranged and Programmed Events to Alter Subtraction Performance of Children with Learning Disabilities[1]

TOM LOVITT, DEBBY SMITH, JOHN KIDDER,
and ROXANNE EVISON

When a pupil is not responding correctly or efficiently to academic materials, the teacher, obviously, must select a remediation technique. Broadly speaking, two remediation strategies are available—the involvement of either programmed or arranged events.

Programmed events are those the teacher schedules on a noncontingent basis. Temporally, programmed events can occur before, during, or after the pupil's responding. Examples of each type of programmed event are instructions before responding, background music during responding, and confirmation after responding.

By contrast, arranged events are those which are scheduled on a contingent basis—if the pupil behaves in a certain way, something will consistently happen. The occurrence of an arranged event, then, is dependent on the pupil's behavior; whereas the mere passage of time or the completion of some assignment, regardless of the quality of performance, can dictate the involvement of a programmed event. Arranged events, since they are contingent on behavior, can occur only *after* a response.

[1]This research was supported by N.I.E. Grant Number OEG–070–3916(607). Reprinted by permission from D. Smith, T.Lovitt, and J. Kidder, Using reinforcement contingencies and teaching aids to alter subtraction performance of children with learning disabilities. In George Semb (Ed.), *Behavior Analysis and Education*. Lawrence, Kansas: Univ. of Kansas Press, 1972.

Many events can be contingently or noncontingently scheduled. They may, depending on their relationship with the target behavior, function as either programmed or arranged events. Pupil charting, for example, can be scheduled as a programmed or an arranged event. If the teacher has the child chart his rate in oral reading each day regardless of his performance, charting is a programmed event. If, however, the child's correct rate must exceed a certain rate, e.g., 100 per minute, before he can chart his performance, the charting is scheduled as an arranged event.

Generally, teachers are more apt to schedule programmed than arranged events. Some teachers probably schedule 25 programmed events for each arranged event that is planned. To assist the child having a difficult time computing arithmetic responses, teachers have used such programmed events as cuisinare rods, number lines, the abacus and other teaching devices. Instructions and mnemonic aids have also been provided noncontingently to assist pupils to perform more satisfactorily.

Occasionally, arranged events have been scheduled in attempts to improve computation skills. Some teachers have given stars or other small prizes contingent on correct math papers, while others have delayed recess until a paper is completed perfectly.

In order to design individualized and productive settings for their pupils, teachers should develop a large and varied repertory of both programmed and arranged events. Furthermore, the teacher, in his efforts to modify behaviors, must be able to discriminate pupil behaviors to the extent that his initial selection of a programmed or arranged event is generally effective in promoting student learning. If, however, the initial teaching event does not effectively influence the target behavior, the teacher must be capable of selecting another programmed or arranged event and proceeding with his instruction.

Most teachers, since they have a penchant for programmed events, initially select a programmed event to alter pupil behavior. If that event proves nonfunctional, they select other programmed events. If a child cannot solve the problems in one text at a given level, the level is reduced, then another series is tried, then flash cards are used, then a number line is provided. Some teachers are constantly engaged in a quest for the panacea program—the one that works. From time to time, of course, if a number of techniques are tried, something is bound to be effective. (It is a bit like running a mass of correlations: A few are certain to be significant.) Quixotic searches for perfect programs could, however, require months.

Many pupils could have the behavior requested by the teacher, but are unwilling to perform. Some are more attracted by other stimuli. Certain pupils are more reinforced by staring out of windows than by completing their math assignments. Others seem to enjoy playing games with their teachers.

They know that certain teachers are reinforced by instructing pupils and do not particularly want to reward them. Still other pupils see no point in doing their math; they fail to grasp the relevancy of it all. With children that actively resist instruction, teachers could alter programmed events until doomsday, and to no avail.

On the other hand, the rare teacher who has an arranged event affinity (generally a misplaced operant psychologist) can be found. This teacher believes that anything can be taught if only the effective reinforcer can be found and contingently arranged with the desired behavior. As his programmed event-prone counterpart impetuously grasps for the ideal material or procedure, so the arranged event merchant chases the elusive motivator. Such a teacher, attempting to instruct a child to borrow (e.g., $26 - 8 = \square$) might initially arrange a setting that will provide the pupil with 1 minute of music listening time for each 10 correct answers. If that failed, the ratio might be reduced to 5:1, then 1:1. If those changes also failed to stimulate correct responding, the consequence itself might be altered from music to television, to candy, to praise. It could be that the child has no part of the required behavior in his repertory. In such a case the manager could arrange countless contingencies without affecting the pupil's behavior.

Certainly, in the first case where the behavior was *in* the child's "system," and several programmed events were ineffectively scheduled, the involvement of an arranged event—something to alter the pupil's motivation— might have been more functional. Likewise, in the second case, where the behavior had never appeared as a part of the child's repertory yet several arranged events were scheduled without effect, a programmed event such as modeling or instruction should have been initially scheduled. These are obvious instances. Teachers and researchers must actively search for other, more subtle cues that tell them when to schedule which approach.

Following are descriptions of two experiments. Both studies dealt with subtraction. The first study demonstrates how, under certain conditions, an arranged event can effectively influence a pupil's rate and accuracy of responding. By contrast, the second project serves to illustrate how, under different circumstances, programmed events in the form of instructional aids can positively alter rate and accuracy of answering problems.

Both studies were conducted in the curriculum research classroom at the Experimental Education Unit (EEU), University of Washington. In this class were six children, ages 8–12. Three of the children were referred from special classes, three from regular. The class was directed by two full-time teachers. In addition, several graduate students were in the class on a part-time basis. The purpose of the class was twofold: (1) to serve as a location for conducting educational research, and (2) to serve as a facility to train educational researchers.

EXPERIMENT I

The pupil in this study was an 11-year-old girl who was referred to the EEU primarily because of reading problems. She was first enrolled at the EEU's curriculum research class in the summer of 1970 on a part-time basis. That summer she was tutored in reading by a graduate student in special education. Throughout the 1970–1971 academic year she was a full-time student.

The managers of this experiment were graduate students in special education. Debby Smith, a doctoral student, ran Study 1 of the experiment from February until June, 1971. Roxanne Evison, a master's student, ran Study 2 of the experiment from June until the end of summer school, August, 1971.

Study 1

Procedures

Each day this pupil was given three sheets of subtraction problems. Each sheet contained 25 problems of a different class. One sheet, coded S1, contained problems of the type, $18 - 9$. The second sheet, S2, had problems of the type $24 - 6$, and the third sheet, S3, had problems of the type $34 - 16$.

The S1 problems were those where the minuends were from 10 to 19, the subtrahends from 0 to 9, and the differences from 1 ($10 - 9$) to 9 ($18 - 9$). There were 45 different problems in this class. The S2 problems differed in that the minuends were from 20 to 98. The subtrahends were single digits, 1 through 9, and the differences ranged from 11 ($20 - 9$) to 89 ($98 - 9$). In all of these problems, borrowing was required. There were 360 problems in this class. For the S3 problems, the minuends ranged from 30 to 98. The subtrahends ranged from 11 to 79; whereas the differences were from 11 ($30 - 19$) to 79 ($98 - 19$). Regrouping was always required. There were 1,260 different problems in this class. For each class of problems five different sheets were constructed. For the S1 class some problems were used on more than one sheet since there were only 45 different problems in the class. The different problems were randomly assigned to the sheets and no problem appeared more than once on any sheet. For S2 and S3, different problems were placed on the five sheets in each class. First, the 125 problems (25 per sheet) of each class were randomly selected from the total number of problems in each class. Then, those problems were randomly assigned to one of the five sheets.

On successive days a different form for each class of problems was used. The order in which the sheets from each class were given to the pupil varied from day to day. On one day the S1 sheet was the top sheet of the three handed the pupil. The next day S2 was on top, then S3.

The pupil was requested to complete each page and to start a stopwatch as she began each page and shut it off when she finished. Periodically, the manager checked the pupil's timing accuracy. These checks initially revealed that the pupil was not an accurate timer. However, as the manager continued to monitor the timing, the girl's accuracy improved. The timings of the manager, when different from the child's, were used to calculate rate. Upon completion, the three pages were collected by the manager, who checked the answers, counted the number of correct and incorrect responses, calculated correct and error rates, then plotted the data.

Throughout this study the manager used scoring sheets to record information regarding each session. On these sheets, one for each class of problems, were recorded the day of the session, the date, number of correct and incorrect answers, time to complete each sheet, correct and error rates, and the percentage correct score. After the study was completed all the daily papers were rechecked to determine whether the girl's responses were accurately checked, and each entry on the scoring sheets was rechecked. The data appearing on the graphs and tables were based on rechecks.

Throughout the study the pupil was given no feedback as to which problems were incorrect. The only feedback she received was during the phases when the withdraw contingency was in effect; then, she was simply told how many problems were incorrectly answered. Also, during withdraw conditions, she was told on which sheet the contingency was placed; she was not, however, told when the contingency was removed. The reason no feedback was given and that no teaching was provided was that the manager had observed, on occasions prior to this study, that the pupil could perform the S1 and S2 class problems. The manager did not, however, know what to expect when the girl worked the S3 problems.

The design of this study was a multiple base line. During the first phase, no arranged contingencies were in effect. Following this base line, a withdraw contingency was successively scheduled on each sheet. This contingency, which specified that for each incorrect answer 1 minute of recess time would be lost, was arranged first on S1. Then, after 5 days, it was also placed on S2. After another 10 days, the contingency was additionally placed on S3. The contingency remained in effect for all three sheets for another 12 days.

The contingency was to be withdrawn from each sheet after 4 consecutive perfect days were observed. Since 4 perfect days were first noted on S2, the contingency was removed first from that list. After 3 more days, 4 consecutive perfect days were also recorded for the S1 problems, thus the contingency was in effect for only the third sheet. Although 4 consecutive no-error days were recorded for S3, the quarter ended; thus no time was left for a withdraw phase.

Results

Two sets of graphs have been included to explain the results of this study. The first chart reveals percentage of accuracy throughout the six conditions of the study. Since each sheet contained 25 problems, each problem was worth 4%. If 12 problems were correctly answered, the correct percentage could be 48 (12 × 4).

Three percentage charts are placed on one figure; one chart for each class of problems (see Fig. 1).

The second set of charts provides rate information. One chart is included for each class of problems and shows the girl's correct and error rates per session (see Figs. 2, 3, and 4). On both sets of charts, percentage and rate, the reader will note some gaps between plots. These spaces indicate that no data were obtained on some days because of weekends, field trips, or absences.

A table that contains summary data about the study is included. This table provides information about the number and description of the experimental conditions, the number of sessions in each condition, correct and error rate means, and correct and error rate standard deviation scores (see Table 1).

First, the girl's performance on each class of problems will be explained in terms of percentage; then her performance will be described in terms of correct and error rate.

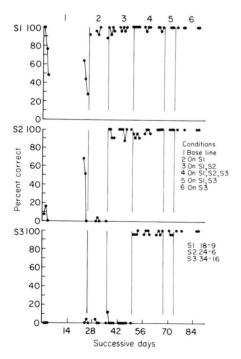

Fig. 1. *Experiment I (Study 1): Percentage of correct scores for three classes of subtraction facts across six experimental conditions. Spaces between data points indicate no data gathered on those days because of weekends, holidays, or other interruptions.*

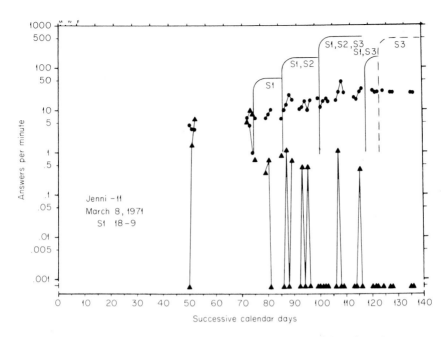

Fig. 2. *Experiment I (Study 1): Correct and error rates for the S1 problems throughout six experimental conditions. The solid lines that separate conditions indicate that a variable was directly associated with the problems on that sheet. A broken line indicates a variable was associated with another set of problems.*

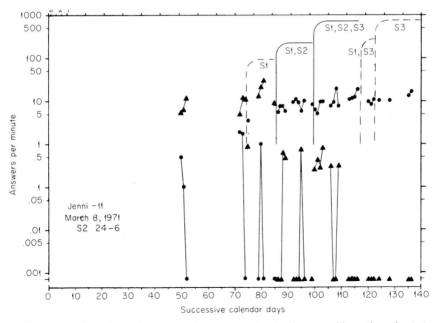

Fig. 3. *Experiment I (Study 1): Correct and error rates for the S2 problems throughout six experimental conditions.*

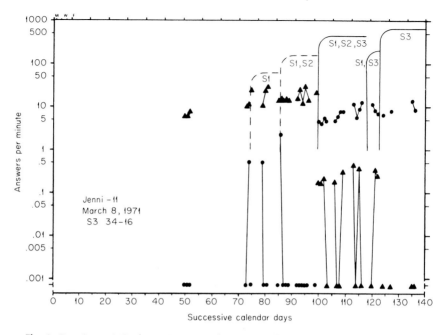

Fig. 4. *Experiment I (Study 1): Correct and error rates for the S3 problems throughout six experimental conditions.*

During the base-line phase, the girl's performance was very poor. On the S1 problems only 1 100% day was noted; none were recorded for the S2 problems. Meanwhile, on 4 of the 5 days, her percent scores were zero on the S3 problems (see Fig. 1).

When the contingency was placed on the S1 problems, the pupil's performance was immediately affected. Throughout Conditions 2, 3, 4, and 5, when the 1-minute loss per error contingency was arranged for S1, her performance was perfect on 20 of 30 days.

When the contingency was arranged for errors on S2, her performance was again immediately influenced. Throughout Conditions 3 and 4, when the withdraw contingency was scheduled, her performance was perfect on 13 of the 22 days.

When the contingency was placed on the S3 problems, her accuracy was once again immediately influenced. Throughout the final three conditions of the study, when the contingency was imposed on S3 problems, her accuracy was 100% for 10 of 19 days.

On S2, when the contingency was removed (Conditions 5 and 6), her performance was perfect for 7 consecutive days. When the contingency was removed from S1 (Condition 6), her performance was perfect for 5 consecutive days.

TABLE 1
Summary Rate Data for Experiment I (Study 1)

Condition		S1					S2					S3				
			Mean		S.D.			Mean		S.D.			Mean		S.D.	
Description	N	C	E	C	E	N	C	E	C	E	N	C	E	C	E
Base line	6	3.97	5.50	1.92	4.08	6	.73	9.35	.91	3.72	5	.10	8.69	.22	2.61
On S1	5	7.76	.54	1.81	.37	5	.93	16.01	1.58	12.71	5	.10	21.70	.22	9.13
On S1, S2	10	15.81	.29	4.80	.43	10	8.08	.19	2.04	.32	10	.21	18.91	.67	6.86
On S1, S2, S3	12	23.80	.12	9.92	.35	12	10.84	.29	4.61	.33	12	7.09	.16	2.97	.17
On S1, S3	3	26.90	.00	2.68	.00	3	9.93	.00	1.76	.00	3	9.16	.21	2.59	.18
On S3	5	26.00	.00	2.23	.00	4	13.10	.00	3.34	.00	4	8.80	.00	2.58	.00

35

During the base-line condition, when rate was considered, her mean error rates on each sheet were much higher than her mean correct rates. It may also be noted that her error rate standard deviations in this condition were higher than her correct rate standard deviations (see Table 1).

When the contingency was imposed on S1, her mean correct rate doubled, whereas her error rate fell drastically. Correct rate standard deviation now surpassed error rate standard deviation. On the other two sheets in this phase (Condition 2) her error rates doubled. Error rate standard deviations on S2 and S3 continued to be higher than their correct rate counterparts.

In Condition 3, when the withdraw contingency was also arranged for S2, her mean correct rate rose considerably, while her average error rate fell from the preceding phase. Her correct rate standard deviation was now greater than her error rate deviation score. Her mean error rate and error rate standard deviation scores on S3, the sheet not covered by the contingency, were higher than the mean correct rate and correct rate standard deviation scores.

During Condition 4, when the contingency was placed on S3, in addition to the other two sheets, her mean correct and error rates were markedly influenced. Now, for the first time, as was the case when the contingency was invoked on the other lists, her correct rate standard deviation score was greater than that figure for her error rate.

When the contingency was removed from S2 (Conditions 5 and 6), her correct and error rate mean and standard deviation scores remained about the same as before the contingency was lifted. A similar observation can be made regarding her performance when the contingency was removed from S4 (Condition 6).

Discussion

When the withdraw contingency was imposed first on S1, then S2, then S3, the effects were immediate. When placed on S1 in the second condition, her percent score rose from 28% on the last session of the preceding phase to a 92% on the first day of the withdraw condition. Similarly, her performance on S2, when the contingency was scheduled, rose from zero to 100%, and on S3 from zero to 96% (see Fig. 1).

These prompt changes, however, were noted on only the sheet where the contingency was scheduled; changes on the other sheets did not occur. In Condition 2, when S1 performance was influenced, the pupil's scores on S2 and S3 remained as low as they had been during the base line. When the contingency was arranged for S1 and S2 in Condition 3, her performance on S3 continued to be poor. A further observation based on these data was that performance on S1 and S2 continued at a high level when the withdraw contingency was removed.

As explained earlier, three types of problems were scheduled for this girl.

That these problems were of three different classes was substantiated by the girl's performance. Her mean correct rate in the final condition on the S1 problems (the easiest) was 26.00 responses per minute. Her mean correct rates in this final condition for the S2 and S3 problems were 13.10 and 8.80 (see Table 1). Although her error rates were always zero in the final condition for all sheets, her correct rate means were quite different. By comparison, it should be pointed out that when the percent chart is studied, the girl's scores in the final phase for each type of problem are identical—100%.

Criterion rates for the three classes of problems had been obtained by having a number of normal 12-year-old pupils compute the problems. The correct rate scores of these children were rank ordered, and the 75th percentile score was used as a criterion. This same procedure was used in Experiment I (Study 2) and in Experiment II to determine criterion rates. The criterion rates for S1, S2, and S3 were 12, 8, and 7. The girl's performance in the final condition of this study surpassed those criterion rates.

Study 2

Procedures

The procedures used in this study were similar to those of Study 1. One difference between the two studies was that in Study 2, four classes of problems were presented each day, whereas in Study 1, three classes were used.

Four sheets, each containing 25 problems of a different class, were assigned to the girl daily. S1, S2, and S3 contained problems of the type described in Study 1. S4 contained problems of the type, $453 - 35$. A more complete description of the S1, S2, and S3 classes was presented in Study 1. For the S4 problems, the minuend was from 130 to 998, and the subtrahend from 11 to 79. The differences ranged from 111 to 979. These problems were like those of S2, except for the numeral in the hundreds column. Regrouping was required only in the units column. There were an "infinite" number of problems in this class.

There were several forms for the four classes (S1, S2, S3, S4). The same procedure as in Study 1 was used for distributing the problems on five different sheets. The ordering of the sheets (S1, S2, S3, S4) was similar to that explained earlier.

As in Study 1, the girl timed her performance on each sheet. When finished, she summoned the teacher, who checked the answers, counted the number correct and incorrect, and charted the rates. As in Study 1, the teacher checked the girl's timing on several occasions. For reliability, all the daily sheets and each entry on the scoring sheets was rechecked after the experiments.

During the first 3 weeks of this project, no instructions or feedback were scheduled, nor was a reinforcement contingency arranged. Then, during successive phases, the same recess contingency used in Study 1 was arranged; for every incorrect answer, one minute was taken off recess.

This contingency was initially placed on the S4 problems, since the girl's mean error rate in the base-line phase was highest on that class of problems. Thereafter, the withdraw contingency was successively placed on S1, S2, and S3. In the final condition of the study, the withdraw contingency was involved for all four sheets.

The multiple base-line design used in Study 2 differed from that arranged in Study 1. In the first study, after the base-line period, the contingency was scheduled for one sheet, then for two and then three: It was not removed from one sheet and imposed on another. In Study 2, after the base line, the contingency was imposed on one sheet, then removed from that sheet and placed on another, until the contingency had been placed on each of the sheets, one at a time.

Results

The results of this study will be explained as they were for Study 1. First the data will be presented in terms of percentage, then the data will be described in terms of rate.

At the beginning of Condition 1, which was 3 weeks after the final condition of Study 1, the girl's accuracy from the preceding quarter was maintained. For the first 5 days she missed only two problems on S1, one on S2, none on S3, and two on S4. Her performance, however, began to deteriorate throughout the remainder of the 3-week condition. On the final day of the phase her percent scores on the four sheets were: S1, 52%; S2, 0%; S3, 0%; and S4, 0% (see Fig. 5).

During the second condition, when the withdraw contingency was placed on S4, her performance was promptly influenced. On 5 of the 8 days of this condition, her scores were 100%. Meanwhile, on S1 and S2, her performance throughout the condition generally deteriorated. On S3 during this condition, she scored zero on 7 of 8 days.

In Condition 3, the contingency was placed on the S1 problems. On 3 of 5 days her accuracy was 100%. At the same time her performance was generally poor on the other three sheets: Three of 5 scores on S2 were zero; 5 of 5 were zero on S3; and 2 of 5 were zero on S4.

Throughout Condition 4, the withdraw contingency was arranged for only the S2 problems. Her performance was excellent on this sheet. Accuracy was also quite good on the S1 problems. On the S3 problems, her scores were always zero, while on the S4 sheet her scores were erratic.

During the fifth phase of the study, the contingency was scheduled for the S3 problems. On all 3 days of this condition, her S3 scores were 100%. Meanwhile, her scores on the other sheets were rather poor, except for S1, where she scored 100% on 2 of the 3 days.

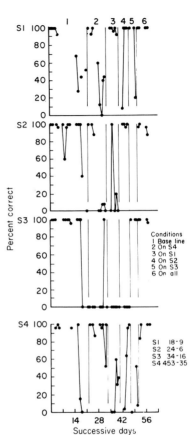

Fig. 5. *Experiment I (Study 2): Percentage of correct scores for four classes of subtraction facts across the six conditions of Study 2.*

Throughout the final condition, the contingency was imposed on all four sheets. During that time very few problems were incorrectly answered: none on S1, 5 on S2, 1 on S3, and 4 on S4.

When response rates were considered, the girl's mean correct and error rates for the four sheets during Condition 1 were as follows: S1, 14.90 and 8.00; S2, 9.21 and 2.65; S3, 5.53 and 1.91; and S4, 8.22 and 10.71. In three of the four cases the error rate standard deviations were higher than those for correct rate (see Table 2 and Figs. 6, 7, 8, and 9).

In Condition 2, her mean correct rate on S4, where the contingency was arranged, nearly doubled from the preceding phase. The mean error rate was .28. On the three other sheets, mean error rates surpassed average correct rates. On S4, error rate standard deviation was much lower than the correct rate score; the opposite was the case on the other three sheets.

TABLE 2
Summary Rate Data for Experiment I (Study 2)

| Condition | | | S1 | | | | | S2 | | | | | S3 | | | | | S4 | | | |
| | | | | Mean | | S.D. | | | Mean | | S.D. | | | Mean | | S.D. | | | Mean | | S.D. | |
No.	Description	N	C	E	C	E	N	C	E	C	E	N	C	E	C	E	N	C	E	C	E
1	Baseline	9	14.90	8.00	6.12	12.15	14	9.21	2.65	6.53	5.00	13	5.53	1.91	3.19	4.62	7	8.22	10.71	5.68	17.96
2	On S4	8	15.53	17.11	10.32	18.49	8	4.96	13.02	6.28	12.09	8	.47	11.35	1.34	5.27	8	14.58	.28	6.46	.44
3	On S1	5	23.44	.63	6.87	.89	5	2.16	18.12	3.30	12.00	5	.00	21.06	.00	10.56	5	7.06	18.94	8.53	11.63
4	On S2	4	17.88	3.05	12.21	6.10	4	9.07	.10	.62	.20	4	.00	26.00	.00	8.30	4	11.47	4.86	8.70	6.43
5	On S3	3	17.90	4.83	12.50	8.37	1	.00	34.00	.00	.00	3	5.46	.00	.80	.00	3	5.60	37.66	6.00	23.43
6	On all	4	22.12	.00	4.03	.00	4	12.87	.64	3.15	.68	4	4.72	.04	.55	.09	4	12.25	.37	4.19	.75

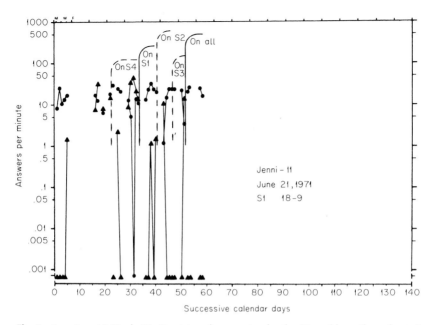

Fig. 6. *Experiment I (Study 2): Correct and error rates for the S1 problems throughout six experimental conditions.*

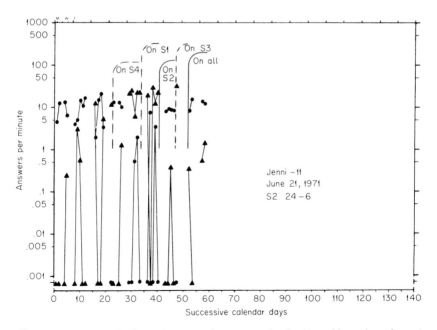

Fig. 7. *Experiment I (Study 2): Correct and error rates for the S2 problems throughout six experimental conditions.*

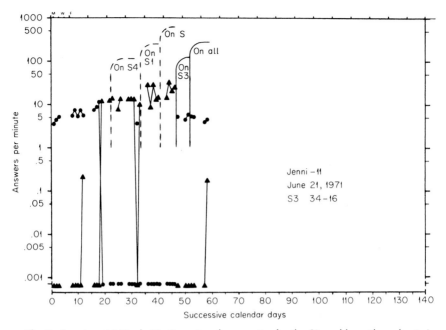

Fig. 8. *Experiment I (Study 2): Correct and error rates for the S3 problems throughout six experimental conditions.*

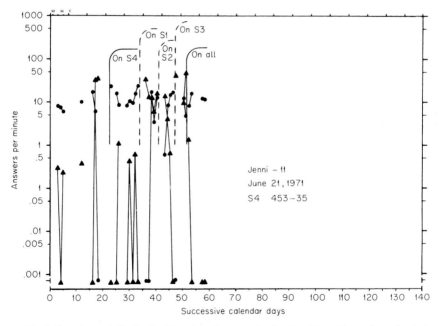

Fig. 9 *Experiment I (Study 2): Correct and error rates for the S4 problems throughout six experimental conditions.*

42

In Condition 3, when the withdraw contingency was arranged for S1, her mean correct and error rates greatly improved from the preceding phase. Meanwhile, mean error rates on the other three sheets were greater than average correct rates. Error rate standard deviation was lower than correct rate standard deviation only on S1.

In Condition 4 (contingency placed on S2), the pupil's mean correct rate on S2 increased by four times from the third condition. Her error rate standard deviation on S2 was lower than for her correct rate. On two of the other sheets, mean correct rates were greater than average error rates. Error rate standard deviations were also lower than for correct rate on two of the other three sheets.

Throughout Condition 5, the contingency was scheduled for S3. Her mean correct rate for those problems changed from .00 in the preceding phase to 5.46, while her mean error rate dropped from 26.00 to .00. During this phase the error rate standard deviation on S4 only was higher than the correct rate equivalent.

During the final phase, where the contingency was arranged on all lists, her mean correct rate performance improved on three of the four sheets from the preceding phase. On S3, where the contingency had been in effect in the preceding phase, her mean correct rate was slightly less. In every case, the error rate standard deviation was lower than for the correct rate.

Discussion

In every instance when the contingency was scheduled, an immediate effect was noted. Successively, as the contingency was imposed, performance on first S4, then S1, S2, and S3 was promptly improved.

During the final phases of Study 1, when the withdraw contingency was removed from S1 and S2, accuracy on those sheets maintained. In fact, when Study 2 began during the summer quarter after a 3-week vacation, the girl's accuracy was very good on the S1, S2, and S3 sheets that were scheduled throughout the spring. Quite a different pattern of behavior was noted in the second study when the contingency was removed. Throughout Study 2, when the contingency was removed from a sheet, performance on that sheet deteriorated. In Condition 3, when the contingency was removed from S4, her mean correct rate not only fell below what it had been in the preceding phase, but below the base-line rate. The data in Condition 5 were very similar when the contingency was removed from S2. Her performance was the poorest it had been throughout the study. Although her mean correct rate for the S1 problems in Condition 4 was less than in the preceding phase when the contingency was removed, her performance was poorer during other conditions.

In this study the criterion rates were: S1, 12; S2, 8; S3, 7; S4, 12. The criterion rates for S1, S2, and S3 were the same as those used in Study 1. During the final phase her mean correct rates for the four types of problems were: S1, 22.12; S2, 12.87; S3, 4.72; S4, 12.25. When the final condition mean scores for S1 and S2 from the two studies were compared, they were very similar. Her mean score on the S3 problems in Study 2 was significantly less, however, than that score during Study 1. All average scores except the S3 were above the criterion rates.

In the second study, these criterion rates were not considered in moving from one condition to another as they were in Study 1. The different experimental conditions were rather arbitrarily scheduled.

EXPERIMENT II

The subject of this study was a 10-year-old boy who had been at the curriculum research classroom of the EEU for 1 academic year. He had been referred to the class because of academic deficiencies from a special education class in the Mercer Island School District.

This experiment was conducted by Debby Smith, a doctoral student at the EEU, University of Washington. The study ran from October, 1970 until the end of spring quarter, June, 1971.

The authors had two purposes for conducting the study: (1) to obtain data about within and across response class generalization; and (2) to gather data regarding the effects of some traditionally used arithmetic teaching aids.

Procedures

Each day the pupil was given several sheets of subtraction problems to perform. $S1^a$ and $S1^b$ contained 20 problems, whereas $S2^a$, $S2^b$, $S3^a$, and $S3^b$ contained 25 problems. A description of these classes of problems was provided in Experiment 1.

For each class, different problems were randomly assigned to one subclass or the other, e.g., $S1^a$ or $S2^b$. Then five different sheets were formed using the same process described in Experiment I. The scheduling of the various sheets within the classes and the order that the different classes were presented was also the same as that described earlier.

Each sheet was separately timed by the pupil. As he began a sheet he started a stopwatch; when he finished, he stopped it. Periodically the manager checked his timing, and the checks indicated that the student was an accurate timer. The pupil wrote the time in minutes and seconds on the top of each page.

When the student completed the sheets, the manager corrected each one. She counted the number of correct and incorrect answers, divided each by the time to complete the sheet, obtained correct and incorrect rate measures, then plotted these rates.

Scoring sheets identical to those described in Experiment I were used in this study. On these were recorded the day and date of the session, number of correct and incorrect answers, time to complete each sheet, correct and error rates, and the percentage correct score. After the study, each entry on these sheets was rechecked.

The pre-experimental strategy was as follows: (1) Obtain base-line measurement from five sheets, two of the class currently being taught, two of the next class, one of the class after that. (2) Schedule a teaching aid with one sheet of the class currently being taught (e.g., $S1^a$) and measure performance on all sheets. Do not associate the aid with the sheet of the same class (e.g., $S1^b$), since one purpose is to measure within-class generalization. (3) Obtain measurements of the "next" response class, to determine the extent of across-class generalization. For example, as the pupil is "taught" the $S1^a$ problems, measurement is obtained on $S2^a$ and $S2^b$, the next class. Moreover, when the focus is on $S2^a$, measurements will be obtained on $S3^a$ and $S3^b$, the class after that. (4) When criterion rates are reached on the sheet where the aid is used (e.g., $S1^a$), withdraw the aid to determine if performance continues at a satisfactory level. (5) If performance is satisfactory, focus attention on the next class of problems (e.g., $S2^a$) and use a different teaching aid with that sheet. At this time, schedule a second sheet of the third class ($S3^b$) in order to obtain within-class generalization for that class of problems. This scheme should be followed through several classes of problems. (6) After criterion on a sheet is reached and instruction is shifted to a different class, measurement will continue to be gathered periodically on the former class of problems. In this way the experimenters will obtain data about retention and will be able to schedule review sessions if the pupil's performance deteriorates.

The criterion correct rates for the six sheets were: $S1^a$ and $S1^b$, 12 per minute; $S2^a$ and $S2^b$, 8 per minute; and $S3^a$ and $S3^b$, 8 per minute. In addition to these correct rate criterion, zero error rates were specified as a part of the performance objective. Criterion performances were defined not only by the rate dimension, correct and incorrect, but by time. Throughout this experiment criterion rates had to be achieved for three consecutive days before a new experimental condition was scheduled.

The study consisted of 11 conditions (see Table 3). Condition 1 was the base line; during this time no instructions, confirmation, or contingencies were scheduled. Throughout the second condition the pupil was given 18 paper clips. Each day, prior to the boy's working the $S1^a$ problems, the manager handed him the clips and gave one example on their use in solving problems. He was shown how, if the problem was $18 - 9 = \square$, to take nine clips away from the pile, then count the remainder. This later figure was the answer.

Although the plan was to have the child use paper clips in Condition 2

TABLE 3

Summary Rate Data for Experment II

| | | S1[a] | | | | | S1[b] | | | | | S2[a] | | | | |
| | | | Mean | | S.D. | | | Mean | | S.D. | | | Mean | | S.D. | |
No.	Description	N	C	E	C	E	N	C	E	C	E	N	C	E	C	E
1	Base line	2	.00	5.83	.00	1.18	2	.00	4.50	.00	.70	3	.00	7.59	.00	1.22
2	Clips on S1[a]	9	5.25	.16	2.27	.20	9	5.50	.14	2.50	.17	9	.41	4.06	.24	1.97
3	Clips off S1[a]	10	13.60	.05	2.20	.17	16	13.28	.18	3.22	.28	14	.10	8.56	.14	3.12
4	Abacus on S2[a]	3	5.10	.00	.95	.00	2	7.05	.00	1.34	.00	9	6.89	.00	2.73	.00
5	Abacus off S2[a]	2	9.95	.39	.50	.22	2	9.20	.22	1.13	.31	8	11.48	.14	6.03	.20
6	Instruct on S1[a]	4	15.07	.00	5.17	.00	4	13.32	.57	3.84	.75	4	10.95	.23	.83	.26
7	Instruct off S1[a]	10	18.53	.12	4.53	.37	10	16.54	.10	5.02	.31	18	12.37	.16	3.39	.28
8	Rods on S3[a]	2	10.40	.00	1.41	.00	1	14.30	.00	.00	.00	6	1.11	14.11	.95	4.06
9	Rods off S3[a]	—	—	—	—	—	—	—	—	—	—					
	Abacus on S2[a]	—	—	—	—	—	—	—	—	—	—	10	3.49	.18	1.86	.26
10	Abacus off S2[a]	—	—	—	—	—	—	—	—	—	—	2	1.80	11.50	.28	4.38
11	Instruct on S2[a]	—	—	—	—	—	—	—	—	—	—	2	7.78	.00	2.14	.00

TABLE 3 (cont.)

No.	Description	S2^b N	S2^b Mean C	S2^b Mean E	S2^b S.D. C	S2^b S.D. E	S3^a N	S3^a Mean C	S3^a Mean E	S3^a S.D. C	S3^a S.D. E	S3^b N	S3^b Mean C	S3^b Mean E	S3^b S.D. C	S3^b S.D. E
1	Base line	3	.00	6.20	.00	2.10	3	.00	4.80	.00	1.21	—	—	—	—	—
2	Clips on S1^a	9	.56	3.93	.26	2.17	9	.00	6.72	.00	2.16	—	—	—	—	—
3	Clips off S1^a	14	1.05	7.23	.43	1.65	14	.00	9.33	.00	3.07	—	—	—	—	—
4	Abacus on S2^a	8	7.08	.09	1.15	.14	8	.00	8.65	.00	2.28	—	—	—	—	—
5	Abacus off S2^a	8	10.28	.12	1.86	.17	8	.00	12.97	.00	2.14	—	—	—	—	—
6	Instruct on S1^a	4	9.47	.00	1.32	.00	4	.00	13.90	.00	1.30	—	—	—	—	—
7	Instruct off S1^a	15	11.65	.07	1.66	.20	19	.00	13.50	.00	1.93	6	.00	15.15	.00	4.71
8	Rods on S3^a	6	1.09	14.75	1.01	6.04	11	1.91	.57	.95	.34	12	.18	6.30	2.79	.22
9	Rods off S3^a / Abacus on S2^a	10	5.77	3.02	2.96	5.44	3	.00	8.80	.00	2.58	1	.00	6.80	.00	.00
10	Abacus off S2^a	2	1.76	11.45	.48	5.72	—	—	—	—	—	—	—	—	—	—
11	Instruct on S2^a	2	7.85	.00	3.60	.00	1	.00	5.75	.00	.00	—	—	—	—	—

until performance criterion (3 consecutive days when the correct rate surpassed 12 and error rate was zero) was reached, the manager of the study believed the clips were inhibiting correct rate performance. The manager speculated that the clips had served their purpose by assisting the boy to master the basic subtraction facts, but were now retarding his speed. Thus the aid was removed prior to his attaining the performance criterion.

Condition 3 was the withdrawal of the clips from S1^a. This condition ran through the autumn quarter, through Christmas vacation, and ended after the first day of winter quarter.

Condition 4 began the second day of the winter quarter. Throughout this condition an abacus was provided to the boy as he worked on the S2^a problems. During this phase, the manager worked one problem for the boy each day, using the abacus. He used the aid only on the S2^a problems. The correct rate criterion on these problems was 8 per minute. As was the case with the S1^a problems, the manager felt that the aid had served its purpose and after several sessions was inhibiting the boy's speed. The abacus, therefore, was removed before the correct rate criterion had been achieved.

In Condition 5, the abacus was removed from the S2^a problems. Although during this time the boy's performance on the S2^a problems reached criterion, his accuracy on the S1^a problems began to deteriorate. Throughout Condition 6, therefore, attention was refocused on that sheet. Each day, before he worked on these problems, instructions were provided. The instructions comprised the following steps. First, the manager wrote out a problem like 18 − 9. Second, she asked the pupil to say the answer. If he answered correctly she said "good"; if not, she told him the answer. Third, she asked if he needed to cross out anything (to borrow). If he answered correctly, she said "good"; if he said that it was necessary, she explained why it was not. In a short time, he again reached criterion rates on the S1^a problems.

In Condition 7, the instructions were no longer used for the S1^a problems. In Condition 8, cuisinare rods were given the boy while he worked on the S3^a problems. Although his performance on the S3^a problems improved, his performance on the S2^a problems began to worsen. In Condition 9, therefore, the rods were taken off the S3^a problems and the abacus was again given the child as he worked on the S2^a problems.

During Condition 10 the abacus was removed from S2^a. His performance was adversely affected; therefore, the final phase of the study was initiated. At this time instructions were provided for the S2^a problems. Instructions consisted of the following. First, the teacher wrote out a problem of the type, 24 − 6. Second, she asked the pupil to solve it. If he was successful, she said "good"; if not, she computed the problem for him. Third, she asked the pupil to explain the borrowing process (cross out 2, replace it with 1, place 1 by 4). If he could comply, she said "good"; if not, she explained the steps. Further conditions would have been run, but the school term ended.

Results

A table and two sets of charts are used to explain the data of this study. Table 3 contains summary data from the 11 conditions of the study. Included in the table is a label for each condition, the number of days each condition ran (N); mean correct and error rates, and correct and error rate standard deviations. These data are provided for the six sheets of problems used in the study.

One set of charts describes the data from each sheet of problems in terms of percentage. The reader will recall that the first two sheets of problems, S1ᵃ and S1ᵇ, contained 20 problems. Therefore, each problem had a value of five percentage points. Sheets S2ᵃ, S2ᵇ, S3ᵃ, and S3ᵇ contained 25 problems. On those sheets each problem was equal to four percentage points.

All six percentage charts are shown together so that the reader can view the data on all charts simultaneously throughout the 11 conditions. Thus the reader can study such matters as within- and between-class generalization (see Fig. 10).

The second set of charts refers to rate—correct and error. One chart for each sheet of problems is provided (see Figures 11, 12, 13, 14, 15, and 16).

The data will be discussed first in terms of percentage, then in terms of rate.

In the first condition, the pupil's percent correct scores were zero on all five sheets. In Condition 2, when the paper clips were provided for S1ᵃ, his performance on that set of problems greatly improved. Throughout that condition, he missed no more than one problem a day on S1ᵃ. Similarly, his performance was excellent on the S1ᵇ problems. Meanwhile, on the S2ᵃ problems his performance only improved slightly from the base-line phase. Scores throughout this phase ranged from 4 to 72%; most were 4 or 8%. On S2ᵇ his scores ranged from zero to 40%; his median percentage score was 12. His scores on S3ᵃ were always zero.

During Condition 3, when the paper clips were no longer provided for S1ᵃ, his performance continued to be excellent. On 10 of 12 days his scores were 100% on S1ᵃ. On 14 of 18 days in this same phase, his scores were 100% on S1ᵇ. However, his scores on S2ᵃ deteriorated from the previous phase. On 8 of 14 days his scores were zero. On S2ᵇ, his scores ranged from 8 to 16%. All scores on S3ᵃ in this condition continued to be zero.

In Condition 4, an abacus was given the boy as he worked on the S2ᵃ figures. His scores were 100%, 9 of 9 times in that phase. On the companion sheet, S2ᵇ, his scores were generally perfect throughout the phase. His performance on the S1ᵃ and S1ᵇ problems throughout this phase continued to be good. S3ᵃ scores were all zero.

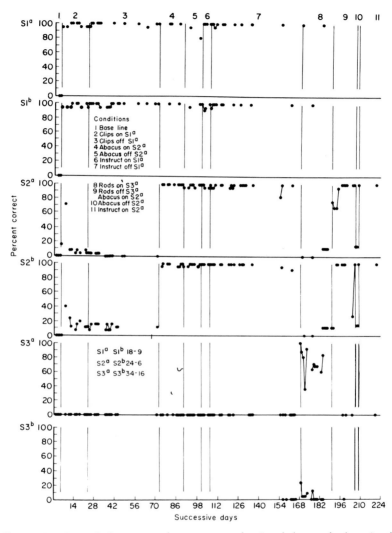

Fig. 10. *Experiment II: Percentage of correct scores for six subclasses of subtraction facts for 11 experimental conditions.*

In the fifth phase the abacus aid was withdrawn from S2ᵃ. On 5 of the 8 days in that condition his performance continued to be 100% on the S2ᵃ problems. On S2ᵇ his scores were also 100% in five of eight sessions. On the 2 days his performance was measured on S1ᵃ, his scores were 95 and 80%. On S1ᵇ they were 95 and 100%. All S3ᵃ, scores were zero.

During Condition 6, the focus was once more on S1ᵃ. Now, instructions were provided daily prior to his working the S1ᵃ problems. His four scores during that phase on the instructed sheet were all 100%. On S1ᵇ no more

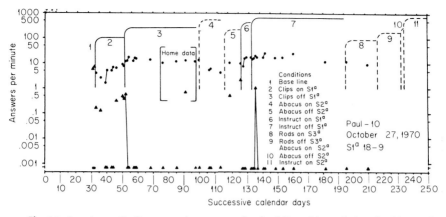

Fig. 11. *Experiment II: Correct and error rates for the S1ᵃ problems during the 11 experimental conditions.*

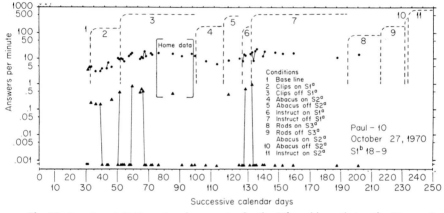

Fig. 12. *Experiment II: Correct and error rates for the S1ᵇ problems during the 11 experimental conditions.*

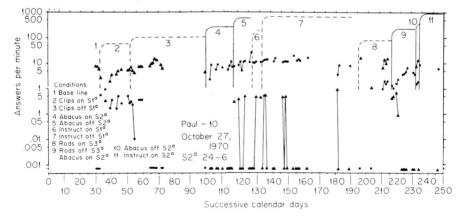

Fig. 13. *Experiment II: Correct and error rates for the S2ᵃ problems throughout the 11 experimental conditions.*

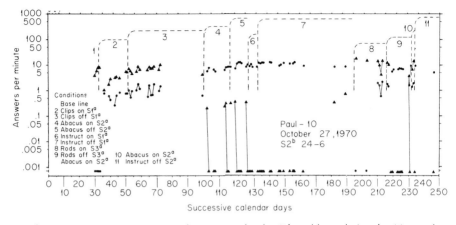

Fig. 14. *Experiment II: Correct and error rates for the S2^b problems during the 11 experimental conditions.*

than two problems were incorrect on a day. Meanwhile, on S2^a and S2^b his scores were generally 100%. Once more, all S3^a scores were zero.

In Condition 7, the instructions were removed from S1^a. All but one of his S1^a scores were 100% throughout this phase. The same was true for his S1^b scores. On S2^a his scores were 100% for 13 of 18 sessions. They were 100% for 13 of 15 sessions for S2^b. Throughout this phase all scores on the S3^a and S3^b problems were zero.

During Condition 8, instruction was centered on S3^a. Throughout this phase, as the boy worked on the S3^a problems, he was given a set of cuisinare rods to use. He was instructed in the use of the rods and given one ex-

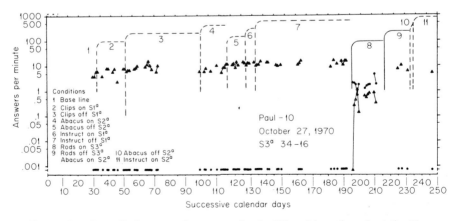

Fig. 15. *Experiment II: Correct and error rates for the S3^a problems throughout the 11 experimental conditions.*

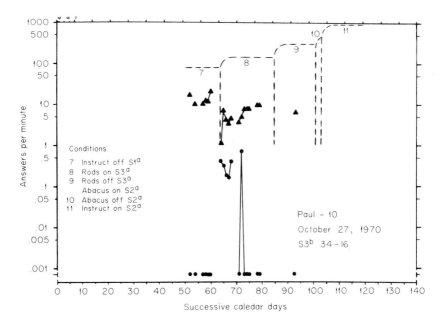

Fig. 16. Experiment II: Correct and error rates for the S3[b] problems for five experimental conditions.

ample each day. On the first day of that phase, his S3[a] score was 100%; thereafter, his accuracy varied. His scores ranged from 36 to 100% with a median percentage of 72. On S3[b] his scores ranged from zero to 24%, his first-day score. His two scores on S1[a] and one score on S1[b] were 100% in this phase. Meanwhile, on S2[a] and S2[b], his scores were drastically reduced from the previous phase. For the first 2 days of Condition 8, his scores were zero on both sheets. During the next 4 days, he answered only three problems correctly on both sheets each day.

Since performance on S2[a] worsened in Condition 8, the focus throughout Condition 9 was again on that sheet. The rods were withdrawn from S3[a] in this phase, and the abacus was once again given to the lad as he worked the S2[a] problems. His percent scores on S2[a] increased steadily in this phase, and on the final six sessions his scores were all 100%. Although 3 poor days were noted regarding his S2[b] performance, his scores were 100% on 7 of 10 days. Measurements were not taken on S1[a] and S1[b] during this phase. On S3[a] and S3[b] his scores returned again to zero.

During Condition 10, the abacus was once more removed from S2[a]. This condition ran only two days, since the pupil's accuracy was very poor. Only four problems were answered correctly on both days on S2[a] and S2[b]. No measurement was obtained for the S3[a] and S3[b] problems in that condition.

In the final phase, the focus returned to $S2^a$, and instructions were provided daily prior to his answering those problems. During that brief phase his scores on $S2^a$ and $S2^b$ were all 100%. On $S3^a$, measurement was obtained only once; that score was zero.

In regard to response rate, the Condition 1 correct rates for all sheets were zero; whereas the mean error rates across the sheets ranged from 4.50 to 7.59. During Condition 2, the boy's mean correct rate on $S1^a$, where paper clips were used, was 5.25. The mean correct and error rates on $S1^a$ and $S1^b$ were nearly identical in that phase. His mean error rates declined on $S2^a$ and $S2^b$ and rose on $S3^a$.

In Condition 3, where the paper clips were removed from $S1^a$, his mean correct rate performance on $S1^a$ and $S1^b$ more than doubled. On $S2^a$ the mean correct rate decreased and the mean error rate increased. On $S2^b$ both mean rates increased. Error rate continued to increase on $S3^a$.

In Condition 4, the focus was on $S2^a$. Now, as may be noted (Table 3), his mean correct and error rates on $S2^a$ and $S2^b$ virtually reversed. On $S1^a$ and $S1^b$, although the pupil's scores were 100%, his mean correct rate dropped considerably from the preceding phase. Mean error rate performance on $S3^a$ dropped slightly.

When the abacus was pulled off $S2^a$, the boy's mean correct rates on $S2^a$ and $S2^b$ accelerated. Mean correct rates also increased for $S1^a$ and $S1^b$. Meanwhile, on $S3^a$ his mean error rate reached 12.97 incorrect problems per minute.

In Condition 6, when the focus was again on $S1^a$, his correct rates rose to a point they had been during Phase 3 and, in addition, his mean error rate on $S1^a$ fell to zero. On $S2^a$ and $S2^b$, his mean correct and error rates remained about the same as in the preceding phase. Error rates on $S3^a$ continued to increase.

In Condition 7 (instruction removed from $S1^a$), mean correct rates on $S1^a$, $S1^b$, $S2^a$, and $S2^b$ all reached their respective highs. Across the four sheets, these mean rates ranged from 11.65 to 18.53. The boy's mean error rates on $S3^a$ and $S3^b$ were 13.50 and 15.15 incorrect problems per minute. It should also be pointed out that correct rate standard deviation scores on the first four sheets were very high during this phase.

In Condition 8, the pupil's mean correct rate for the $S3^a$ problems was 1.91 problems per minute, while his average error rate was greatly reduced. On $S3^b$ his mean correct and incorrect rates were .18 and 6.30. On $S1^a$ and $S1^b$, his mean correct rates fell. On $S2^a$ and $S2^b$, his mean correct and error rates virtually switched from the preceding phase.

Another observation that could be made regarding $S2^a$ and $S2^b$ performance at this time is that during Phases 7 and 8, the total mean response rate (correct plus error) for the two lists was nearly identical, although his performance was far superior, in both cases, during Condition 7 than during Condition 8. During Condition 7, his total response rates for S2[a] and S3[b] were 12.53 and 11.72. During Condition 8, they were 15.22 and 15.84.

In Condition 9, the abacus was reinstated for S2[a], and the rods taken away from S3[a]. Performance on these two lists was immediately influenced. His mean correct rate increased and mean error rate decreased for S2[a] (also for S2[b]), while the opposite occurred for S3[a].

The last two conditions were concerned with S2[a] and S2[b]. No S1[a], S1[b], or S3[b] measures were taken, and only one was obtained for S3[a]. In Condition 10 (abacus removed from S2[a]), his S2[a] and S2[b] performances were immediately and seriously retarded. When instruction was scheduled for S2[a] in the final phase, however, his performance on those and the companion problems was once again excellent.

Discussion

In several instances, within-class generalization was noted. Regarding S1[a] and S1[b], when, in the second condition, attention was directed toward the S1[a] problems, the boy's performance improved not only on that sheet but also on S1[b]. Within-class generalization also occurred in Condition 6 when the teaching focus was again on S1[a].

Within-class generalization was also noted when the focus was on S2[a]. In Condition 4, when the aid was given while working on the S2[a] problems, not only was the accuracy on those items positively influenced, but the boy's performance on S2[b] similarly improved.

Within-class generalization between S2[a] and S2[b] was again noted in Condition 9, when the abacus was, for the second time, offered the lad while he worked on the S2[a] problems. In Condition 11, such generalization was noted for a third time. A modest amount of within-class generalization occurred in Condition 8. When attention was focused on S3[a], some slight improvement was noted on the S3[b] items.

Meanwhile, little, if any, across-class generalization was observed. As the pupil's performance on S1[a] and S1[b] improved in Condition 2, his performance on S2[a] and S2[b] was only slightly influenced. No change was noted on S3[a], the third class of problems. Similarly, in Conditions 4, 9, and 11, when performance on S2[a] and S2[b] was influenced, accuracy on S3[a] and S3[b] was unaltered.

A similar finding—the inability of a pupil to generalize across classes of mathematics problems—was noted by Lovitt and Curtiss (1968). That study comprised three experiments, each dealing with a different class of subtraction problems. In the first phase of Experiment I, it was noted that the child's accuracy was poor. In Condition 2, he verbalized the problems before writing the answers. This proved to be an effective technique. In the final condition, he was not required to verbalize the problems. Accuracy was maintained in that phase. Experiment II was then begun, and a different class of problems was used. During the base line his performance was again poor; he didn't generalize from the previous experiment. The same verbalization technique was successfully used, then withdrawn. When the third experiment began his performance was again very poor; once more he had failed to generalize across classes of problems.

Throughout the experiment, three teaching aids were used. In Condition 1 paper clips were used on the S1ᵃ problems; in Conditions 3 and 9 an abacus was given to the pupil as he worked on the S2ᵃ problems. Cuisinare rods were given to the lad in Condition 8 as he worked on the S3ᵃ problems. There were effects in every case. It should be further noted that in two instances when the aid was removed in a phase following the use of the instructional device, the boy's performance continued to be excellent. In Condition 3, when the paper clips were removed from S1ᵃ, and in Condition 5 when the abacus was withdrawn from S2ᵃ, his performance held up. In fact, it can be observed that the pupil's correct rate in the removal phase in these two instances was higher than when the aid was scheduled.

Performance, however, did not hold up when the abacus was removed from the S2ᵃ problems in Condition 10. At that time, correct rate fell and error rate rose. Also, performance did not hold for the S3ᵃ problems when the rods were removed in Condition 9.

In addition to the three teaching aids that were used, instruction was scheduled for two sheets of problems. In Condition 6, instruction was provided for the S1ᵃ problems; instruction was also used in Condition 11 for the S2ᵃ problems. In both situations the effects were positive. Only in the first instance was the instruction removed in a subsequent phase. In Condition 7, when instruction was no longer used for the S1ᵃ problems, the boy's accuracy remained at the level achieved in the previous phase. Since a quarter ended during Condition 11, when instruction was arranged for S2ᵃ problems, there was no opportunity to withdraw the instruction, hence evaluate its effect on those problems.

A form of interference was noted during Condition 8 of the study. At that time attention was focused on S3ᵃ. The pupil was given cuisinare rods to use as he calculated those problems. The teacher had keyed on the S3ᵃ problems, since mastery had been reached on the other problems. During this phase, although some improvement was noted on the S3ᵃ problems, his accuracy on S2ᵃ problems greatly deteriorated. S3ᵃ problems were like $34 - 26 = \square$; whereas the S2ᵃ problems were like $24 - 6 = \square$.

On the S2ᵃ and S2ᵇ problems in this condition, the boy began to make two types of errors. One form of error was the same as that noted in Condition 1: He borrowed in reverse. Occasionally, his answer to a problem like

24 – 6 would be 22. The other type of error was more complex. He would borrow from the tens column and then subtract in reverse. When this type error was committed, his answer to the problem 24 − 6 would be 12. When teaching was again directed toward the S2[a] problems, he quickly ceased making either type of error.

Of some interest in this study was the data kept by a parent. Since the experimenters desired to continue the study throughout the winter quarter but were concerned that the gains noted in the fall quarter might deteriorate during the Christmas vacation, one of the managers taught the boy's mother to administer two of the math sheets at home. She taught the mother to schedule the sheets, give the boy clips to use while calculating the S1[a] problems, count the number of his correct and incorrect answers after he was finished, time his performance, calculate correct and incorrect rates, and plot the data. On four occasions during the Christmas vacation, the mother obtained data on S1[a] and S1[b]. In the figures, these "home data" are bracketed and are so labeled. An inspection of these data reveal that his rates at home on the two subclasses of problems were about the same as they had been at school.

The general procedures used throughout this project have implications for teaching as well as research. Sometimes this is not the case. In many research studies the primary interest is the analysis of a single independent variable or the investigation of a component of the learning process, such as discrimination or generalization. Ordinarily, the intent of research is not to validate or design a strategy through which the subject matter could be systematically taught.

This research was concerned with generalization. As previously discussed, the design was set up so that data regarding within- and across-class generalizations were obtained. The design used throughout this study is also compatible with educational purposes. First of all, three classes of problems were generally scheduled. These classes could be described by the temporal interest in their development—current, past, future. When instruction was focused on the S2 class of problems, those were of *current* concern. Measurements were also being obtained on the S1 class of problems. Since they had previously been mastered, they were the *past* problems. By obtaining measurements on past problems, the examiners were able to study retention. In addition, measurements were being obtained on the S3 class of problems, those that would be taught next. Thus measures on *future* problems were being gathered. By obtaining data on the future sheets, the examiners were able to study across-class generalization.

Two sets of current problems were scheduled, one where instruction was focused, the other where only measurements were obtained. Such a scheme allowed the experimenters to study within-class generalization.

In this experiment, daily measurements were obtained on the current and future sheets, while intermittent measurements were gathered from the past sheets. For reasons of economy, teachers could measure only the current sheets on a daily basis and obtain intermittent measurements on the past and future sheets.

Another procedural feature of this experiment was that checkpoints used for making programming decisions were established. Often in classrooms, such points are lacking, hence decisions are made rather arbitrarily. The decision points in this study were based on criterion or normative rates. The derivation of these rates has been explained previously. Criterion rates could certainly be obtained in ways other than the method used for these experiments. Unless, however, they are obtained and used, the scheduling of classes of problems, moving from one response class to another, could be rather capricious.

One checkpoint in this study indicated when to stop using a teaching aid. In certain phases of the study, a teaching aid was used by the pupil as he worked a specific sheet. This aid was used until criterion rates were reached, then removed. (Exceptions to this and the rationale for the exceptions have been explained earlier.) A second checkpoint was in the condition following the withdrawal of the teaching aid. This phase was to run until criterion was achieved without the aid; then the instructional focus would be on a new set of problems.

Other checkpoints dealt with past problems. Since performance on the previously learned problems was periodically measured, the manager could tell when performance began to deteriorate and when review was necessary. The pre-experiment plan was that if either correct or error rate deviated from the criterion rates for 2 successive days while being reviewed, attention would be redirected to those problems. This plan was followed for S1[a] in Condition 5. Attention was also redirected to S2[a], but not as soon as it should have been. Review should have been scheduled in Condition 7 after 2 high error rate days were noted. The next time 2 successive poor performance days occurred was early in Condition 8.

Future research could extend the strategy used here and attempt to provide other checkpoints. For example, a system could be devised that would inform the teacher when to shift from one form of remediation to another. The research here merely indicated when to move from one class of problems to another at the time criterion was reached. A more sophisticated scheme would inform the teacher when, prior to reaching criterion rates, she should do something. In other words, a system could be developed which suggested that if the correct rate or error rate was not at a specified level, the current instructional technique should be replaced by a different teaching procedure.

In summary, the procedures used in this study to research aspects of the generalization process could be adopted by teachers to instruct basic computation skills. Although the skill measured in this study was subtraction, similar procedures could be used with the other three arithmetic processes. Research is under way at the curriculum research classroom with all four computational processes.

GENERAL DISCUSSION

In these experiments the data were presented in two ways, percentage and rate. A few comments will be made about the relative ease of reading percentage and rate charts and the type of information revealed in either form.

Percentage charts are perhaps easier for most people to understand, if for no other reason than that they are more frequently used. They are often kept by teachers to evaluate spelling and reading comprehension performance.

Percentage is finite; the entirety of anything is equal to 100%. Therefore, one half equals 50%; one fourth equals 25%. In order to calculate a percentage score, two figures are required: number possible and number observed (percent = number observed ÷ number possible).

Although only one percentage score is reported, either the number observed or the number not observed (in academic terms, either correct or incorrect), a reciprocal is implied. For example, if the pupil's correct percentage is 80, his error percentage is 20. As either percentage, correct or incorrect, goes up, the other goes down. Percentage, when used to explain academic performance, provides an index of quality.

Rate is a less common measurement than percent. Occasionally, teachers use rate to chart silent reading and typing performance. To calculate rate, two figures are required—the frequency of the responses and the time to execute those responses (rate = frequency ÷ time). Traditionally, when rate is used, a single rate is plotted. For silent reading, the rate includes *all* words "read," whether correctly or incorrectly perceived. For typing, the rate is based only on the correctly formed words. In the charts used in these experiments, correct *and* error rates have been plotted simultaneously. With this information, the interpreter of the data knows the speed at which correct and incorrect responses have been made.

When correct and error rates are simultaneously plotted, the interpreter is furnished with a third figure in addition to learning the speed at which both types of responses were made. The relationship of the two rates, correct and incorrect, provides a percentage of correct responding. If the two rates are totaled for a given day and divided into that day's correct rate, a percentage correct score is revealed. Thus when two rates are concurrently plotted, three figures of descriptive data are provided, two relating to speed or efficiency, the other to quality. Percentage charts, by contrast, supply only the qualitative dimension of performance.

This difference is quite apparent in the rate and percentage charts that are included here. If, for example, the reader compares the rate and percentage charts for the S1[a] problems in Conditions 4 and 6 (Experiment II), he will see that, on the percentage chart, the boy's scores were identical in both phases! Every score in the two phases is 100. By contrast, if the reader examines the rate data for the same problems throughout the same two conditions, he will see that while the pupil's error rates were zero for every session, his correct rates in Condition 6 were, on the average, three times faster than during Condition 4. Such differences between percentage and rate are obvious during other conditions for other sheets throughout the experiments.

Another difference between rate and percentage should be pointed out. As mentioned earlier, when correct percentage is given, incorrect percentage is implied, since the two equal 100%. Thus, the two scores are reciprocal; as one goes up, the other goes down. This is not true for correct and incorrect rates. Either rate is free to vary, independent of the other. Throughout several days, for example, correct rates may all be the same, whereas error rates might steadily decline. Dozens of other rate combinations are possible, since one rate is not dependent on the other.

When rates are used to specify behavioral objectives, a more sophisticated performance criteria can be described than if only percent is used. As the reader will recall, the performance criteria throughout the studies called for zero error rate. In other words, 100% accuracy was expected. Such a specification of terminal performance is standard (Mager, 1962). However, when correct rate is also used to specify performance criteria, a different dimension is added: The matter of proficiency is considered. If we again consider the fourth and sixth conditions of the rate chart for S1[a], it is apparent that the pupil was more proficient in Condition 6 than in Condition 4. Thus, if the dimensions of proficiency and quality are both to be considered when behavioral objectives are detailed, specifications concerning both correct and incorrect rates must be made.

This type of goal specification certainly allows for more flexibility than if percent is used. For if percent is used to describe terminal performance and 100% is the top score, no score could be higher. When correct rates are used to specify objectives, a ceiling is not always imposed. Only in cases where performance is controlled by some feature of the program or where certain physiological factors inhibit speed would there be upper limits. Throughout this study, depending on the class of problems, correct rate criteria differed.

A primary objective of this research was to point out that two remediation strategies are available for altering behavior (specifically, behavior in subtraction): programmed and arranged events. As suggested in the introduction, teachers should develop expertise in scheduling both; for if they rely on one set of events more than the other, they are probably less effective teachers than they could be. It was also suggested in the introduction that the professional teacher would be the one who could best discriminate student performance to determine whether arranged or programmed events would be more appropriate. This research suggests some pupil behaviors to consider in deciding whether to use a programmed or arranged event and whether to establish a noncontingent or contingent relationship.

First of all, a careful error analysis is required before a functional remediation program can be incorporated. A mere counting of the responses, correct and incorrect, will not generally inform the manager which instructional technique he should enlist. In the first experiment, the girl's errors followed no apparent order, except that occasionally she wrote down answers in consecutive order, e.g., 22, 23, 24. It was also noted that occasionally she erred on none of her problems. The first observation, that sometimes she simply wrote numbers in order, indicated that she was not making mistakes because of some misunderstanding. The second observation, that at times she could be accurate, signified that she could be precise when it appeared profitable to do so. On the basis of these observations, it was hypothesized that she would be amenable to arranged-event-therapy. As for the selection of an arranged event, it was decided to use recess time, since earlier in the year she had been required to earn recess by her performance in reading and this contingency had proved effective. In Experiment I, minutes were taken away contingent on errors, whereas in the reading study they were given contingent on correct answers.

In Experiment II, an error analysis in Condition I revealed that the boy subtracted in reverse. Consistently, for example, his answer to $13 - 5$ was 12, and invariably his answer to the problem $12 - 8$ was 16. In the units column, he subtracted the top numeral from the bottom numeral and brought the numeral in the tens column down—a type of mistake commonly made by children.

Unlike the girl in Experiment I, this pupil's mistakes were predictable. He had his own rule which, although consistently applied, was faulty. Other studies had been conducted with this lad where programmed events such as simple instructions were functional in altering his behavior. In a reading study, for example, when he was told simply to "read a little faster," he generally did. Thus this boy seemed a good candidate for some programmed event.

To conclude, teachers must acutely and consistently observe and analyze the behavioral patterns of children in order to prescribe the most effective instructional technique. They must be informed about the speed (or proficiency) and quality of the performance; about pupil error patterns that could be caused by erroneous rules; and, of course, about the motivational system of the child (which events or circumstances are reinforcing to him).

Often, if the effort to determine the most effective instructional technique is precisely administered, if the diagnosis focuses on exact components of a pupil's behavior, designing or selecting an instructional technique is, if not obvious, rather simple. Many times, if the diagnosis has consisted of a systematic appraisal of the important elements of pupil behavior, the pupil will "tell" the manager which instructional plan to follow. Some aspect of his performance will clearly inform the teacher as to which tactic to schedule.

The teaching procedures used in these two experiments were quite simple. In Experiment I, a rudimentary 1:1 withdraw contingency was arranged; in Experiment II, some fundamental instructional aids were programmed. Such techniques are available to all teachers; little expense is involved. In fact, although in Experiment II, the manager purchased the abacus, she made the cuisinare rods from scrap lumber. In addition, the administration of the techniques used in these experiments is rather straightforward. The teacher desiring to use the instructional events discussed here would merely need to be systematic in the involvement of the techniques; he would not need to read a complex instructional manual or attend an expensive workshop.

We believe that efforts should be directed toward the simplification of all instructional components—designing direct methods for diagnosis, devising uncomplicated procedures for instruction, developing functional routines for evaluation—instead of proposing highly complex and erudite educational systems. If such a Populist approach toward education is followed, more people will be able to teach; hence more individuals will learn.

REFERENCES

Lovitt, T. C., & Curtiss, K. A. Effects of manipulating an antecedent event on mathematics response rate. *Journal of Applied Behavior Analysis,* 1968, **1**, 329–333.

Mager, R. F. *Preparing instructional objectives.* Palo Alto, Calif.: Fearon Publishing, 1962.

Smith, D.D., Lovitt, T.C., & Kidder, J.D. Using reinforcement contingencies and teaching aids to alter subtraction performance of children with learning disabilities. In G. Semb (Ed.), *Behavior analysis and education.* Lawrence, Kansas: Univ. of Kansas Press, 1972.

Case History of
a Behavior-Modification Project
in a Public School

DAVID PHILLIPS

The project described here began in 1968 and lasted for 3 years. It was a demonstration project, not an experiment in the usual sense of the term.

The main objectives of the project were (1) to redesign the "special education" program so as to accelerate the rate of progress of these students and to place them back into "normal classrooms," (2) to individualize instructional materials for an entire elementary school, and (3) to retrain the teachers, using a behavior modification approach.

Many educational innovations have been tested in "lab schools" or other rarified environments. Many of these have demonstrated success in meeting their objectives. These settings do not contain all of the variables that impede change in public schools. Thus the final pragmatic test of a program is to attempt its implementation in a public school. This approach assumes that operating outside of the "lab school" system ultimately will be less effective.

The project was conducted in a public elementary school containing 750 children, grades kindergarten through sixth. In addition, the school contained approximately 75 ''special education'' children who had been diagnosed as (1) socially maladjusted, (2) emotionally disturbed, or (3) retarded.

Our approach to retraining a teacher was to find a teacher who apparently had a very aversive classroom situation, a complete lack of control, and no relief in sight. Assistance was offered in the form of an aide (a person trained in behavior modification). This offer was accepted and, in about a week, the teacher of this class (third grade special education) was asking for instruction and more help. She was enthusiastic about what she saw, not about what was offered.

Using fairly standard (and not very efficient) training techniques of didactic instruction and on-the-job training, this formerly frustrated teacher was gaining precision in her control of the class and beginning to have the time to teach. The basic principles we taught and demonstrated were positive and negative reinforcement, extinction, punishment, fading, shaping, stimulus control, and scheduling. The outline of studies completed by teachers is presented in the appendix.

SPECIAL EDUCATION

The area of special education is an extremely important facet of public education. Many standard public school approaches to this problem have had large effects on the school but little effect on the learner. Complex classification systems have been introduced with the hope that this would somehow lead to remedial procedures. Unfortunately this has not always occurred. In some states it is profitable to classify, i.e., label, a child as disabled in some way. The state reimburses the school district for the child's teacher, and far too often the program offered is worse than the standard or normal program. One of the obvious weaknesses is the self-fulfilling prophecy aspect! This child has a problem and we cannot expect as much from him so we will not teach as much, and sure enough, he doesn't learn as much. Another weakness in the system is that all too often it is an excuse for a teacher who merely is unwilling to spend the extra time and hard work with the problem child. The teacher has the child tested, a staff meeting is held, and eventually the child is removed from her room. Sure enough, it helps the teacher, but what does it do for the child? Another very serious problem is the quality of many learning disability programs. Many of these are understaffed, lack trained personnel, or simply function as baby-sitting programs. Little effort is made to build a solid educational program based on empirically derived principles, beginning with the empirically determined entering skills of the child, relative to the academic program being used.

Problem

Our project attempted to overcome some of these traditional problems in a public elementary school in a financially feasible manner. The main objective was to prevent rather than remediate learning problems, and the program used a distinct behavioral approach in restructuring the procedures. The school population was primarily lower middle class in composition. One of the first objectives of the program was to accelerate the progress of special education children, who had been grouped together in a "special education" class, so that they could be phased back into the normal system.

Another basic assumption of our program was that when children do not learn, it is because they have not been taught. Instead of looking for learning problems, we looked for teaching problems: What were we doing wrong? The more traditional approach was, What is wrong with the child? With a few exceptions it was felt that most learning disabilities were a function of previous teaching disabilities.

There was little interest in standardized diagnostic tests or in labeling the students. Instead, when a child demonstrated a learning or social problem, we attempted to remedy that specific deficiency directly. We made no inferences about hypothetical internal malfunctions, feeling this was of little value because the teacher can only work with observable events and external stimuli, no matter what the hypothesized internal problem.

The special education teachers in the school were given training in a seminar on the use of behavioral principles in an educational setting and on-the-job training, which was much more effective. The special education class of problem children was placed on a point system, where each child's improvements in academic and social behavior earned points that were redeemable for privileges and goodies at the classroom "store." This was done to immediately reinforce and strengthen desirable changes in children's behavior. The educational materials in reading, language, and mathematics were individualized by the teacher or purchased. Advancement was contingent on demonstrated mastery of each step.

One of the major questions that is usually not considered is, What, specifically, are the skills that should be taught? In our remedial situation, the answer depended on the subject being taught in the classroom. We would teach specific skills in which the child was having difficulty or teaching precurrent behaviors in which the child's deficiency prevented him from progressing.

Before the project began, the behavior of the special education children was such that regular classroom teachers would not readily accept them as students in their classes. After approximately 12 weeks in our new program, the students had improved to the point where they were acceptable to the normal classroom teachers. They were then phased into normal classrooms and placed by age so that they were with their peers. Approximately 10% of the school population (75 students) could be classified in the various categories of special education used in public schools. The categories in our "normal" classroom ranged from Downs syndrome to psychotic, with many other classifications in between. The most prominent was the so-called socially maladjusted. Our subjective opinion was that, with the exception of a few, they were behavior-problem children who for the most part were academically retarded. This was the main criterion for their placement into special classrooms.

The former special education teachers then began a new supportive services center where all children in need of academic help could be referred for 45-minute blocks of time each day. These services were not restricted to "labeled" children, as was formerly the case. A paraprofessional was hired and trained to assist the two teachers. Each teacher could refer any three children at any one time for these services. If a teacher felt she had more than three children who needed help, she had to decide on the three most needy. The teacher then had only to specify what the problem was. Arrangements were made to tutor the child during the period when the child was involved with the problem material.

The supportive services center was a regular classroom that had been divided into separate small areas with bookcases, bulletin boards, etc. The students were tutored individually or in small groups, depending on their particular deficit or their progress in tutoring. The objective was to accelerate them as quickly as possible and phase out the tutoring so that other children could be served. The materials used in the center were mainly the same materials the children were using in the room.

If reading behavior is regarded as complex operant behavior (i.e., under the control of its consequences) then the general strategy for remediating reading deficiencies is to identify the specific responses that need strengthening (or weakening) under specific stimulus conditions followed by specific consequences. This would hold true for mathematics, also.

One of the major problems was finding functional reinforcers for the children. That is, we needed some consequent stimulus event that would increase the rate of the response it followed. Edibles were used with some children, but social reinforcers and reinforcing events were the main classes of reinforcers used. Points were immediately dispensed in the form of marks on a piece of paper, and these were turned in at the end of the period for the back-up reinforcers mentioned earlier.

The point system was adjusted for each child. In some cases where certain precurrent skills have not been mastered, materials were programmed on the spot to teach these skills. In all cases the objective was to get the children to work as independently as possible. The tutoring center worked with up to 65 children per day. The academic program in reading and math for the entire school has been changed from a traditional textbook approach to an individualized format. The reading materials from the first grade begin with the Sullivan Programmed Readers and progress into the Individually Prescribed Instruction (IPI) reading program through the sixth grade. The math program is the IPI program from grades 1 through 6. The individualization of the curriculum for the entire school played a large role in remediating and preventing learning problems. The teacher's role changed from purveying information to the class to tutoring children who had difficulty. This allowed us to place *academically* retarded students in a class without creating difficulties for the teacher. This gave the teacher time to work with individuals who really needed her attention.

This program has been helpful in overcoming most of the teaching problems in the school. Not all problems have been solved, certainly, but the school has been able to reduce greatly the number of children who were functional nonreaders and eliminate the need to group problem children together.

Standardized achievement tests have not been used in an attempt to evaluate the program. Rather, data on individual children and the percentage of time they spend "on task" has been collected under several conditions. For the purposes of this paper, I will not present individual data on error rates, etc., but rather indicate the general results for the children formerly in the special education program. The major finding was that the relative academic retardedness declined for the students in our program, i.e., either the gap between these students and the median for their age group was reduced or, at worst, it remained about the same in terms of progress in the program. Under traditional circumstances we would have predicted an ever increasing gap of academic retardation. Many of these former special education students are now operating around the median for their classes, and the discriminative function of their labels has been removed.

It should be stated that, in spite of our enthusiasm, we have not eliminated all of the problems, and that there are a few children with whom we have had little success. However, our gains reinforce us for these programming activities.

Another major objective of this demonstration program was to individualize the reading materials. This elementary school was fairly typical of many schools in the area with 20–40% of the children leaving the fourth grade at least 2 years behind in their reading achievement scores. In addition, there were many behavior problems in the school. The principal felt that something had to be done and that many of the behavior problems were a function of children's not being able to work satisfactorily with their traditional materials. In order for the teacher to have the time for those in need she would have to reduce the time she spent with those who did not need special help. Individualized materials accomplished this and allowed the teacher to concentrate on problem learners rather than squandering her time on the entire class.

The application of behavioral principles to teaching reading takes the form of programmed instruction. This behavioral approach to reading instruction is not particularly new. Probably the most familiar "programmed" reading series is the Sullivan Programmed Reader. Programming is essentially the specification of terminal objectives and the careful sequencing of skills so that prerequisite skills are always provided. Other distinguishing features are that programs have built-in feedback systems and are empirically tested so that weak points in the program, reflected by high error rates, are modified. Perhaps one of the most beneficial aspects of programming any subject matter is that the process demands that one specify the objectives to be taught in very concrete, measurable terms. This procedure has not been a central aspect of the traditional textbook approach. As Robert Mager has pointed out, if we don't know where we are going we can never know if we have arrived. Establishing behavioral objectives is an often neglected aspect of curriculum design. Most public school administrators apparently accept the objectives of the publishing firms. Many times it appears as though the publisher did not have any specific objectives clearly in mind. Acceptance of the publisher's objectives also occurs when purchasing programmed readers. However, in a programmed series additions and deletions of specific skills are easily made, whereas in a textbook where the objectives typically are not specified, this is a very cumbersome task.

The program was initiated with an attempt to resequence the Ginn reading series into a continuum of skills, progressively more difficult and complex, and their prerequisites. This task became formidable, and alternatives were sought. The McGraw-Hill Programmed Readers were purchased and an attempt to use them in our kindergarten classes was made. The kindergarten children did not have the necessary entering skills to begin in the program. Consequently, we began in the first grade with the McGraw-Hill Programmed Readers. A survey was made of the skills necessary to work with these readers, and these became the initial objectives in our kindergarten program. This new program began by our borrowing parts from several experimental programs, especially instructional techniques from the Engelman–Becker Program (Distar), then writing our own materials until we had a complete sequence of skills that assumed almost no entering skills in reading; basic relational concepts such as on, below, etc., or fine motor skills such as drawing lines, circling, placing an X on, etc. This program was in continual evolution. It was programmed in the sense that the terminal objectives were specified, skills were sequenced and data gathered concerning its effectiveness skill by skill. Initially the children were pretested on each skill to be taught. If the child did not demonstrate 100% mastery in a skill, then work in that skill area was provided.

The kindergarten program began with teaching the children the sounds of various letters in a small group setting, using techniques developed in the Engelman–Becker Program. The teacher verbally followed a very specific format of modeling sounds, asking for responses from individuals and from the group, and using very specific correction procedures when necessary. Letters were shown to the children, and visual discrimination skills were systematically taught. Four initial sounds were taught, and also the sight vocabulary words A and I. The children were not taught the names of the letters, only the sounds. Sound blending was taught, as was rhyming. Initial visual discriminations were made easier by the use of supplemental cues, which were later faded out. Seat work supplemented the small group work and provided practice in skills covered in the group. However, because beginning kindergarten children cannot read directions, they worked in small groups on the same skill at the same time. Verbal instructions were given to the group. Each skill was contained in a separate booklet of dittoed pages stapled together. Children varied in the time they took to finish, so they could automatically proceed to alternate reinforcing activities (such as play) when the task was completed and checked by the teacher or aide.

Children experiencing any difficulty were tutored through the problem areas. Because progress in the program required demonstrated mastery on post tests following each skill, the progress of each student could be monitored very closely.

Initially the academic portions of the K program were very short. Periods were approximately 5 to 10 minutes in length at the beginning of the year and were slowly extended, so that the children learned to work for longer and longer periods. By midyear the students worked from 20 to 30 minutes without interruption, and by the end of the year from 30 to 45 minutes. It should be pointed out that the children were very enthusiastic and motivated during these periods, and were in no sense badgered into it. The children received a great deal of attention contingent upon task completion, "trying hard," and appropriate social behavior. Therefore they liked school and liked learning to read.

As previously described, the first grade began with the McGraw-Hill Programmed Readers. Children experiencing problems were given special tutoring in order to overcome the reading problems. No standardized diagnostic tests were used, nor were any inferences made about hypothetical causes of reading problems. When a child was having difficulty, we assumed that something was wrong with our prior instruction; the use of "labels" was totally absent. The children progressed through the Programmed Readers with varying speed. Progress charts were kept so that we might detect students who required assistance. The teachers supplemented this program with other language activities as they saw fit, as long as it did not conflict with the scheduled program. Grade levels were used, but academic progress was continuous and grade levels reflected only age groups. The students typically completed the Programmed Readers in the third grade, though obviously there were great differences in this.

At the conclusion of the above program, the Individually Prescribed Instruction (IPI) program began. This language program moved away from basic skill-building into more complex concepts. The IPI program was developed by Research for Better Schools and the University of Pittsburgh and was obtained on an experimental basis. We have made extensive revisions in the content and have a built-in system to correct the more obvious problems. The format of this program required the use of clerks in the class. First the child was pretested and placed in the general topic areas in which he was deficient; then another pretest was used to place him at the precise level within the skill area. A "prescription" was made for the child which usually could be completed within the class period, and as soon as the work was completed the child took it to the clerk, who scored it. The student then took the scored work to the teacher, who evaluated it and made another prescription that might either advance the child in the program or require more in the same area. The general topics covered were library skills, reference skills, literal comprehension, interpretive comprehension, and evaluative comprehension. This program was also supplemented as the individual teachers desired. Within this school, all of the special education students had been placed back in the normal classrooms. Consequently, their range of abilities and achievement was increased. Individual instruction made this possible.

Evaluation of such a program is difficult. Many desirable controls of laboratory investigations are impossible within the realities of the public school educational setting. Subject variables, for example, cannot be adequately controlled, for children *cannot* be randomly assigned to schools and often not even to teachers. In addition, measuring instruments are often not maximally suited to the purposes of evaluation.

Consider a typical situation: a comparative evaluation of the relative success of two curriculae in meeting the objectives of a particular educational system. At first glance evaluation may appear relatively simple. The solution would appear to be usage of curriculum A with one group of children, usage of curriculum B with a comparable group, with subsequent testing of all children on one or more indices of achievement to compare performance. The solution, however, is much more complex. One problem stems from the fact that different curricular programs do not necessarily teach the same skills and may not necessarily have the same educational objectives. Results of an achievement test may therefore be very misleading. Any test chosen for the comparison may potentially be biased more favorably toward one curriculum than toward the other, and this bias may be extremely difficult to pinpoint. In consequence, if a difference between the groups tested does occur, it cannot be readily ascertained whether the test was biased in favor of one set of materials, or whether those materials were in fact more effective.

The potential effect of such variables upon the results of evaluation must be recognized, and confidence in the results modified appropriately. Educational decision making is a complex and vital process; no single segment of data can be accepted as conclusive. The process must be a continuous one, with each unit viewed in perspective of the entire continuum.

More appropriate evaluations consist of diagnostic instruments which test the specific concepts being taught. That is, the tests should be used to evaluate the program and must stem from the program itself. Thus, standardized tests are not viewed as very helpful. The results of diagnostic testing should specify what was not taught well and what to do to remedy it within the program.

Unless the two curricula were developed to teach precisely the same concepts and skills in two different formats, the comparisons between them are fairly useless except for public relations reasons. In spite of these difficulties, a number of our initial investigations and observations have yielded information that is favorable to the program.

One of the first observations that is readily apparent is the teachers' enthusiasm about the program. In this respect, the program is an unqualified success. Teachers report that for the first time they felt as though they were "really teaching," and would be reluctant to revert back to traditional classroom teaching techniques. Initially several of the teachers were reticent about coming into the program. Some were openly negative in their attitudes. However, once involved and trained they rapidly became enthusiastic.

In spite of our reluctance to use standardized measures of academic gains for comparative purposes, the school system routinely used the California Achievement Test (CAT), and we made several comparisons of our programmed classes and comparable classrooms in the same school initially not using the program. The results were consistently in favor of our program. Although the gains were significant, they were not overwhelming. However, we placed little value on these results. The most appropriate evaluation measure is progress within the program. Another important variable to consider is that by individualizing, we were able to place students severely academically (former special education students) back into regular classrooms and deal with them more effectively. Although it is too early to tell, it appears as though nonreaders are almost nonexistent from the first grade up, as opposed to a sizable percentage (40%) before the program began.

The evaluation of the program in some areas admittedly rests on faith. For example, we feel it is better to individualize materials, and that this concept does not need testing. Unfortunately there is little agreement as to what is most important to teach, and the content being taught is open to functional analysis. However, the program appears to prevent many learning problems from developing.

Ultimately a program should be evaluated in terms of its objectives, which should be specified behaviorally. What are the skills the students can demonstrate at the end of the program that they could not at the beginning? If we follow this line, then in order to evaluate a program we must specify behaviorally what its objectives are. Next we should examine the rate at which skills are acquired and the variables that affect this rate. An evaluation of this sort is very complex, but provides the data necessary to achieve the objectives most efficiently.

In order to determine the objectives that are desirable, a functional analysis of higher-order skills should be undertaken as well as an analysis of the skills required in the environment in which the child is living.

Behavior Modification

I. *Define the problem objectively and in behavioral terms.*
   A. Specifically state the problem, i.e., the child is *out of his seat* or says, "*I don't like school,*" etc. Do not use generalizations such as, "The kid fools around too much," or "has a bad attitude." You cannot effectively deal with these generalizations, you *can* however, deal with specific behaviors.
   B. What do you want the child to do? How does this differ from the current behavior, i.e., is it a problem of more, less, or different behavior?
II. *Obtain an objective measure of the strength of the current behavior.* In order to assess any treatment we must know the strength of the behavior before the treatment. Observe and record systematically.
   A. *Measurement techniques:* frequency counts and durational measures in most cases. How many times does the behavior occur in a minute, hour, etc., or how long does it last after it begins?
   B. *Data recording:* graphs of rates and frequencies. Draw a simple graph depicting the frequency or duration for each observation period.
III. *Attach some consequence to the behavior,* i.e., behavior is a function of its consequences. If you want to change the behavior, change its consequences.
   A. *Identify a likely reinforcer or punisher.* If you want to increase a behavior, reinforce it. If you want to weaken a behavior, punish it or withhold reinforcement.
      1. Be sure that the reinforcer or punisher is in terms of the subject's behavior, not yours, i.e., what reinforces you may not reinforce someone else, and vice versa.

B. *Set a behavioral criterion for the consequence:* Specifically, what the person must do before he gets reinforced or punished.
   1. Begin with small steps toward the terminal performance. Do not demand too much too soon. Reinforce approximations to the desired final performance.
C. *Arrange the details of the contingency.* How is the consequence presented? By whom and how?
   1. A *direct* contingency: Immediately follow the behavior with the consequence. A child gets a problem correct; you consequate by saying, "Good."
   2. An *indirect* contingency: A "token" or "point" system whereby some symbol signifying reinforcement is given, with the consequence delivered at some later time. A child gets a problem correct; you consequate it by giving a token that will be exchanged for some reward at a later time.
IV. *Assess the effectiveness of your contingency:* If it is not working as anticipated, change it.
A. *The importance of continued measurement.* Without continued measurement, you cannot assess the effectiveness of your contingency.
B. *What to do if the contingency appears to be ineffective.* This can be established by measurement of the behavior.
   1. There may be an error in consequence identification. Perhaps the consequence chosen is not an effective reinforcer or punisher. If not, change it.
   2. The initial criterion for reinforcement may be too high. You may be asking for too much too soon. Reinforce approximations to the desired behavior.
   3. The delay between the behavior and the consequence may be too long. Delayed reinforcement or punishment will most likely be ineffective. To be effective the consequence must immediately follow the behavior.

APPENDIX: APPLICATION OF BEHAVIORAL PRINCIPLES TO CLASSROOM SETTINGS

Brief studies completed by elementary teachers on the effective use of behavioral principles are presented. These studies were conducted by teachers as part of a class requirement. They were taking an in-service graduate course on behavior management offered by the University of Illinois Educational Psychology Department. David Phillips was instructor.

The studies are presented as they were prepared by the teachers and reflect the attempt to systematically apply behavioral principles to a classroom setting. The teachers involved had no prior knowledge of behavioral principles and thus were representative of most teachers. The course was a 14-week seminar, and the project was the culmination of the techniques and theory learned.

A wide variety of problems were approached and dealt with, using behavioral principles. No attempt was made to produce "experimentally pure" studies with careful controls. Rather, a more pragmatic approach was taken whereby the teachers tackled the problems in the classroom as efficiently as possible.

A brief outline of typical procedures used in dealing with behavior problems is presented. One of the purposes of this paper is to acquaint the reader with the kinds of problems faced and the techniques used in dealing with them.

Behavior and Its Consequences

Most of the behavior that teachers deal with is controlled by its consequences. Whatever immediately follows a given behavior will definitely affect the probability of that behavior occurring again. If you say "Please pass the salt" and the salt is passed to you, you have been rewarded for asking by receiving the salt. You are more likely to ask for it that way in the future. If you say "Thanks," you reward the one who passed the salt and he is more likely to pass it in the future because of the reward. Similarly, if a child exhibits deviant behavior and the teacher draws attention to it (by nagging, scolding, reprimanding, etc.), the child is very likely going to do it *more* in the future. Her attention is reinforcing the very behavior she wishes to eliminate! The best way to eliminate this behavior is to remove the attention (reinforcement), ignore the behavior and reinforce some other behavior that is incompatible with the deviant behavior. In other words, praise the child when he is behaving properly and ignore the deviant behavior.

This may seem very trivial, but in general most of our behavior is controlled in the same way. Much behavior is under the control of subtle interacting consequences, and thus it is not always obvious or clear what the controlling variables are. The basic principle is: *Behavior is a function of its consequences.* Thus if we want to change behavior, we must change the consequences.

Essentially, we can either *increase, decrease,* or *maintain* behavior. Behavior strengthening and maintenance is a result of reinforcement. Behavior weakening is a result of punishment or extinction. The following outline covers the essential principles of behavior modification and how they may be applied.

Behavior Modification in the Classroom

I. Most classroom problems are of two general types: academic problems and problems of classroom management

A. *Problems of inadequate academic performance*

    1. Students who have the necessary academic skills but sometimes not participate

        a. Example: On the basis of achievement, you feel reasonably sure the child is capable but puts forth no effort

        b. Example: The difficulty in obtaining class participation when the material is too difficult or uninteresting

    2. Students whose poor academic achievement results from a lack of prerequisite academic skills

        a. Example: The student who lacks a specific skill, i.e., cannot multiply because he cannot add

        b. Example: The student who lacks more general skills, i.e., has not learned to read because he has not learned to pay attention

B. *Problems involving classroom management*

    1. Relatively weak behaviors which should be strengthened

        a. Example: The student who is withdrawn and generally noncommunicative. Class participation behaviors should be strengthened.

        b. Example: The class that is slow to get ready to work. On-task behaviors should be strengthened.

    2. Students with strong undesirable or disruptive behaviors which should be weakened and/or eliminated entirely

        a. Example: The student who is "deliberately" disruptive. These disruptive behaviors should be eliminated.

        b. Example: The noisy classroom. The noise level should be lowered by reinforcing more quiet behavior.

II. Strategies for solving academic and classroom management problems

A. *Contingencies designed to strengthen desirable academic or classroom behaviors*

    1. Have you specified the behavior of interest in precise behavioral terms?

    2. Do you have an accurate estimate of the current behavior? That is, have you measured? This must be done in order to determine the effectiveness of any program to change behavior.

    3. How to find a reinforcer: on the basis of past experience or advance knowledge; or, simply ask the children, "What do you like?"

      a. Will grades work? To some children grades are too far re-
moved in time to be effective.

      b. Other reinforcers: Ask your subjects, "What do you like
or what would you work for?" (For example, privileges,
activities, or goodies?)

4. Which behavior are you going to start with? That is, what behavior must occur before you reinforce the child—some ap-
proximation of the desired behavior.

      a. Are all the necessary prerequisite skills well learned, or is
some remediation necessary? Do not demand some performance the child simply cannot do because no one has
taught him before. Remediate the skill if necessary.

      b. Be sure to make your first criterion for reinforcement some-
thing that the student can do relatively easily. If you ask for
a difficult performance initially, you may readily get failure.
Reinforce for a correct performance.

5. Is the contingency going to be direct or indirect (a point system)?

      a. Example: an academic strengthening problem involving
the shaping of prerequisite behaviors: reading readiness
skills. Reinforce these behaviors with praise or another direct
reinforcer.

      b. Example: classroom motivational systems in public schools:
a token reinforcement system is indirect. The tokens are
turned in later for a variety of reinforcers.

B. *Contingencies designed to weaken undesirable behavior*

1. Specify the behavior of interest in precise behavioral terms.

2. Do you have an accurate estimate of the current behavior? Have
you measured its frequency or duration?

3. Deciding on the contingency: Three ways to weaken behavior.

      a. Extinction—this amounts to removing the reinforcement
that is maintaining the behavior.

      b. The reinforcement of incompatible behavior strengthens
behaviors that are incompatible with the deviant behavior,
e.g., sitting down is incompatible with standing up.

      c. Punishment—removing a reinforcer or presenting an aver-
sive stimulus. These procedures, when made contingent on
a specified response, will weaken it.

         1. Why punishment is not necessarily the best procedure,
even though it may be the fastest. It produces side effects
such as avoidance and escape behavior and may result
in the increase of aggressive behavior: The person may
tend to avoid the situation in which he is punished, e.g.,
a classroom or school.

C. *How do you know if you have succeeded?*
1. The importance of continued measurement. This is the only way you will know if you are making progress.
2. Some likely pitfalls in educational contingencies.
    a. Misidentified reinforcers. We all too often assume that what reinforces us will reinforce others—this is not always the case. Also what reinforces us at one time may not be a reinforcer at another time, e.g., food may be a good reinforcer before a meal; however, directly after a meal food is not likely to be an effective reinforcer.
    b. Standards for reinforcement are initially too difficult for some students—the heterogeneity problem. Individualize the standards for reinforcement. Reinforcement for improvement, not for one standard of performance.
    c. The teacher's standards keep increasing as the student's performance improves. You are succeeding, but do not notice it. As the student's behavior improves, it is easy to forget the improvement you have made and demand more all the time.
D. *Relativity of the consequences*
1. The behavior you have either strengthened or weakened is not permanent. This is true of *all* behavior. We behave according to the consequences. For example: If you reinforce and increase on-task behavior in a child, and next year he goes into a class where the teacher gives him attention for fooling around, he will come under the control of these new consequences and will begin to fool around more. Almost all of our behavior is like this.

Summary

1. Identify and define behavior.
2. Measure.
3. Place consequence on the behavior.
4. Continue measurement.
5. Try again if not achieving anticipated result.

The following material is concerned with observation graphing. Graphing is a convenient way to summarize your results. Included are: general observation techniques; instructions to observers; coding categories and symbols which have been used (you need not limit yourself to these), an observation sheet, and a summary graph card.

General Observation Techniques

1. Specify the behavior you are going to observe very precisely, always in terms of observable behaviors. A general class of behavior may be

used, such as "on task" or "off task" if you have defined "on task" so that it may be reliably observed.

2. Behavior which is of a single-response nature may be recorded with a frequency tally over a measured period of time, e.g., hitting, pinching, etc. Other types of behaviors, which are composed of many separate responses and endure over an extended period of time, should be recorded in short 10–15-second intervals. Behaviors in this class are such things as "on task," thumb sucking, talking, etc. This type of recording may be done as follows: Take a sheet of paper, draw a series of cells on it (like large graph paper). Use this for recording. Observe for 10 seconds. If the person exhibits the behavior of interest, place a mark in the cell. This recording is done for 10 seconds. So, you are observing for 10 seconds and recording for 10 seconds, then observing again and so on. Do not record during the 10-second observing period. This technique calls for the use of a stopwatch taped to a clipboard, or some similar arrangement.

3. The frequency of observations will vary according to many things like practicality, etc. However, be consistent and observe under the same conditions every observation period. For example, you might observe every morning from 9:30 to 10:00. This assumes the same teacher, children, and classroom each time.

General Instructions for Observers

1. Do not talk to any children at any time: in schoolroom, hall, or yard, including before and after actual school hours.
2. Do not let children either see or hear you talking to their teacher or observer. Questions on recording can be written and discussed later.
3. Do not make any differential responses to children. Do not laugh at children, answer children, or change position of head or eyes, if addressed. Do not turn and look at any child when you hear a noise. Make the minimal response necessary to see the child you are recording.
4. When observing sit silently and as immobile as possible in the most convenient observer chair. Change location quietly only when absolutely necessary.
5. Do not engage in any social behavior with children either on entering of leaving school or classroom. Do not respond to children in halls.
6. The goal is to become a piece of furniture. You are not to be a variable with reference to the children's behavior. "Neither discriminating nor reinforcing be."

Observation Sheet

Observer_____ Teacher_____

Subject _____ Date _____

Time _____ School _____

Observation interval length :   10 seconds, 20 seconds, 30 seconds etc._____

Observed behavior :_____

_____

S	Observations							Comments	Symbols used

Summary Graph Card

You may fill in your own units of frequency and time on the vertical and horizontal axes. For example, on the graph shown, there was one 20-minute observation period per day for 20 days. Ten days were recorded before treatment so we can assess the effectiveness of the program. We were observing "on-task" behavior and reporting the result in terms of percentage of intervals during which "on-task" behavior occurred for the full 10-second interval.

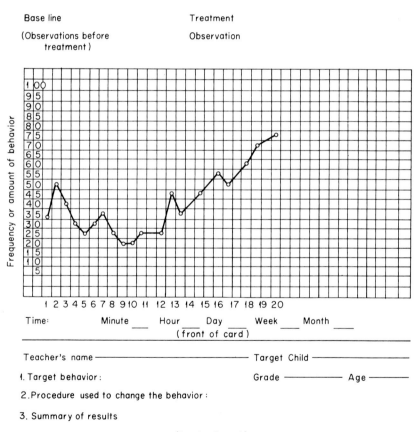

Base line   Treatment

(Observations before   Observation
    treatment)

1 2 3 4 5 6 7 8 9 10 11 12 13 14 15 16 17 18 19 20

Time: Minute ___ Hour ___ Day ___ Week ___ Month ___
                              (front of card)

Teacher's name ——————————————— Target Child ———————————

1. Target behavior: Grade ————— Age —————

2. Procedure used to change the behavior:

3. Summary of results

(back of card)

Study 1

Target Behavior

Selection of target behavior was difficult, as I have one of those rare classes, a first grade, in which it is almost impossible to find undesirable behavior. I chose David, whose problem was different from usual deviant behavior. By licking, touching, and rubbing, David irritated his lips and surrounding areas with such frequency that his mouth area was constantly red and raw-looking. He frequently complained that his mouth hurt, asking that I put some medicine on it. Though I had suggested that his refraining from licking and touching would help, I did not pursue correction of the problem. The terminal behavior I sought was cessation of the irritating behaviors that resulted in David's sore mouth.

Time Span of Experiment

I was pressed for time with only 13 possible observation days before Christmas vacation. Therefore, I limited my observation to one solid block of time before the holiday break. I realize this short time is not ideal and may cast some doubt on the results; however, this was a practical limitation.

Observation Personnel

At the time of the experiment I had a junior participant from the University of Illinois in my classroom preparing for student teaching. She was the only observer available in our building. After my discussing the principles of this course, she was extremely interested and eager to serve as my observer again, a built-in shortcoming to the study. If two observers were used it would have been possible to establish reliability of the observer. However, this was not possible.

Recording Procedure

Time plan. Three days base line, 10 days extinction; 30 minutes each day, same time and class activity; 10 seconds observing—10 seconds recording.

Code categories:

Symbol	Definition
1	licking lips and surrounding area,
p	pencil in or on mouth and surrounding area,
f	fingers in or on mouth and surrounding area,
a	arm or sleeve rubbing mouth area

Procedure to Weaken Target Behavior

Explanation to target child of the experiment and terminal behavior desired

Vocal praise when undesirable behavior was absent: i.e., "Your mouth is looking better, David." "You are remembering very well."
My facial expressions of a smile or a wink, a hug when he was refraining

Vocal praise, to the whole class, of David's positive efforts

Getting the class to help David accomplish his goal through their praise

Results

In 3 days of base-line observation, the undesirable behavior registered 82%, 81%, and 68% at the observed time. At the introduction of extinction procedure on the fourth day, the percentage dropped to 29%; fifth day to 18%; and the sixth day to 4%. Illness of both teacher and observer prevented data collection on Days 7 and 8. Post checks were made on Days 11 and 13 to be sure the extinction pattern was durable. Such post checks resulted in 5% and 2% of undesirable behavior. The percentage dropped so quickly that contingent reinforcement beyond praise was unnecessary in order to effect weakening of the undesirable behavior (see accompanying graph).

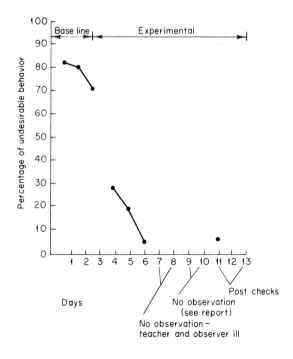

After a 2-week Christmas vacation, I observed David's mouth area to be normal. His reward is a normal mouth, which he is most happy about. He is proud of our cooperative effort and says he is determined it will not happen again.

Study 2

Target Behavior

Choosing a target child presented a problem in my case. My class is a high-achieving group of middle primary students. Therefore, the group has no serious problems.

Lucy is a 6-year-old child who scored well above 150 on the California Test of Mental Maturity. Her achievement scores also placed her far above the average middle primary student. She was chosen as a target child because she seldom completes assignments. Her time is usually spent staring off into space, doodling on her paper, or wiggling in her seat. Therefore, the target behavior in this case was for Lucy to sit still, face forward, eyes on paper, and complete the assigned task.

Time Span of Experiment

Lucy was observed for approximately 20 minutes a day for 8 days. Behavior was observed for 10 seconds and then recorded for 10 seconds. The behavior which was observed was time on task. Time-on-task behavior was defined as sitting appropriately in seat, eyes on paper, and apparently working on the assigned task. The data also indicated gross physical movement. The observations were made during the reading period. This is a time when Lucy has a specific set of tasks to complete. Previously, Lucy displayed much deviant behavior during this period and seldom completed the assigned task during the time allotted.

Procedure

After 4 days of base line, I changed my daily program. I opened each day with a discussion of good work habits. I praised the children for stating correct behavior in a concise, positive manner. I also began giving Lucy praise and attention contingent on the target behavior; I ignored all behaviors incompatible with good work habits.

The following graph presents the percentage of time spent in gross physical movement. As this figure indicates, the subject responded immediately to differential reinforcement. She began to display excellent work habits. Especially noticeable was the marked decrease in gross physical movement. Occasionally, she would revert to her old patterns of behavior. At that time, I used a simple comment, such as "I like the way Susie is sitting and working." Lucy would immediately begin working well again.

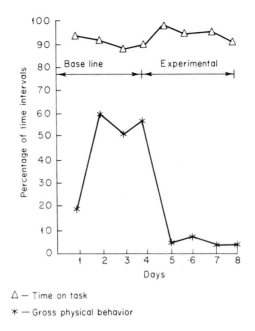

$\triangle$ — Time on task

$*$ — Gross physical behavior

Lucy's work habits have improved a great deal, especially in reducing her gross physical movement. In addition to her increased time on task, the work produced has been more accurate. Although there are no data to illustrate an attitude change, Lucy has expressed more of an interest in reading.

Study 3

Target Behavior

The behavior I sought was for Tim, a second grader, to read or to do whatever task he was given without arguments as to which book he should be working in, or without comments concerning Darrin, a classmate of his. The behaviors to be modified or eliminated were the almost constant queries or comments concerning Darrin. Tim's preoccupation with "which book Darrin is in," "which pencil Darrin uses," "which chair Darrin sits in," "which side of the table Darrin sits on," etc., was extremely disruptive to the learning situation.

Recording Procedure

A trained observer using a stopwatch and clipboard observed 10 seconds and recorded 10 seconds for approximately 30 minutes per day. A check mark was used for any comment or question about Darrin or other students that had no connection with the lessons we were doing. Such comments as "Is this the book Darrin is in?", or "Is this the story Darrin is on?" were not acceptable and received a check mark.

Experimental Procedure

Tim was told the "Rules of the Room" were: (1) Each person works in the books he is given. (2) He doesn't worry or ask about other people's work. (3) He does the best he can. I tried to explain to Tim how some people were stronger and could run faster, while perhaps other people could read faster or in harder books, but all we wanted was that each person do his best and not be concerned with what the others were doing. My project was a little different from the regular classroom situation, since I work with the children one at a time. I could not praise others to shape Tim's behavior, since this preoccupation with others was the very behavior I was attempting to eliminate.

Praise was used as a positive reinforcer for any work done correctly. To weaken the unwanted behavior of questions and comments about Darrin, they were ignored (as much as possible) or answered with a very short answer and a displeased look when he insisted on an answer. Reinforcing comments such as "good," "fine," "very good," and "you are doing very well" were made whenever possible.

Results

This procedure has been very effective (see accompanying graph). Tim has reached target behavior with only an occasional query concerning Darrin. His homeroom teacher stated that he is also more cooperative in his homeroom.

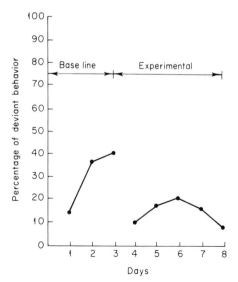

Study 4

Target Behavior

My subject was Louis, 9 years old, a second grader. I wished to decrease verbalizations by Louis that I considered undesirable, i.e., blurting-out behavior was constituted of comments he made aloud to himself, classmates, or the teacher without having first been called on. I did not count as "blurts" whispered conversations with a neighbor; but rather, only his random remarks, often only one or two words, which were audible to all in the room.

Recording Procedure Used

My observer recorded the number of "blurts" (undesirable verbalizations) occurring within 30-minute periods each day for 13 days.

Procedures Used to Modify the Behavior

I ignored any comments that were blurted out. I praised hand raising and talking only when called on. I praised listening and waiting to be called on.

During the 4-day base-line period, I continued to treat Louis as I had all year. I felt it would render the results of the experiment invalid if I instituted any of the behavior modification procedures before base-line data had been gathered. Therefore, I at times reminded Louis, either privately or in front of the class, not to talk without being called on. On occasion I responded to Louis' blurts, especially when he had given a comment or answer that I had been seeking. Therefore, on Day 5, when the time came to begin extinction of Louis' blurting-out behavior, I had to discipline myself to be sure that at all times I ignored his blurts and gave attention only to the desired behaviors.

On the first of the 9 experimental days (Day 5), I posted a chart in front of the room, enumerating the following three rules:

1. Raise your hand if you wish to talk.
2. Wait to be called on.
3. Listen while others talk.

I purposely listed as few rules as possible while still managing to cover the essentials. I felt that the task might seem easier to master if it did not involve numerous rules.

The entire class read the rules together and discussed each rule, being careful to follow the rules during our discussion. Louis seemed especially anxious to please me and had his hand up constantly. On this first day and for a few days following, I called on Louis every time he raised his hand and as soon as possible after he raised it. After Day 7, I found that by stressing rules 2 and 3, I could lengthen the interval between the time Louis raised his hand and the time I called on him, and still maintain the reduction of "blurts."

At first I praised Louis' slightest hand-raising movement. However, not much shaping was required. Louis was eager to receive positive attention. I praised Louis (and others) whenever they applied the rules, and referred to the rules in my reinforcing comments. Aside from the usual "goods" I used such comments as, "I called on ———— because he had his hand up" or "I like the way ———— always listens while others are talking." Whenever possible I named Louis in the comments. I praised good raisers, good waiters, and good listeners. In regards to the effectiveness of vicarious reinforcement on Louis, I found that it worked best if I could praise someone for an incompatible behavior at the *exact* moment when Louis was blurting out.

The whole class cooperated, too, by not responding to any comments blurted out by classmates. For example, during show and tell, if a classmate had a comment or question, the "shower" would not acknowledge it unless he had first called on that classmate. We recited the rules each morning, and when necessary or applicable, we reviewed the reasons for the rules and evaluated our class progress.

Results

I feel that I learned and accomplished much through this first project. Not only was my target behavior realized, proving to me the effectiveness of the ignore-and-praise combination, but fringe benefits were gained also. I became accustomed to giving praise freely and sincerely. And I am training myself not to acknowledge deviant behavior by means of any verbal, facial, or physical response. Although my primary goal was to stop Louis' blurting out and to get him to raise his hand if he wished to speak, good listening habits for the whole class resulted from this experiment. Toward the end of the 13 days, after the basics of raising-hand-to-talk had been mastered, I pursued the skills further by branching off into connecting areas. All children learned to listen while classmates or teachers were talking. If a comment was made that repeated what another had just finished saying, I ignored it. I employed the use of such questions as "What do you think of what ———— said?" or "Please tell me what ———— just said."

The following graph vividly illustrates my results. By ignoring the undesirable behavior and giving positive reinforcements to behaviors incompatible with it, the blurting-out behavior was drastically reduced from a high frequency of occurrence. Perhaps over a longer period of time, the blurting-out behavior could be totally extinguished.

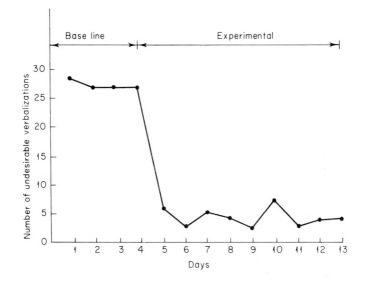

Study 6

Target Behavior

Steve, a 10-year-old fourth grader, tests at average ability. He was chosen for this study because he exhibited many behaviors incompatible with good work habits. During the morning reading period he disturbed others in his group by talking and leaning over their desks. Much of his time was also spent in daydreaming or working at something other than reading, such as coloring a sheet of paper. Daily reading assignments were never completed. Therefore *the target behavior* was that Steve not disturb others or daydream, but rather work continuously on his reading.

Procedure

To keep a record of Steve's behavior an observer came to the room for 30 minutes each day for 9 days. Behavior was recorded in 10-second intervals; observe for 10 seconds, record for 10 seconds. The observer recorded time on task; not talking and working on assigned reading task. The 9-day observation period was divided into 5 days base line and 4 days experimental. Following 5 days of base line, Steve and I visited, and discussed his poor work habits. Steve expressed a desire to improve. We set up a point system based on a set of positively stated rules for the reading period. The rules set up were working quietly and independently, and only on the reading assignment until the given assignment was completed. I explained that points would be contingent on compliance with these rules. The points would earn a mutually agreed upon reward.

I began reinforcement by rewarding with praise comments and points during a specified interval. When deviant behavior occurred, it was ignored and no points were given.

Results

The accompanying graph shows the data gathered during observation. For the first 5 days of base line, Steve shows a high rate of deviant behavior —off task as much as 65% of the time. Reinforcement began on Day 6 and, as the figure shows, his deviant behavior was just as high as on the previous days. I analyzed these data and came to the conclusion that perhaps the fixed-interval schedule required too long a work period before reinforcement occurred. I was reinforcing on a 15-minute interval. Therefore, on Days 7, 8, and 9, I reinforced on a 5-minute fixed ratio schedule. As the figure shows, the deviant behavior showed a marked decline. Steve was now off task only 18% of the time. As I changed no other aspects of the program, I attributed the results to the changed schedule of reinforcement.

On Days 7, 8, and 9, Steve's behavior showed improvement. He was more attentive to the task at hand, worked more quietly and independently. His mother reported to me that there has been a change in his attitude. He is greatly encouraged by the feeling that someone cares about him.

Steve is a long way from the desired end behavior; however, the improvement shown is encouraging. I intend to continue the program and reinforce successive approximations of the desired terminal behavior. Eventually the interval of reinforcement will be increased and more work will be required for reinforcement. I plan to work for completion of assignments as a next step. Since Steve responds favorably to praise, I intend to continue this form of reinforcement and fade out material rewards.

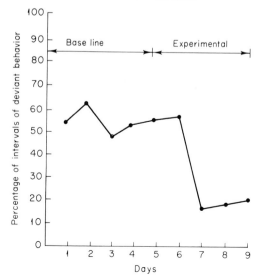

Study 7

Target Behavior

In my classroom, it was very difficult to choose a behavior that needed some modification, as I had already shaped the children to the desired behavior at the beginning of the school year. My group of children is the so-called "sharper" class of second graders. They are all from strong middle-class and upper middle-class families; therefore, they were more easily shaped to the desired middle-class standards.

The child I chose was a 7½-year-old boy. Verdell tended to be boisterous if he was not already in a quiet, orderly atmosphere. After riding the bus to school, he was sometimes this way. Sometimes when he came into the class-room in the morning, he would take a "whirl" through the room before taking off his coat at the closet. Then, he would talk loudly and wander aimlessly around the room. Since my pupils spend the first 20 minutes in the classroom working quietly at their desks—finishing reading-group work or math workbooks, reading a book, writing creatively, or quietly playing a game with their neighbors—to eliminate Verdell's deviant behavior was the goal.

Recording Procedure

Base-line data were secured by having an observer on 4 days for 30 minutes each day at the beginning of the school day. Verdell's deviant behavior occurred less than 10% on any one of the 4 days of base line (see accompanying graph).

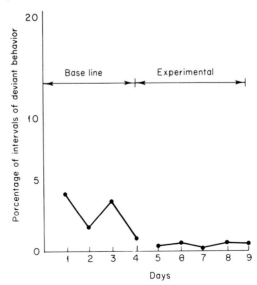

Experimental Procedure

After the Christmas vacation, I told Verdell that if he could get six marks or points within the first 30 minutes of school each morning, I would let him finger-paint at the easel. I checked him at intervals of every 5 minutes. I said to him, "The only way you can earn a point is by staying in your seat and doing something quietly." In other words, the privilege of finger painting was contingent on earning the six points, and earning the points was contingent on his doing something while sitting at his desk.

At first, the privilege of finger-painting was not altogether reinforcing to him. Verdell is the type of individual who does not like to do things unless he knows his peers are envious and want to do the same thing also. In other words, he really did not try too much to get the six points. Then some of the other children started asking me if they could finger-paint. I said, "No, this is just for Verdell." After this, the finger-painting suddenly became a real privilege to Verdell.

Results

The experiment was done on 5 days for 30 minutes each day at the beginning of the school day. During this time, the deviant behavior became almost zero (see graph).

Since then, I have initiated this rule of finger-painting with the remainder of the class. I thought I had a "perfect" class before the project, but now it is even more "perfect." The finger-painting easel is very reinforcing to even the "very best" of my children. I am amazed—it's like magic!

Study 8

Target Behavior

The subject for this project was an 8-year-old fourth-grade boy. He and a third-grade girl come daily to my room for 40 minutes of Type A tutoring in arithmetic.[1]

The behavior to be modified was the utterance of words or noises not relevant to the arithmetic tasks assigned. Acceptable verbalization, as defined for the observer, was questions about work or saying answers and problems aloud. Unacceptable verbalization was grunts and various other guttural sounds, giggles, whistles, sobbing, humming, and comments such as "goodie" and "yah." Target behavior was silence or acceptable verbalization 80% of the time.

[1]Type A is a term used to designate children diagnosed as socially maladjusted.

Recording Procedure

The observer sat behind the subject. She observed for 10 seconds, then recorded for 10 seconds, using a stopwatch and clipboard. Data were gathered for 30 minutes each day.

Experimental Procedure

Five days of base-line observation were done, during which I continued my previous practice of ignoring the deviant behavior of the subject. On the sixth day the experimental program was initiated. Both children were given copies of a chart (see following chart). The three rules were discussed with them. It was explained that for each 5 minutes that they followed the rules, an X would be placed in a box on the clock representing that time interval, and these points could be used to earn rewards. The reinforcers were then shown to them and consisted of things they had suggested, such

Rules

1   No talking unless it is about arithmetic.
2. Sit in seats unless asked to come to board.
3. Raise hands in group discussions.

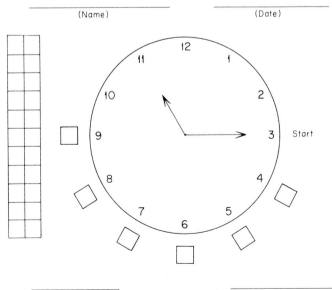

(Name)   (Date)

Start

Today's points   Points saved for tomorrow

as play dough, darts, a toy truck, a ring, coloring books, a doll, and candy. A chart showing the points needed to earn each reward was included.

On the third day of the experimental period, I began to give additional points for work completed. They could earn two points for a perfect paper and one point for not more than two errors. A point was also given for five correct responses to flash cards. These points were recorded in the boxes to the left of the clock. Each day the points were totaled, and the children chose whether to use them or save them for a reward that required more points.

Results

The following graph shows the effect of the experimental program on the child. As his deviant behavior decreased, his time on task increased and his work output increased from one-half paper to two or three papers completed daily.

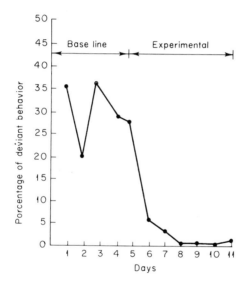

Study 9

Target Behavior

The target child for this study was a 5-year-old kindergarten girl named Mattie. She was chosen for this study because her thumb-sucking often interfered with her ability to communicate verbally.

Recording Procedure

During the base-line and experimental periods, an observer watched Mattie for 10 seconds, then recorded her observations for 10 seconds, then observed again, etc. The criterion for scoring was that the thumb be in Mattie's mouth at least up to the knuckle for the entire 10-second observation period in order to be scored as thumb-sucking. During the base line, the teacher tried to discourage thumb-sucking by frowning at Mattie when she had her thumb in her mouth or by physically removing the thumb from Mattie's mouth by pulling her hand away. Base line was terminated before the desired 5 days because of Christmas vacation.

Experimental Procedure

Thumb-sucking appears to be self-reinforcing, and it was felt that praise alone would not be a strong enough reinforcer in extinguishing the behavior. To determine what material reinforcers would be most effective, the teacher asked Mattie to help select them. Mattie said she liked toys such as balls, clay, small dolls, and doll baby bottles. She could receive these prizes by earning points (at least five points per toy), which she could exchange for a prize.

The teacher set a timer that would ring at 3-minute intervals the first day of the experimental period. This interval was gradually increased to 10 minutes. Mattie could earn one point every time she did not have her thumb in her mouth when the bell rang. Points were recorded by filling in one block on a piece of graph paper every time Mattie was exhibiting appropriate behavior (not sucking her thumb) when the bell rang. The rest of the class was instructed to ignore the bell, and everyone, including me, was to ignore the thumb-sucking. If Mattie had earned at least five points by dismissal time she could choose a prize or save her points until the next day and try to earn more points toward a larger prize.

Results

The results of this study are presented in the two graphs that follow. The average incidents of thumb-sucking during the instructional period of the

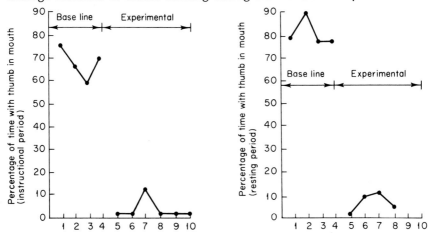

day was 64% during base line and 2% during the experimental period—a decrease of 62%. During rest period, thumb-sucking went from an average of 81% for base line to 7% during the experimental period—a decrease of 74% (right graph). It was noted that thumb-sucking was highest on Day 1 for base line and Day 7 for the experimental period (left graph). Both of these peaks occurred during a televised phonics lesson.

On the eighth day, Mattie decided to work toward a doll in a bathtub. She did not earn the needed 10 points that day, so she decided to take a lesser prize instead of waiting until the next day to earn more points.

Study 10

Target Behavior

The subject for this behavior-shaping experiment was Sally, age 8 years, 4 months, one of nine children in a preprimary Educable Mentally Handicapped (EMH) class. Because of her generally disruptive and uncontrollable classroom behavior, the school principal suggested Sally for behavior shaping. The teacher, Mrs. K., had been concerned enough and perplexed with Sally's behavior to suggest to the principal that Sally be placed in a special program for aggressive children. Mrs. K. described Sally as bullying and terrorizing other less assertive children in the classroom. Her physical aggressiveness both in the classroom and on the playground created frequent crises that resulted in heightened attention from and contact with the teachers involved. She was often impudent and stated that the teacher couldn't tell her what to do. Lack of self-control included unrestrained talking in class to other children, to herself as she worked, and to the teacher, often in a demanding and insulting manner.

For purposes of the assigned project, it was decided to focus on Sally's inappropriate talking and, more specifically, her responding to questions that were directed to other children, random blurting out in class, either in a general way or to someone in particular, mumbling to herself, and talking or whispering to other children.

Mrs. K. was cooperative in agreeing to the project, but expressed doubts about the effectiveness of behavior-shaping and operant-conditioning techniques. She had been involved in a student-teaching situation in which m&m's had been used, and her attitude toward this technique was negative. Furthermore, last year when she had assumed an intermediate EMH class as a replacement teacher at midyear, she found that behavior shaping by using concrete rewards had created a situation in which the pupils were so dependent upon concrete reinforcement that they would not perform without some tangible reward. Mrs. K. felt that because these children would be attending junior high school the following year, such extreme dependence upon extrinsic rewards was inappropriate, and she refused to continue with the token system then in effect.

Consequently, although Mrs. K. agreed to cooperate with the experiment, she insisted that no m&m's or token systems be used. She was at a distinct disadvantage compared to other teachers who were initiating behavior-shaping programs in their classrooms at the same time because she had neither the theoretical background nor the acquaintance with pertinent research to appreciate the potential of operant conditioning; nor did she have the personal commitment to make it work. Rather, she was in the position of implementing, in a rather rote fashion, some specific control techniques suggested by the observer–experimenter.

Recording Procedures

On each of 3 successive days, Sally was observed between approximately 9:55 and 10:25 A.M. in order to record base-line behavior. Each 10-second observation interval was followed by 10 seconds of recording, whether or not inappropriate talking had occurred. This half-hour period was divided roughly into two segments. During the first 15 minutes, Mrs. K. met with five children for a reading group at the rear of the room while the four other children, including Sally, worked at their desks on prescribed papers from their individual work folders. During the last 15 minutes, the four children met with the teacher for their reading instruction, while the other five children returned to their seats and worked on daily assignments.

Experimental Procedures

After 3 days of base-line behavior had been recorded for Sally, the teacher was asked to post on the blackboard four rules that the class was to repeat with her each morning and at the start of each afternoon. The rules were: (1) I will sit quietly when I work at my desk. (2) I will keep my eyes on my own papers. (3) If I need help, I will raise my hand and wait quietly for the teacher to come. (4) When I know an answer, I will raise my hand and wait until the teacher calls on me. Mrs. K. was asked, in addition, to use the following classroom control techniques in an effort to reduce the frequency of Sally's inappropriate talking. (1) Ignore Sally's blurting out by not looking at or saying anything to her rather than reminding her to be quiet. (2) Use no special urging when she lags or behaves as if she is not going to participate. Simply ignore her and proceed with the activity. (3) Throughout the day, frequently praise other children in the classroom who are working quietly and staying on task. (4) When you are working with the other reading group, look for opportunities to make such comments as "I like the way Sally is working quietly at her seat," as well as praising other children doing seat work who will then realize that you are keeping an eye on them.

On the next 10 school days, daily observations during the same half-hour period continued with the introduction of four classroom rules and the four classroom control techniques.

Results

On the first day of the experimental period, Sally responded in a verbally belligerent manner by announcing that she wasn't going to obey any rules and that she did not have to mind anyone except her mother. Nevertheless, some behavior shaping did occur in that on the same day: Sally raised her hand repeatedly for teacher help although in some instances her impatience in waiting resulted in such comments as "I raised my hand, and I'm not going to wait all day." During the experimental period, Mrs. K. felt that the experimenter simply by her presence in the classroom exerted a control which vanished when she left the room. For example, on one occasion, Sally verbally attacked Mrs. K. in a highly personal and offensive manner as soon as the experimenter left the room. Mrs. K. tried to ignore these comments but was told that a time-out period behind an isolation screen was entirely appropriate for such occasions.

As shown on the following graph, the percentage of Sally's inappropriate talking during 3 days of base-line observations ranged between 17% and 39%, with an average of 27%. During the 10-day experimental period, percentage of inappropriate talking during the daily half-hour periods of observation ranged from 2% to 44%, with an average of 18%. Talking behavior fluctuated widely, particularly during the last 5 days immediately preceding Christmas vacation. The general level of excitement and anticipation of classroom parties, Christmas programs, and other holiday-related

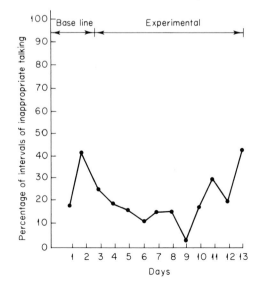

activities were variables that might explain the highest percentage of inappropriate talking, 44%, recorded on the final day of the experimental period. In addition, on several days, two or more observers were in the classroom and Mrs. K. felt that the level of pupil distractibility increased appreciably.

Concurrent with fluctuations in frequency of inappropriate talking, changes were observed in Sally's behavior in general. It had been observed during base line that two or three teacher reminders were often required to engage Sally in some structured group activity. On the first day of the experimental period, Mrs. K., in adopting one of the prescribed techniques, omitted any special urging if Sally did not respond to initial directions and proceeded with the planned activity. When Sally was called for in her reading group, she continued sitting at her seat while the other three children went promptly to the reading table. After one child made a comment concerning Sally's absence, which Mrs. K. ignored, all children in the class ignored Sally, thereby effectively isolating her, and proceeded with their reading group. Sally, still seated, turned her head frequently toward her reading group, then turned her whole body halfway around in her chair and stretched her neck to see what they were doing. Finally, she was on her knees on her seat attending closely to her group's activities. During this 15-minute period, there were only two instances of inappropriate talking. During the remaining 9 days of the experimental period, Sally went promptly to her reading group on the first call from the teacher.

Although during the base-line period no record was kept of the number of praising comments made by Mrs. K., the frequency of praising remarks was recorded during the experimental period. The number of praising comments, including those directed both to Sally and to other children in the class, ranged from two on the first 2 days of the experimental period to 12 on the third day. The average number of praising comments during the daily 30-minute observation periods over the 10 days was 6.9. The experimenter felt that this classroom control technique could have been used to greater advantage by Mrs. K. It seemed not so much resistance to the method but rather that Mrs. K. was put into the position of assuming an unfamiliar pose in a classroom situation, i.e., actively looking for and verbally praising appropriate behaviors. In addition, the effectiveness of the contingent praise technique was weakened somewhat late in the second week of the experimental period, because Mrs. K. began issuing undeserved praise comments—noncontingent reinforcement. For example, a praise comment from Mrs. K. at the reading table to Sally doing seat work sometimes followed too closely some inappropriate talking or other noise, so that Mrs. K. was in effect intermittently reinforcing deviant behavior. Such a situation illustrates why a teacher must be careful to reserve praise for a situation that warrants it. Otherwise, children will quickly observe that teacher attention and praise are not contingent on approved behavior.

Conclusions

Any conclusions derived from this project are highly tentative, because both base-line and experimental periods were too abbreviated and contained too many extraneous variables to produce any clearly valid or reliable results. However, findings do agree in kind with previous similar research, which shows that with a change in classroom control techniques a teacher can produce significant behavioral changes within the classroom.

Study 11

Target Behavior

For approximately three quarters of the school year the student, John, had mostly just put in his time in math class. He usually did not do his work either in class or at home, and he sometimes bothered the other students around him. He was off task much of the time, and the teacher had almost given up on him.

The target behavior was defined as (1) being in his seat; (2) working on whatever the class was doing, e.g., homework, quiz, listening; and (3) not bothering other students.

Procedure

After the base line was established, the teacher informed John that she was concerned about him and his progress. She explained to him that since all students were different and had different needs, perhaps he would be interested in a special program she had thought of to help him. She described the program to him, and he said he would be interested. For each 5-minute interval that he was on task, he would earn a point. A total of 10 points was possible in one period. If he earned six points, he received an "A" for the day; five points, a "B," etc. This would be a good way for him to raise his grade and succeed. He was told at the end of each interval whether he received a point.

Results

During base line, he had been on task only a very small part of the time. After the program started, he missed receiving an "A" only one day. In short, he improved immensely. His on-task behavior was reinforced by good daily grades, better grades on quizzes, and as I hypothesize from my subjective point of view, because he felt successful at a task for a change.

Discussion

Initially, it was somewhat hard to convince the teacher to try the project, because she thought that since the student "really hadn't done much of anything that he was supposed to all year," he probably could not be helped in a regular classroom environment. As the project progressed, the teacher became so interested and excited that she began using the idea with several other students, with some on the same point system and some getting to go to lunch early as a reinforcement.

One of the problems with the measurement of the behavior in the project was that the teacher felt that she could not deal with any interval smaller than 5 minutes. She said it would take up too much of the time she should be spending teaching. On numerous occasions, though, a smaller interval would have been better and more sensitive, because the teacher said that John had been on task almost all of the time during the 5-minute interval but had done one thing during the interval, for which he had lost the point. This problem caused the data to fail to truly reflect the change in John's behavior.

An interesting sidelight occurred when the teacher first began to mark base line. The whole class noticed her periodically marking a card. Most of the members of the class thought she might be watching them, so the behavior of the entire class vastly improved, even though there was no specific system of reinforcement established. The "assumed" reinforcer was the student's grade.

Had we had time to continue the program, the "cost" of an "A" would have increased, since John had received an "A" seven out of the last eight times. Actually, it probably should have been increased earlier, but we wanted to make sure that he felt he could be successful, and we did not strain the ratio. Social reinforcers and better grades because of his increased effort should have eventually maintained the on-task behavior as natural reinforcers in the environment.

The one day during the experimental stage on which John did not receive an "A" was the day of the school "hop," and all of the students were very excited over it. This may be the reason he did not do as well that day.

Overall, the teacher was very impressed with the change in John and others of her students, an she began to talk to other teachers in the building about the program. Nothing can convince teachers faster than another teacher experiencing success with a program and passing the idea along.

Study 12

Target Behavior

Pamela, age 13, had bitten her nails to the point where they were almost nonexistent. She could be seen biting them or the skin surrounding them while she read or watched TV. In observing her to get a base line, I found that she averaged about 50% of the observed time with her fingers in her mouth. Eliminating this was the target behavior.

Procedures

A token worth 10¢ was given to her each time she manicured her nails, which consisted initially of caring for her cuticles twice daily. She was paid at the end of the week. When Pam put her fingers in her mouth, she had to close her book for at least 5 minutes or the TV was turned off, depending on which activity she was engaged in at the time. Pam was also promised a chance to see a certain movie at the end of 2 weeks if she reduced the nail-biting.

Results

I was startled to find that it took only two book closings and one TV plug pulling to stop the nail-biting—at least in my presence (see accompanying graph). The manicuring was done religiously before leaving for school and before going to bed. Pamela was surprised to find $2 in her purse at the end of the week ($1.40 + .60 bonus for stopping so quickly). She received $1.48 the next week plus the movie trip, $.70 last week, and the thrill of seeing her nails grow is keeping her going.

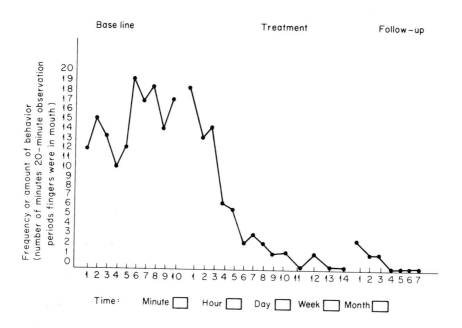

Study 13

Target Behavior

Paul was a child of 5 years. The target behavior I wished to extinguish was his tantrums whenever he was asked to do something that he did not want to do; either performing a task, or self-care help, or stopping an activity in a group or alone. Paul's tantrums can be described as kicking, crying, banging his head, and throwing objects. These behaviors occurred in various combinations and in a varying degree.

Procedures

When the behavior occurred, I said, "Stop it." If Paul did not stop, he was taken to the time-out room and placed in the room without comment. The door was closed and held if necessary to keep him in the room, and not opened until Paul had been quiet for 2 minutes. Then he was returned to the activity with no comment, so as not to reinforce being in the room. After 2 or 3 minutes of appropriate activity, he was reinforced with social praise and a hug or a pat for playing nicely.

Results

Paul's base line indicated 5–7 tantrums daily; time period from 7:00 A.M. to 9:00 P.M. When treatment began, tantrums increased to 10 the first

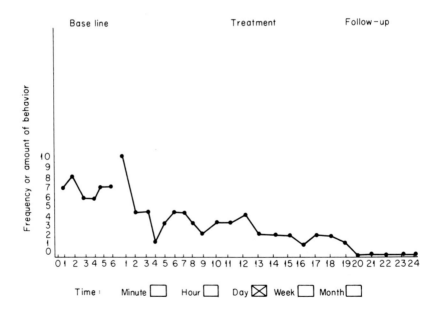

day: However, over a period of 21 days decreased to none on the last 4 days of record (see the graph on page 102). In addition, Paul's overall behavior was one of a happier child: He smiled more, entered into activities willingly, and ate appropriately at meals, used a napkin, and did not throw food or dishes. A bit of whining remained, but the verbal cue to stop has not been needed except on rare occasions.

Study 14

Target Behavior

I wanted to help my daughter, Becky, age 8½, to achieve better behavior at home. The self-care and home-helping tasks were: (1) combing or brushing hair; (2) brushing teeth; (3) hanging up clothes; (4) putting away shoes; (5) studying for Sunday School; (6) setting the table; (7) emptying the wastebaskets; and (8) making the bed. These tasks were identified as behaviors which, when performed without "reminders," would help to reduce tensions in a busy multiple-scheduled graduate-school household. (As a result of our discussions, I am now better able to identify specific "target behaviors"; however, I treated the ones in this study as collectively desired behaviors.)

Procedures

Becky was provided with an acetate-covered picture chart, a red marking pencil, and a soft cloth to use as an eraser. The chart could record daily per-

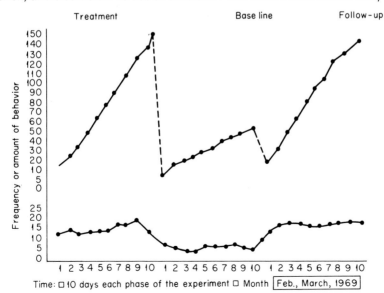

Time: □ 10 days each phase of the experiment □ Month │Feb., March, 1969│

formances of the eight tasks for 7 consecutive days. Initially, Becky received a penny for each task when she performed it. After 3 days, pennies were awarded at the end of the day when the chart was reviewed. Finally, she was rewarded with a choice of "presents" at the end of the week for having 100 accumulated points.

Results

The results were impressive! Becky worked for the reward (penny) and enjoyed the recognition (praise) accorded her upon the completion of her tasks. As shown in the graph on page 103, she performed more than three times better during those phases of the experiment when she was systematically reinforced for the performance of desired behaviors. (Becky liked "earning" her own pennies, and spending or saving them as she wished.)

Study 15

Target Behavior

I wanted Grady to work in either his social studies or spelling folder, and to take his turn in seeing the aide for having work checked and obtaining necessary materials.

Grady constantly showed passive resistance to class activities. His high-frequency behavior was sitting and staring, and thus withdrawing from the classroom atmosphere. He did not socialize with his peers and would not listen to adults (i.e., when instructed to work on the materials, he would simply look and not follow the instructions).

Recording Procedures

Using a watch with a second hand and a clipboard, I observed 10 seconds and recorded 10 seconds for approximately 10 minutes a day for a total 10-day observation. An X was used to indicate any time that Grady was off task during a given 10-second interval. Off-task behaviors exhibited included sitting and staring, wandering aimlessly around the room, intentionally remaining at the end of the line to see the aide, hiding his head in his desk, and aimlessly pretending to look for materials.

Experimental Procedure I

Grady was told that he was expected to work in either his social studies or spelling folder (and at other times of the day, in his math and/or reading folders) and to assume responsibility for seeing the aide to have his folder checked and to get the needed materials. I showed him the timer and explained to him that I would set it for varying amounts of time. Each time the bell rang, he would receive one point to be marked on a card on his desk if he was on task. I also explained that 10 points could be traded for a candy bar. However, since Grady would not accept the points (he hid or destroyed the cards) and was not interested in the candy bar, I found it necessary to try another procedure.

Experimental Procedure II

I informed Grady that instead of working for a candy bar, he could work for free time during Reward Time. (1 point = 1 minute free time). It was at this point that I introduced him to negative reinforcement, i.e., removal of an aversive stimulus to increase desired behavior. I explained to Grady that when he did not work, John, a classmate, would come over and annoy him until he went to work. To rid himself of John, he needed only to go to work. John was instructed to slide his desk over when Grady went off task and to ask him to go to work, get his book, etc.

Praise was not used for Grady because it was found to be ineffective. John was verbally and tangibly reinforced for his part in the experiment.

Results

Negative reinforcement has been very effective with Grady. It has helped him increase his target behavior (see following graph). Grady has produced more work during Experiment Period II than at any time since he entered my classroom. He has, in fact, taken the lead in his social studies group. In terms of the data collected from this study, Grady's on-task behavior averaged 34% during the base-line period. This average was increased during Experimental Period II to 88%.

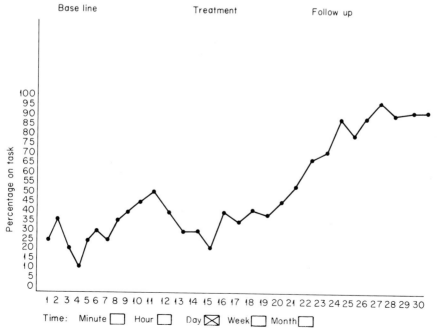

Measurement and Analysis of Classroom Behavior

EMILIO RIBES-INESTA

Education is fundamentally a process directed at the development of new and more complex forms of behavior. Education, a process that is carried out on multiple levels, provides the different members of a culture with the behavioral repertoires necessary for social and individual evolvement in agreement with the norms and goals of that culture.

The responsibility to educate is delegated, although not exclusively, to an ad hoc institution generically called a school. This institution is converted into the social agency specialized in educating the individual members of the culture, providing them not only with specific repertoires for different tasks that benefit the community as a whole, but also with those behaviors which are indispensable for living in a group.

Educational philosophies have traditionally been inspired by ideologies alien to an experimental science of behavior. The recent development of the experimental analysis of behavior, and of an applied technology with vast implications, makes possible a rigorous evaluation of the advantages and disadvantages of formal educational systems and their objectives in the light of data obtained under laboratory conditions.

The distinctive features of the experimental analysis of behavior are: (1) the determination of the environmental variables that enter into a functional relation with the behavior (either of an individual subject or of a group); and (2) a marked emphasis on measuring the behavioral and functional variables in the natural situation. An experimental analysis of the educational setting, the traditional paradigm of which is the classroom, necessarily requires both characteristics. It is our purpose in this paper to describe the instrumentation of procedures for behavior measurement in the classroom and to analyze some of the data obtained from the use of these measuring instruments.

EVALUATION OF RELEVANT BEHAVIORS

The measurement techniques of behavior analysis in natural environments have been characterized to date by stipulating, to a certain extent, a priori relevant response dimensions.

In the elaboration of complex measures (behavioral scales)—(Becker, Madsen, Arnold, & Thomas, 1967; Buell, Stoddard, Harris, & Baer, 1968; Patterson, 1969)—the main procedure has consisted of informal observation, which leads to the definition of response categories in the recording scale. A behavioral scale attempts to be a multi-use instrument in different natural environments that possess common elements. In this way, behavioral categories are formulated and topographically defined as response classes, which may appear in the aforementioned natural environment in some functional relation with stimulus constellations. Once the categories are established, the scale is submitted to a continuous refining process in regard to the definition of each of the categories. Its prolonged use makes this a permanent process.

As part of a pilot project for developing a preschool program that could be extended to primary school, we have initiated a series of exploratory studies of classroom behavior in elementary, kindergarten, and nursery schools at Xalapa and Mexico City. The beginnings of the project have been directed to a new tactic in approaching the construction and refinement of a behavioral scale especially designed for the classroom situation. It should be made clear that this scale is not to be used by the teacher or other nonpsychologists. It is rather intended to be a measuring instrument designed for descriptive studies that will allow for an experimental analysis of the determining variables of classroom behavior, either for analyzing the present structure of the educational environment or for evaluating new forms of programming the school environment.

The construction of the behavioral scale covers three well-defined steps:

1. Development of an *unspecific* scale
2. Construction of a *specific* scale from the data obtained with the unspecific scale
3. Calibration of the specific scale through the intermittent use of the unspecific scale.

Next, we shall describe the general procedure followed in the three steps for constructing the behavioral scale.

Unspecific Scale

The unspecific scale has a double function. In the first place, it allows the recording of behaviors occurring without stipulating a priori categories. The resulting categories may be divided into high-rate and low-rate behaviors, according to their actual rate of occurrence in the natural setting. Recording high-rate behaviors gives the basis for establishing a behavioral scale a posteriori, with categories generated by formal, reliable observation of the behaviors of multiple subjects in a wide sample of situations that define a classroom setting. Moreover, the unspecific scale affords the fundamental elements for elaborating a functional analysis that will allow the development of an ulterior controlled experimental analysis of the situation being recorded. These elements constitute the three-term contingency relationship: antecedent stimuli (S^D), response classes (R), and consequent reinforcing or punishing stimuli (S^R and S^P).

The type of unspecific scale used foresees the recording of three aspects:

1. What behavior occurs
2. Where it occurs
3. Who is present when it occurs

Recording the behaviors that take place provides us with a direct index of the behavioral categories most relevant to the situation being assessed. The place where the behaviors occur tells us about the physical background conditions that may have discriminative and/or dispositional properties. Finally, recording what people are present permits us to obtain information about the discriminative and reinforcing functions of the behavior of others in the natural environment.

Recording is carried out through an instantaneous temporal "flash" sampling system, which samples different subjects in a successive way according to a previously established sequence. This permits us to have an objective record of the group situation, but with individual measures. The particular value of the temporal sample depends on the number of subjects who constitute the situation to be recorded, so that there is a sufficient number of observations per subject in each session.

The measurement of the behaviors that takes place, the physical location where they occur, and the people present at that moment permit a more sophisticated analysis of the subjects' behavior in terms of conditional probabilities. From the total number of samplings, the percentage of samplings in which a given behavior occurs indicates its overall probability. Its conditional probability can be calculated in terms of the discriminative properties of the physical location, the people present, and the physical location *plus* the people present. The percentage of samplings in which a behavior in a determined place occurs with respect to the total number of occurrences of that behavior gives us its conditional probability. The same happens when the calculation is made in terms of the people present, or in terms of both aspects: physical location and people. The relevance of this information is self-evident: It provides a different approach to intervention in the environment. Instead of altering the overall probability of a response through the manipulation of certain types of consequences when the behavior takes place, the occurrence of the same behavior may be prevented by prior intervention in the discriminative conditions that control it. Which of these intervention tactics is more effective and susceptible to implementation in a natural environment is something to be tested in the future.

Specific Scale

The specific scale is constructed from the data obtained by applying the unspecific scale. The elaboration of this scale includes three steps. The first consists in tabulating the frequency of occurrence of each of the behaviors exactly as the individual observers recorded them. Tabulating the frequencies of occurrence only takes into account the column of the recording sheet that corresponds to "what behavior occurred," irrespective of the physical situation or the people present when the behavior took place.

Second, once the frequency of occurrence of the observed responses per group of individual observers is tabulated, the responses are selected in two categories: high-rate behaviors and low-rate behaviors. The functional relevance of high- and low-rate behaviors is also evaluated, with the purpose of eliminating response classes that are of no interest to the behavioral program to be developed. Once the behaviors are selected, the third step follows.

Here, the categories are defined from the labeling given by the different individual observers. The redefinition of the categories, which takes place in group discussions, includes two aspects: The first consists in standardizing the labels of the different categories of the unspecific scale in order to omit different names for common responses—i.e., to look at, to see, to pay attention to, etc. The second aspect refers to the definition of the categories themselves, considering the problems of judgment that may arise and the previous observers' experience.

This process has two advantages over the traditional method of constructing behavioral scales. The behavioral categories are specified a posteriori, after the *formal* observation of the subject's behavior in the natural environment in which the scale is later to be used. In this way, the categories that are included reflect the behaviors most relevant to the situation being recorded, avoiding extreme contamination of the scale by the particular verbal repertoires of those who construct it. Besides, it becomes unnecessary to redefine the categories continuously while the instrument is being used, since the redefinition of these categories constitutes a step previous to the scale use.

Calibrating the Specific Scale

Every empirical measurement should have three characteristics: validity, reliability, and sensitivity. The problem of the validity of a direct behavioral measurement is solved by the definition of the category to be measured. The reliability is determined by the extent of agreement among independent observers recording the same event. Finally, sensitivity refers to the precision with which the scale may reflect the changes that take place in time in the behavior being observed.

A behavioral scale is used before and after applying any technique of environmental intervention. If the intervention technique is effective, we may assume that it will alter substantially the behavior of the subject toward whom the intervention is directed. In some instances, the change in the behavior observed could be so great that the scale in use would not be able to measure the new repertoires or interactions taking place. In such cases the scale has lost sensitivity as a measure of this particular situation.

How could the original sensitivity of the scale be maintained? The process to be described is just being evaluated. Various periods of observation are sampled in which specific and unspecific scales are used simultaneously by independent observers. If the unspecific scale records responses different from the categories of the specific scale, a low correlation between both scales will be obtained, which means that the specific scale is no longer sufficiently sensitive; that is, it does not record what actually happens in the situation being measured. If we have high correlation between the scales, we can conclude that the specific scale continues to provide the necessary sensitivity.

In those cases where interscale correlation is low, the specific scale needs to be corrected, either by introducing new categories or by redefining the existing ones. This process, intermittently applied, allows for a continuous calibration of the scale's sensitivity, a factor not taken into consideration in the use of measuring instruments in behavioral analysis. Its use, in the last instance, should be tested through application in different situations and with different measurement scales.

FUNCTIONAL ANALYSIS OF CLASSROOM BEHAVIOR

A functional analysis of classroom behavior requires taking into account the control relation established among various sectors of the physical and social environments and the behavior of one or all of the subjects forming part of the classroom. Among the sectors of the environment that may require control relations with respect to the behavior that prevails in the classroom, we can identify:

1. The physical characteristics of the location
2. The behavior of the teacher.
3. The behavior of classmates or peers

These categories do not exhaust, of course, all the empirical possibilities given by a classroom setting. Nevertheless, they are the most outstanding from a behavioral viewpoint.

These different sectors of the environment may have a three-fold relationship with respect to a given behavior or behaviors: (1) as a reinforcing or punishing stimulus; (2) as a discriminative stimulus; or (3) as a setting event (see Bijou & Baer, 1961).

The purely physical aspects of the environment may have functional properties of dispositional or discriminative type, while the behavior of the teacher and of the classmates may function as discriminative or consequent stimuli, and in some particular cases as setting events—when they alter an already established three-term contingency. The potential functional duality of the physical characteristics of the classroom and the behavior of the teacher and peers raises a series of methodological problems.

In first place, in order to distinguish the discriminative properties from the dispositional control exerted by the physical location, it is necessary to take into account the interactions produced between the location and the control assumed by the behaviors of another person in relation to a given behavior. A setting event is defined in relation to the specificity of the effect of a reinforcer. To find out if a physical characteristic has dispositional properties it is necessary to observe that the reinforcing effect of an event is associated almost exclusively with the physical stimulus; that is, that an interaction exists between the reinforcing stimulus and the setting event. Let us say that the physical properties of the location are a discriminative stimulus when they control a given subsequent behavioral probability, independently of the presence or absence of the specified reinforcer in question or a previous event. A discriminative stimulus may control a variable response probability depending upon the parameters of the particular reinforcer.

To find out if the behavior of the teacher or of a peer has discriminative or consequent (reinforcing or punishing) stimulus properties, it is necessary to develop a special recording system in which the antecedent and consequent stimuli consistent with the behavior are taken into consideration. Even when this type of recording gives very valuable information about the environmental control of the behavior, it presents two shortcomings: First, the observer's training is very prolonged in order to achieve acceptable reliability in the measurements. Second, the action of remote discriminative, punishing, and reinforcing stimuli can be neither discarded nor evaluated, making it very difficult to establish with certainty which are the specific stimuli that control a particular behavior at a given moment.

A third factor, most relevant in natural situations, should also be mentioned. When the behavior of a given subject takes place in the presence of another person, the subject generally exerts at the same time discriminative and reinforcing control over that behavior, since it is not plausible that he would respond solely as a consequence of the behavior exhibited in his presence. Therefore, we find very often that the same person simultaneously has discriminative and reinforcing properties with respect to the same behavior. Even in situations in which the subject behaves neutrally towards a behavior of another, by the simple fact of his being present at the moment when this behavior is reinforced by others, we may deduce that he is going to acquire conditioned reinforcing properties. With this we want to stress that when measuring in practice it is extremely difficult to differentiate between the discriminative and the reinforcing properties of a subject present at the moment a particular behavior is exhibited.

The measurement of different degrees of conditional probability of the occurrence of a behavior in the presence of a physical location, the presence of a teacher, or the presence of one or several students, permits the analysis of the various control relationships that may be established in a relatively complex environment such as the classroom.

Physical Spaces

The analysis of the discriminative or dispositional control exerted by the physical characteristics of the architectural space has just begun to be taken into consideration in the studies of behavior analysis. A physical space may acquire discriminative properties for two fundamental reasons: (1) because it is associated with the reinforcement of an arbitrary behavior exhibited in this space, or (2) because the physical space, due to its architectural features, fosters particular types of behavior that will be followed by reinforcement. It is in this second aspect that it is of primary importance to carry out a careful quantitative analysis of the physical and architectural features that favor the exhibition of desirable behaviors and reduce at the same time the probability of undesirable behaviors. The type of measurement that we propose constitutes a first approach to this problem, which requires a more exhaustive and detailed assessment.

Through an imprecise example, we could illustrate one aspect of the physical structure of the classroom that is relevant to what we are saying. The typical classroom that we know usually consists of a rectangular or quadrangular space of intermediate dimensions. In the front part of the room are the blackboard and the teacher's desk. The students' desks are arranged in rows, so that some of them are closer to the teacher in the front part of the room, while others are farther toward the back. It is to be expected that the differential exposure to teacher's behavior (and as a result to her S^Ds and S^Rs) is not the same for all the various members of the group. This simple difference in exposure to the teacher's behavior, determined by the particular architectural arrangement of the classrooms, should produce in some instances important behavioral differences in the students, both with reference to the acquisition of knowledge and to the social behaviors exhibited in the classroom. Later we shall show some data in thi.s regard. We could extend ourselves somewhat more into how other architectural aspects influence the outcome of the educational process, but that would go beyond the basic topic of this paper.

The dispositional properties of the physical space are more complex to evaluate and require a careful study of the way a physical space interacts with the reinforcing properties of different physical and behavioral events. For the time being, no data exist on this matter.

Teacher's Behavior

There are many studies (Hall, Lund, & Jackson, 1968; O'Leary, Becker, Evans, & Saudargas, 1969) that show the importance of the teacher's behavior in determining individual and group behavior in the classroom. Later we shall give some data on how the behavior of the teacher varies in different sections of the school environment, and how a series of initial observations may be made about the type of behavior being exhibited in the classroom and its relevance to the education objectives pursued.

Students' Behavior

In studies in which the behavior of one or more students has been manipulated (Madsen, Becker, & Thomas, 1968; Hall, Panyam, Rabon, & Broden,

1968), the manipulation has been done primarily through the teacher's behavior. However, it is very important to be able to determine empirically the extent to which behaviors of other classmates exert control upon a student, and vice versa. It is necessary to analyze the feasibility of manipulating the behavior of a group through prescribed contingencies for a single subject, considering the possible specificity of social reinforcers in different subgroups in a classroom setting. It is fundamental to be able to determine empirically the differential responsiveness of several students to the behavior of the teacher and to other peers.

The implications for applied studies of socialization and behavior management in the classroom may be very important. Later, we shall show some data of interest on this particular topic.

PRELIMINARY DATA ON A DESCRIPTIVE PILOT STUDY

We will show some partial data from a descriptive pilot study carried out in several kindergarten and elementary schools at Xalapa, as well as in an experimental academic program with preschoolers being developed in the Maximino Avila Camacho Maternal Center for Children in Mexico City.

In the first place, we shall give some representative data of a second-year classroom of a public school in Xalapa. The data were obtained by direct recording in the classroom by two independent teams of observers during a period of 15 days, with daily recording sessions of an hour and a half. A temporal sampling procedure was used with instantaneous "flash" observations, each 30 seconds, which gave a total of 180 observations per day. Teacher and student behaviors were recorded, using the unspecific scale described earlier: what behaviors were exhibited, where they were exhibited, and who was present when the behaviors were exhibited. The reliability in the recordings varied between 85 and 90% and was computed by selecting at random 10 samples of two observers per day and comparing them.

The data obtained allow for an analysis of the classroom situation from different points of view. Figure 1, for example, shows the percentage of academic behaviors that occurred during the sampling periods in terms of the geographic position of the child in the classroom as well as that of the person or persons present. The academic behaviors include reading, writing, and characteristic classroom activities (drawing, etc.). The stability of the recordings is remarkable, as is the low level of occurrence of academic behaviors in the included situations. In none of the nine observation conditions was the percentage of academic behaviors higher than 20%. It is significant that within this reduced occurrence of academic behaviors, the percentage was slightly higher when the child was in a group of peers than when

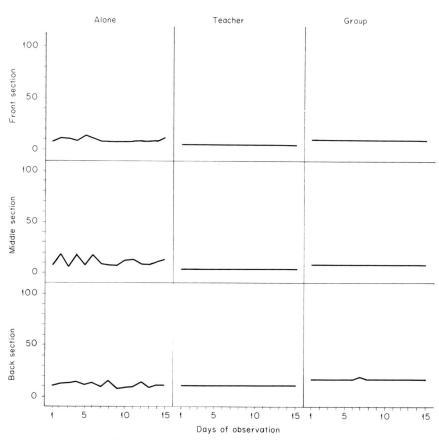

Fig. 1. *Academic behavior in a public school.*

he was alone with the teacher. It tended to present a slight instability when the child was alone at his desk. All this occurred independently of the geographic position of the student in the classroom.

Figure 2 shows the index of occurrence of different behaviors—academic (reading and writing), self-stimulation (entertaining oneself and perseverative behaviors), looking around, and talking—in the children seated in the front part of the classroom, in the presence of the teacher, of a peer, and alone. The percentage of the occurrence of the different behaviors was very low in the recorded situations: It was never higher than 10%. Among these behaviors, looking around and self-stimulation (which includes distraction) seem to be the ones most frequently present. Also, it is evident that the teacher had some type of suppressive property, since in her presence fewer behaviors occurred.

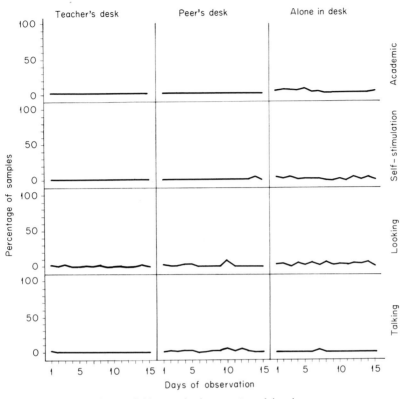

Fig. 2. *Children in the front section of the classroom.*

Figure 3 shows similar data, but refers to children sitting in the middle section of the classroom.

As in the previous case, the levels of behavior that occurred were very low, although the percentages were slightly higher (perhaps because the teacher was farther away). We may observe that the teacher seemed to function as a generalized suppressor, since in her presence the students again exhibited fewer behaviors than when she was not present. On the other hand, the percentage of academic and other behaviors, except talking, increased when the child was alone. Talking appeared only in the presence of a peer or classmate.

Figure 4 shows the occurrence of the four above-mentioned behavior categories in connection with the children sitting at the back of the classroom. It is not necessary to indicate again that the occurrence of the behaviors was very low especially in the presence of the teacher. The percentages here are slightly lower than those for the children sitting in the middle

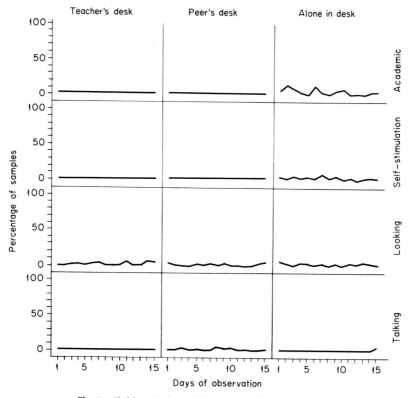

Fig. 3. *Children in the middle section of the classroom.*

of the classroom, and the occurrence of academic behavior seems to be restricted to occasions when the child was alone. The teacher, in this case, seems to control the behavior of looking around better than in the previous cases.

Figure 5 shows the teacher's behavior. Recordings include the four most frequently observed categories: talking to a student, talking to the group, looking at a student, and looking at the group. The data are graphed in terms of the location of the teacher in the sections of the classroom in which the behaviors occurred: the blackboard, the teacher's desk, the front part of the classroom, and the aisle. Other parts of the classroom, where recordings were made very few times with the unspecific scale, were not included. This allows us to infer that the teacher's mobility was very limited, and that therefore the children in the middle and back section of the classroom had little contact and exposure to her.

It may be observed that the behavior that occurs the least is that of looking

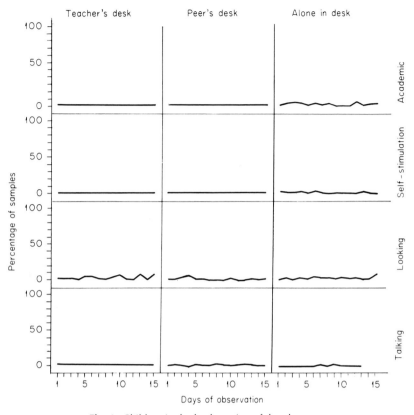

Fig. 4. *Children in the back section of the classroom.*

at the group, in spite of the fact that looking at individual students is not significantly high, either. To a certain extent it could be said that little visual contact between the teacher and students existed, perhaps because the teacher had her back to the group or was seated without facing the students. However, it may also be an artifact of the categories selected, since looking could be included in the category with talking. Talking to a student was the most frequently observed behavior, with the teacher at the blackboard or at the desk. This happened less frequently when the teacher was in the front of the room or walking through the aisles.

Talking to the group occurred more often when the teacher was at her desk or in the front section of the classroom. Looking at one student alone was neither frequent nor of great interest. It is convenient to point out, however, the low percentages of occurrence shown by the students in relation to the teacher's behavior—which also seemed to be extremely poor—

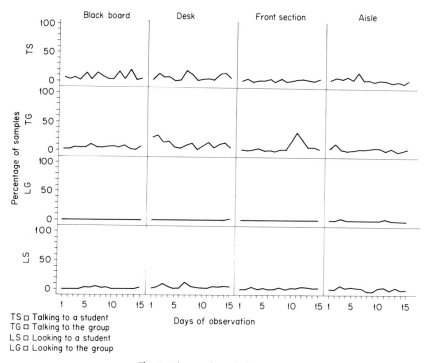

TS □ Talking to a student
TG □ Talking to the group
LS □ Looking to a student
LG □ Looking to the group

Fig. 5. *The teacher's behavior.*

was never greater than 40% of the samples. Later we shall comment on this.

Figure 6 describes some data obtained in an experimental project with children 3, 4, and 5 years old in a nursery school in Mexico City. These are partial data of an extensive academic and verbal project. We have selected them because they illustrate the use of a specific measurement scale, elaborated from an unspecific scale.

Figure 6 describes: (1) the behavior of one child, designated as the "target child," under a differential treatment; (2) the behavior of the children near him in the classroom, designated as "surrounding children"; and (3) the behavior of the teacher. The following categories were recorded for the target and surrounding children: talking to the teacher, aggression, talking to another child, physical contact, and smiling. These categories were elaborated from the inventory of behaviors obtained from the unspecific scale used in the public schools in Xalapa. *Aggression* included every intense physical contact or verbalization, spitting, and teasing; while *physical contact* included every sign of affection, kisses, hugs, nonviolent body contacts, and physical proximity. The following behaviors were recorded from the teacher: talking to a student, talking to the group (about academic matters),

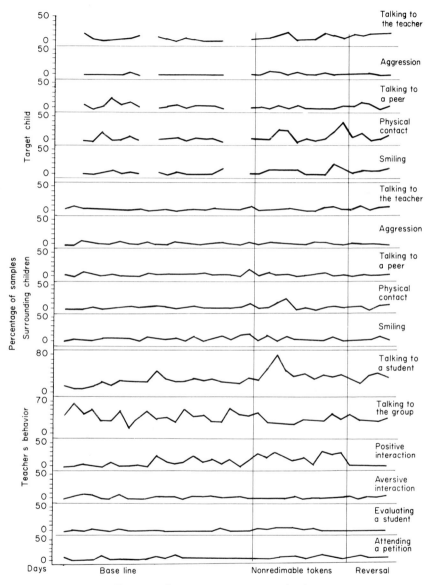

Fig. 6. *Academic project in nursery school.*

evaluating the children (giving points, correcting), answering questions, aversive interaction (scoldings, threats, punishments), and positive interaction (hugging, showing affection, soliciting attention).

The recordings cover 36 days of observation in 1-hour sessions, using flash samplings every 10 seconds, with an overall number of 360 observations per recording session. The reliability approached 90%.

These data form part of an experimental study to evaluate the properties of a token system of academic and social behavior, which includes both the students in the system and students who are not, and the changes observed in the behavior of the teacher. The classroom in question was not a typical situation, since there were only 10 children and a teacher. Figure 6 shows partial data from this study: a situation in which tokens were administered to target children for correct responses in writing, reading, and arithmetic. In this case, the tokens were not redeemed, so no type of reinforcers such as walnuts, snacks, privileges, etc., could be obtained with them.

If we analyze the upper part of the graph, we may observe in the first place the behaviors of the target child. The child showed the following approximate percentages: 10% in smiling, 20% in aggression, 20% in talking to the teacher, 20% in physical contact, and 20% in talking to the other children during the initial base-line period. When tokens were introduced, we may observe an increase in smiling to 20% and in physical contact to 40%. Independently of the changes observed in academic behavior, it is evident that tokens produced an increase (considering the proportional values and not the absolute effects) in two desirable behaviors without affecting the rest of the behaviors. In the period of reversion to base-line conditions—taking away the tokens—the behaviors decreased in percentge again.

Analyzing the middle part of the graph, we observe the behavior of the surrounding children. The percentages obtained for smiling, physical contact, talking to other children, aggression, and talking to the teacher were 10%, 7%, 10%, 10%, and 10% respectively. When tokens were introduced with the target child, a change was observed in the percentage of physical contact of the surrounding children, rising to 20%. This might be a direct effect of the same behavior having increased also in the target child, and it is a very clear illustration of how the behaviors observed in a single subject in a classroom may change the behavior of the rest of the group. In the reversion period, the percentage of physical contact returned to its previous level.

In the bottom part of the graph, we may see the teacher's behaviors. The following percentages were obtained during the base-line period: answering questions, 10%; evaluating a student, 10%; aversive interaction, 10%; positive interaction, 20%; talking to the group, 20%; and talking to a student, 45%. When the teacher introduced the token system with the target child, significant changes were observed: The percentage of times that she spoke to a student was 80%; the percentage of times that she talked to the group was 50%; and the percentage of positive interactions rose to 30%. Passing to the reversion period decreased the behaviors again, and they returned approximately to the same level obtained during the base-line period. Here we may appreciate how the token system, for reasons we shall not go into (see Ribes, Duran, Evans, Félix, Rivera, & Sánchez, 1973), produced important changes in the teacher's behavior, making her most positive by increasing the number of interactions with the students, a remarkable effect if we take into consideration the typical data on the interaction of the teacher in the classroom of a public school. A fact that deserves a more precise evaluation in another study is the extent to which a token system changes the teacher's behavior primarily and, as a derived effect, the behavior of the students in the classroom (Mandelker, Brigham, & Bushell, 1969).

FINAL CONSIDERATIONS

These data, which attempt to give an extremely reduced descriptive framework of the various interactions that take place in a classroom, make us think about several fundamental aspects of the school environment and the educational process.

In general, it is discouraging to observe such a low percentage of academic behaviors occurring in the classroom. Even when the data correspond to one single group in one school, the data obtained in other schools in the same study (not included here because of limitations in space) are similar to those reported here. Unfortunately, this low index is not limited exclusively to academic behaviors, but also affects the general behavior of the students. The fact that the lowest levels occur in the presence of the teacher may indicate two things: that the teacher has punitive properties, and/or that she reinforces passivity (low-rate behaviors). The two possibilities are feasible if we stop a moment to consider what is a good classroom according to the basic educational philosophy in our culture: a silent, orderly classroom with little movement, with children dedicated to the development of routine activities such as repeating aloud or copying.

Verbal behavior, so important for future educational and social development, is preferentially omitted in the presence of other children and is practically nonexistent in the presence of the teacher. On the other hand, the teacher's verbalizations directed to a particular student or to the group are also very much reduced in frequency, even when the data seem to indicate that talking to the student increases in the geographical vicinity of the teacher's desk. The initiative might come from the child and not from the teacher. It is not an ideally programmed environment!

We think that it is important to carry out descriptive studies of this nature with longer periods of observation and a greater variety of situations in order to reach a criterion of statistical representativeness in our schools. However, even though the data are scarce, they seem to present a scene that is not very encouraging with regard to the behavior in a classroom and, consequently, to the educational objectives we are pursuing. The necessity of implementing a behavioral technology that would make education more effective and that could transform the conditions and goals that currently have been imposed should be insisted upon. Measurement instruments and implementation techniques are available. We ought to concentrate on empirical evaluations of new educational objectives and new ways of integrating the process of instruction and socialization.

ACKNOWLEDGMENTS

I would like to acknowledge the collaboration of the group of students (at the University of Veracruz and at the National University of Mexico) who participated in the collection of data for this report, and to give special mention to Vicente Garcia, Enriqueta Galván, Ignacio Castro, Efrén Galván, Lamberto Villanueva, Sylvia Gomar, Leticia Rivas, Guadalupe Hernández, and Cristina Magallanes for their assistance in processing and analyzing the data.

REFERENCES

Becker, W. C. Madsen, C. H., Jr., Arnold, C. R., & Thomas, D. R. The contingent use of teacher attention and praise in reducing classroom behavior problems. *Journal of Special Education,* 1967, **1**, 287–307.

Bijou, S. W., & Baer, D. M. *Child development,* Vol. 1. A systematic and empirical theory. New York: Appleton, 1961.

Buell, J. S., Stoddard, P. L., Harris, F. R., & Baer, D. M. Patterns of social development collateral to social reinforcement of one form of play in an isolate nursery school child. *Journal of Applied Behavior Analysis,* 1968, **1**, 167–173.

Hall, R. V., Lund, D., & Jackson, D. Effects of teacher attention on study behavior. *Journal of Applied Behavior Analysis,* 1968, **1**, 1–12.

Hall, R. V., Panyan, M., Rabon, D., & Broden, M. Instructing beginning teachers in reinforcement procedures which improve classroom control. *Journal of Applied Behavior Analysis,* 1968, **4**, 315–322.

Madsen, C. H., Jr., Becker, W. C., & Thomas, D. R. Rules, praise and ignoring: Elements of elementary classroom control. *Journal of Applied Behavior Analysis*, 1968, **2**, 139–150.

Mandelker, A. V., Brigham, T. A., & Bushell, D., Jr. The effects of token procedures on a teacher's social contacts with her students. *Journal of Applied Behavior Analysis*, 1970, **3**, 169–174.

O'Leary, K. D., Becker, W. C., Evans, M. B., & Saudargas, R. A. A token reinforcement program in a public school: A replication and systematic analysis. *Journal of Applied Behavior Analysis*, 1969, **1**, 3–13.

Patterson, G. R., Programmed steps for family intervention. *Social Learning Project*. Oregon Research Institute. Eugene, Oregon, May 1969.

Ribes, E., Durán, L., Evans, B., Félix, G., Rivera, G., & Sánchez, S. An experimental evaluation of tokens as conditioned reinforcers in retarded children. *Behaviour Research and Therapy*, 1973, **11**, 125–128.

Thomas, D. R., Becker, W. C., & Armstrong, M. Production and elimination of disruptive classroom behavior by systematically varying the teacher's attention. *Journal of Applied Behavior Analysis*, 1968, **1**, 35–45.

The Design of
Classroom Contingencies[1]

DON BUSHELL, JR.

Reports of the systematic modification of classroom behavior have been appearing at an increasing rate since the mid-1960s. Each year, we have seen applications of behavior analysis increase the frequency of desirable classroom behavior and decrease the frequency of behaviors that disrupt the progress of the children or the tranquility of the teacher. Working first with the behavior of single children in specially designed settings (e.g., Staats, Staats, Schutz, & Wolf, 1962), and then with the aggregated behaviors of several children in regularly operating classrooms (e.g., Bushell, Wrobel, & Michaelis, 1968), behavioral researchers have assembled a promising, if young, technology for improving formal school education.

The building blocks of this new technology have been the research studies reported in our journals that repeatedly show how the careful management of contingencies can contribute to the teacher's effectiveness. From the perspective of 1972 it is possible to look back and see the outline of a

[1]The preparation of this paper was supported in part by Grant OEG-O-8-522422-4433 (286) from the United States Office of Education to the University of Kansas Support and Development Center for Follow Through.

pattern in the way these building blocks have been linked. Our early efforts seem to have been devoted to demonstrating that the classroom behaviors of children are indeed altered, for the good or the bad, by the timing and the quality of the teacher attention that follows them (e.g., Harris, Wolf, & Baer, 1964; Madsen, Becker, & Thomas, 1968).

Token reinforcement procedures soon began to provide further support and a degree of flexibility to the developing collection of teaching procedures (e.g., Wolf, Giles, & Hall, 1968). Tokens which the children could earn for performance or progress and then exchange for activities they selected have improved on-task behaviors (O'Leary & Becker, 1967), the accuracy (Glynn, 1970), and the rate of responding (McLaughlin & Malaby, 1971), and they have even altered the amount of teacher attention directed toward children (Mandelker, Brigham, & Bushell, 1970).

Game procedures (Barrish, Saunders, & Wolf, 1969) and self-recording techniques (Broden, Hall, & Mitts, 1971) have now been combined with adult attention and tokens to expand the array of strategies for making the classroom a more favorable learning environment.

More recently, I seem to detect an increase in the amount of attention being given to the analysis of antecedent events such as teacher prompts and curriculum sequencing (Lovitt & Curtiss, 1968). This increase is not detracting from our earlier emphasis on the consequences of both desirable and undesirable behaviors. It is, however, adding new dimensions and complexities to the analysis and improvement of classroom behavior.

The analyses of procedures now under way in our classroom settings in Kansas suggest an increased emphasis on building procedures that lead more directly toward the development of young children's independent study skills—behaviors that will allow elementary children to be less dependent on the continuous attention and support of the teacher. Hopefully, these investigations will add more building blocks to the total collection.

THE QUESTION OF USEFULNESS

As still more research accumulates on teacher training, tutoring, and student achievement, the attention of a wider audience is being drawn to the products of classroom behavior analysis. Still, there are only a very limited number of children who currently enjoy the benefits of a behavior analysis education. Something is missing. For all our scientific thoroughness, much of our work in the United States has missed its mark. As scientists, we have been so reinforced by the opportunity to share our work with one another through the pages of the *Journal of Applied Behavior Analysis* that we have not given enough attention to the concerns of those who do not read *JABA*—those who are the parents and teachers of young children.

In a recent paper, my colleague Donald M. Baer (1971) has suggested that it is time for some changes in the way we conduct our business. He reminds us that the value of our technology to the community will be determined by its effectiveness in solving social problems rather than by the elegance of its methodology or the objectivity of its experimental findings. Demonstrating that changes in reinforcement contingencies can and do increase the rate at which children accurately spell words is not the same thing as demonstrating that children exposed to well-designed systems of classroom contingencies do, in fact, make consistently better gains in school than comparable children with more traditional experiences.

Baer (1971) is pointing out that the continued development of our field depends on the presentation of actuarial evidence from group comparisons as well as functional analyses using single-subject designs:

> In short, the face logic of behavioral analysis is not enough to establish its correctness. Now that it is on the brink of handling massive behavior modification problems with large numbers of children, it can test, rather than assert, the goodness of that logic. It can ask, in an actuarial manner, how often it solves the referring social problem. . . . If in fact it does solve that problem, it has not only demonstrated its value to society, it has also contributed to its own scientific evaluation [p. 366].

BEHAVIOR ANALYSIS IN PROJECT FOLLOW THROUGH

Because I think the need for actuarial data is particularly great in education, I would like to describe how we are approaching the problem in a program for poor children that is supported by the federal government. This special program is called Project Follow Through. The United States Office of Education has given Follow Through funds to a number of local school districts that are trying to improve the education of poor children as they enter kindergarten at age 5, and move through the first 4 consecutive years of elementary school.

Most Follow Through communities use some of their funds to obtain the technical support and assistance of an outside agent called a Program Sponsor. Each of the 20 sponsors who now works with Follow Through projects has developed a technique he believes will improve the school experience of children in inner-city ghettos and rural poverty areas.

At this point, I should explain that we have a problem in public school education in the United States that may not be a problem in other countries. In the United States it is possible to predict how successful a child will be in school if you know the income of his family. Rich children are more successful than poor children. It is also true that communities support their schools by placing a tax on the value of their real estate. Since some communities have very valuable real estate and others do not, some communities provide a lot of money to support their schools, while others can provide very little. The quality of education that children receive is not the same in all United States schools.

Follow Through, then, is a program for children from poor families who live in poor neighborhoods and go to poorly supported schools that are, on an actuarial basis, often ineffective.

Since 1968, my student colleagues and I at the University of Kansas have been the sponsoring group for a number of Follow Through projects throughout the United States. We call our program Behavior Analysis, and we have tried to design a new and more effective classroom by assembling the building blocks created by the experimental analysis of behavior. At the present time we are working with nearly 7,000 children in the 12 communities shown in Table 1. Some of the schools are urban, others are rural. The children are Puerto Rican, black, white, and Indian, but all of them share a level of poverty that predicts they will fail in school unless we are able to make some very basic changes.

When I say they will fail in school, I am referring to the fact that in many schools where we are working, more than 20% of the children who are in the fifth grade do not have beginning reading skills. We want *all*

Table 1

Behavior Analysis: Head Start—Follow Through Projects in Operation 1971–1972

	Location	Grades	Schools	Classes	Children
(U)[a]	Bronx, New York	K-3	2	18	518
(R)[b]	Hopi Reservation, Arizona[c]	H.S.-3	5	31	503
(U)	Indianapolis, Indiana	K-2	4	14	389
(U)	Kansas City, Missouri	K-2	3	20	542
(U)	Louisville, Kentucky[c]	K-2	4	24	605
(R)	Meridian, Illinois	H.S.-3	3	29	606
(R)	Northern Cheyenne, Montana	1-3	3	16	439
(U)	Pittsfield, Massachusetts	K-2	3	8	185
(U)	Philadelphia, Pennsylvania	K-3	3	51	1407
(R)	Portageville, Missouri[c]	H.S.-3	1	17	442
(U)	Trenton, New Jersey	K-3	8	33	841
(U)	Waukegan, Illinois	K-2	1	18	433
	Totals		40	279	6910

[a] (U) Urban.
[b] (R) Rural.
[c] Localization of program control begun.

of our children to be able to read like fifth graders when they reach the fifth grade.

The Elements of a Behavior Analysis Classroom

Because there are many different ways to translate the principles of behavior into a design for a better classroom, I must describe how a Behavior Analysis classroom operates.

Small-Group Instruction

Shaping is a process that requires lots of behavior and lots of consequences for those behaviors. If you were to walk into one of our classrooms you would see four adults and 30 to 35 children. The certified professional teacher would be teaching reading to a small group of six or seven children; a nonprofessional teacher aide would be teaching arithmetic to another small group of children; and the remaining children would be practicing handwriting and spelling with two teaching parents.

The parents who teach in our classrooms are often receiving some kind of welfare support, and typically they have had very little schooling themselves. Nevertheless, we have found that, with proper training, they are excellent teachers. The parents of the children who work with us are first hired for a 6- to 8-week period during the year their child is in kindergarten. These training positions rotate so that we have the opportunity to work with 11 different parents during that first year. The next year, some of these parents will work with us again, this time for a longer period. Each year, as the children progress and the materials become more difficult, the teaching skills of the parents improve. Many of the parents who began with 6 weeks of training in 1968 have now become so skillful they have been hired by the public schools to serve as full-time teacher aides.

I am stressing the role of the parents in our program because I think it is important in many ways. It increases the amount of reinforcement that can be delivered in the classroom, but it also changes the relationship between the neighborhood of the school and the school itself. There is not space here to elaborate, but this is a relationship that badly needs change.

Curriculum Criteria

To make the best use of the opportunity to use small-group instruction, Behavior Analysis classes have selected their curriculum materials according to six criteria which seem to derive from what we know about shaping. If you ask six questions about any instructional sequence, the more often the answer is "yes," the better the sequence is going to be. The six questions that follow are easy to ask, but they are a harsh evaluation of many curriculums.

1. Does the curriculum describe the terminal behavior?
2. Does the curriculum measure the student's entry level?
3. Does the curriculum require frequent student responding?
4. Does the curriculum contain clear criteria for correct responses?
5. Does the curriculum contain check points and prescriptions?
6. Does the curriculum accommodate individual differences?

These questions are challenges to each curriculum, asking that it state its objective in behavioral terms, and that it provide some method of determining the beginning skills of each student so that all are not required to begin at the same point. The materials should provide frequent opportunity for a student to respond in ways that can be directly observed by the teacher, and they should provide a clear indication of when a response is correct so improved approximations of the objective can be quickly reinforced. The materials are also asked to provide for periodic checks on student progress, and appropriate prescriptions for future instruction based on performance at these checks. Finally, and perhaps most important, the materials must be flexible enough to allow different children to work at different rates.

Token Incentives

Even a classroom that provides small-group instruction with carefully selected materials does not guarantee the motivation so necessary to effective learning. Consequently, Behavior Analysis classrooms use a token reinforcement system. The operation of the system is most easily described by explaining what typically happens during a school day. Soon after the children arrive in school, they will begin working with one of the small groups that are studying reading, arithmetic, and writing. As the child responds, either verbally to one of the adults or with marks on paper, the adult is able to provide praise and encouragement very frequently. Praise for progress and improvement is usually accompanied by the presentation of a token. In each group, the adult moves quickly from child to child, in a random sequence, providing correction and help where needed, and tokens and praise where appropriate. The tokens that the children accumulate during an instructional period can later be exchanged for a variety of privileges and activities that they select, according to their individual preferences and according to the number of tokens they have acquired.

Throughout each day there is an alternation between times for instruction and times when the children may exchange their tokens for activities from the changing lists, or menus, of games, art projects, stories, dancing, play-ground activities, singing, and even the opportunity to do extra reading or arithmetic. The fact that the token system allows the children to make inde-pendent decisions about how they will spend their time during a school day introduces a freedom of choice that is unusual in classrooms that are more often characterized by coercion and an absence of appropriate reinforcement.

The Delivery System

All of the elements we have assembled under the heading of Behavior Analysis are supported by experimental evidence of their advantages. These empirical data, however, have come out of rather well-controlled settings that are convenient to the experimenter. In Follow Through, we have the additional challenge of implementing effective procedures under the rela-tively adverse circumstances of regularly operating schools that are many miles from the University of Kansas.

An abbreviated description of our delivery system can be divided into three components: training, local staff development, and data processing. Since 1968 we have consistently moved our training program closer and closer to each participating classroom. Now, special classrooms, designated as training classes, are located in or near each project to provide week-long practicum training for teachers and aides. These settings provide the oppor-tunity to rehearse observation and recording techniques, specific curriculum strategies, planning, and management techniques.

The training classes are undoubtedly very helpful (perhaps essential at this stage), but they cannot provide the day-to-day support that is needed by the teaching teams of four adults in every classroom. To provide this help, we have asked each community to set aside some of its funds to support two training positions for every 10 Behavior Analysis classes. These two trainers, a Staff Trainer who works with teachers and permanent aides and a Parent Trainer who manages the training program for teaching parents, are gradually learning to do all that the outside sponsor was expected to do earlier in the program. Soon we will be able to provide our support on a very intermittent basis and rely on local trainers to maintain the growth and vitality of each project.

The third component of the delivery system, data processing, may be the most important. Over the past 3 years this system has developed to the point that we are now able to monitor the weekly academic progress of every individual child in the program. Moreover, we can determine when a child's progress is falling below the rate needed to reach preestablished targets. Because the data system allows us to see problems as they occur, we can respond with additional training and program refinements when and where they are needed.

SIGNS OF PROGRESS

The effects of Behavior Analysis procedures are determined by experimental evaluations. The effectiveness of our delivery system is established, initially, by the performance of children on standardized achievement tests. Consequently, I would like to share with you some of the current indications that encourage us to believe that Behavior Analysis is capable of meeting the actuarial tests proposed by Baer.

The sequence must begin with one set of non-Follow Through data which indicates that children enrolled in a Behavior Analysis Head Start program run by their mothers made greater gains on the *Wide Range Achievement Test* than a carefully matched group of children in a regular Head Start program. The children in these two groups began with identical entry scores, age, and family income, yet, by the end of the year, the Behavior Analysis (Co-op) children had a substantially greater head start in all three skill areas measured by the test (see Fig. 1).

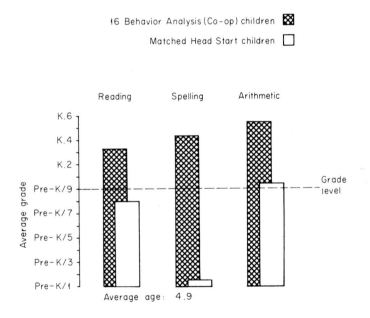

Fig. 1. Wide Range Achievement Test, *end of pre-K average score—Spring 1970.*

The Parent Cooperative Head Start center was located close to the University of Kansas, and the program was supervised by a member of the University staff. Consequently, these data fail to establish that a comparable effect can be achieved in projects that are remote from Kansas and locally managed. Two additional figures address that issue directly.

The first project requiring long-distance support is located in an economically depressed area of southeastern Missouri. Here it was possible to compare the test performance of three groups of children as they entered public-school kindergarten. Figure 2 shows that the poor children who had a Behavior Analysis Head Start performed better than nonpoor children who did not have Head Start, and they were tragically ahead of other poor children who entered kindergarten without prior classroom experience.

These data are supplemented by the performance of Arizona Indian children who entered kindergarten in the fall of 1970. Figure 3 illustrates that, even though they were slightly younger, the children with a Behavior Analysis background began school with an advantage.

Collectively, these data indicate that a Behavior Analysis preschool program makes an important difference for children, a difference that can be replicated in a variety of geographical and cultural settings. Next, of course, we need to know if these kinds of effects are restricted to children of preschool age.

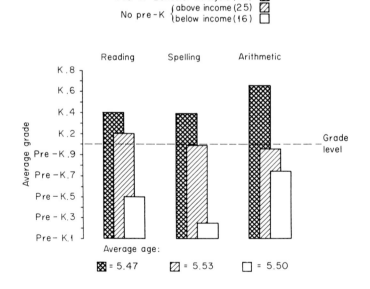

Fig. 2. Wide Range Achievement Test, *entering K average score (rural)—Fall 1970.*

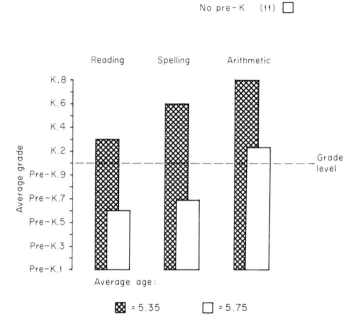

Fig. 3. Wide Range Achievement Test, *entering K average score (Indian)—Fall 1970.*

The *Metropolitan Reading Readiness Test* is widely used in the United States to assess the adequacy of children's backgrounds as they complete the kindergarten year. A high score on this test is taken to indicate that a child is well prepared to profit from first-grade experiences, and a low score forecasts difficulty with first-grade tasks. For convenience, the top of the scoring range is given the category label of "A," the next highest segment of the range is "B," the middle range is "C," and the lower two segments are labeled "D" and "E" respectively.

Figure 4 shows the average performance of kindergarten children from two different school districts both before and after the initiation of their Behavior Analysis programs. District A, a northern middle-sized commercial city, has administered the Metropolitan Test for a number of years as part of its regular evaluation program. In 1969, only 10% of the children from one school scored at the "C" level or higher (indicating adequate preparation for first grade). More than 60% of the children in the same school scored "C" or better at the end of the first Behavior Analysis year, and, by the end of the second year when the teachers were accustomed to the program's procedures, the figure rose to nearly 100%.

Pre – Behavior Analysis Follow Through ☐

First year Behavior Analysis Follow Through ▨

Second year Behavior Analysis Follow Through ▨

Third year Behavior Analysis Follow Through ▨

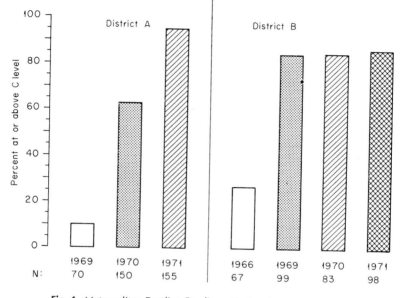

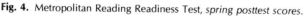

Fig. 4. Metropolitan Reading Readiness Test, *spring posttest scores.*

A similar before–after pattern in District B is additional testimony to the effectiveness of Behavior Analysis at the kindergarten level. The apparent generality of program effects is supported by the fact that, unlike District A, District B is a small, rural community. In District A, the children are predominantly black; in District B they are predominantly white.

Still further encouragement is provided by data from a large midwestern industrial city (see Fig. 5). In this case the *Wide Range Achievement Test* compared performance at the end of kindergarten of poor children in one school with nonpoor children in another. The nonpoor children were selected by this school district as a comparison group because they attend a school that has an established history of scoring at or very near the norms of standardized achievement tests. The poor children who had a Behavior Analysis kindergarten scored, on the average, about one-half year ahead of the norms and the nonpoor comparison group. The poor children, in the

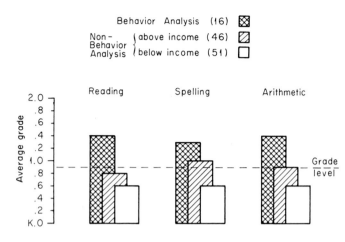

Fig. 5. Wide Range Achievement Test, *spring posttest scores, 1971—Kindergarten.*

same school, who did not have the benefits of a Behavior Analysis program scored below the test norms and the comparison group.

One additional bit of documentation can be added to the accumulating evidence that economic poverty need not determine poor school achievement. The first-grade children in four different schools in a single midwestern university community were given the *Gates, MacGinitie Reading Test* in the spring of 1971 (see Fig. 6). These four schools serve neighborhoods that differ in average family income. The relatively low economic level of the first neighborhood is indexed by the fact that 30% of the children in this school receive a free lunch provided for children of families who are below established income levels. The first-grade children in this school scored 2 months below expected levels in both the vocabulary and comprehension components of the reading test. In contrast, the first graders who were Behavior Analysis students scored well above the expected levels in both areas and were comparable in achievement to children from much more affluent neighborhoods.

In case after case, in large cities and small communities, in neighborhoods that are white, black, and Indian, the evidence is accumulating to deny the inevitability of an actuarial relationship between low income and low school achievement. The poor children in Behavior Analysis classes are progressing more rapidly than their peers in traditional classrooms.

There is another body of actuarial evidence that deserves passing notice. This evidence suggests, not too surprisingly, that children who do not speak English at home will do poorly in English-speaking schools. Teaching parents in Behavior Analysis classes are changing that pattern. Because they represent

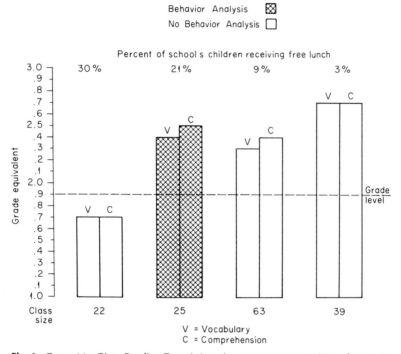

Behavior Analysis ⊠
No Behavior Analysis ☐

Fig. 6. Gates, MacGinty Reading Test, A-1, spring posttest scores, 1971—first grade.

the child's natural language community and extend it into the classroom, they are able to build on whatever communications skills the children bring with them. Where appropriate, our Parent Trainers are bilingual. As they work with the teaching parents they demonstrate that there is no stigma attached to the use of a native language. Instead, they emphasize the importance of getting the child to respond actively, if not in English, in whatever language he is able to use. If the child can respond in Hopi more easily than in English, Hopi is used so the act of responding can be reinforced. When active verbal responding has a well-established history of reinforcement, English-language fluency can develop quickly and, in our experience, easily. Compare, for example, the *Wide Range Achievement Test* scores for two groups of Northern Cheyenne Indian children who have been in Behavior Analysis classes. The performance of the children who are not from English-speaking homes is equivalent to the performance of those who learned English as the primary language at home (see Fig. 7).

Inevitably, a question arises in a form similar to, "Yes, but will it last?" It is a difficult question to answer satisfactorily. Part of the difficulty is

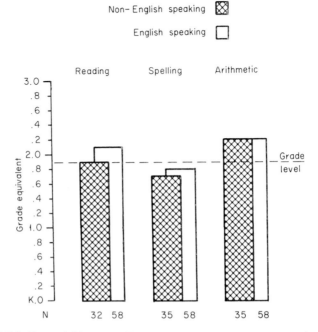

Fig. 7. Wide Range Achievement Test, *spring posttest scores, 1971—Behavior analysis Follow-Through, first grade.*

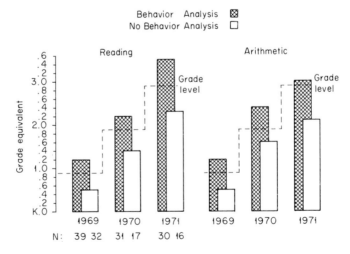

Fig. 8. Wide Range Achievement Test, *spring posttest scores, 1969, 1970, 1971—Kindergarten, first, and second grades.*

that the data are not yet available. This is a temporary problem; the data are accumulating. Another part of the difficulty comes from the vain hope that it is possible to do something magical for children in the primary grades that will forever inoculate them against the effects of inadequate education in higher grade levels. Happily, the children will not lose what they have gained if they leave a Behavior Analysis program. Unhappily, they cannot be expected to continue their high rates of academic progress if they are in classrooms that are less effective.

We have not yet seen our first cohort of Behavior Analysis children complete the 4 full years of Follow Through. At this point, the original group that entered in the fall of 1968 has completed the second grade and will "graduate" from our program later this spring. Even though they are preliminary, there are already some suggestions that the benefits of Behavior Analysis not only last, but accumulate progressively from year to year. The children represented in Fig. 8 live in a ghetto neighborhood of a manufacturing city in the industrial northeastern section of the United States. For 3 successive years the Behavior Analysis children have been demonstrating achievement gains that are moving them farther above expected norms, while a comparison group of children is falling farther below those norms.

It is speculating beyond the available data, but this figure suggests the possibility that Follow Through may be having an influence on the stability of the neighborhoods it serves. Of the 39 Behavior Analysis children tested in 1969, 30 were in the same school 2 years later. Only 16 of the original group of 32 comparison children could be found by school officials after the same interval. It would be an extraordinary bonus to discover that the new relationship between the neighborhood and the school created by the teaching parents is making families less willing to move their residence.

A CLOSING COMMENT

The preceding data must not be misunderstood. In their current, preliminary form they neither confirm nor deny that Behavior Analysis is capable of solving the problem under attack by Project Follow Through. The data are extremely favorable indicators, and they are substantial reinforcers for us at the University of Kansas, but they are incomplete.

There is also considerable room for disagreement over the appropriateness of measuring the effects of a Behavior Analysis program with standardized achievement tests. Our discipline teaches us the value of direct measurement and trains us to be suspicious of indirect evaluations of experimental manipulations. Should we not, then, limit ourselves to the use of criterion-referenced tests that specifically measure the skills we are teaching? For the present, the answer is no. So long as the schools define achievement problems in terms of standardized test scores, that is the measure on which we must demonstrate improvements.

Finally, it must be stressed that none of the data in this presentation alters the continuing need for experimental analyses. By building on behavioral research in classroom settings, we have fashioned a program that appears to make an important difference for the children who are exposed to it. Now we must submit that total program to the kind of component analysis that will begin to specify its critical elements and lead to its further refinement. It will require the combined research skills of all of us, but there appears to be room for optimism that we are beginning to test, rather than merely assert, both the logic and the social value of behavior analysis in education.

REFERENCES

Baer, Donald M. Behavior modification: You shouldn't. In E. A. Ramp & B. L. Hopkins (Eds.), *A new direction for education: Behavior analysis 1971.* Lawrence, Kansas: The University of Kansas, Support and Development Center for Follow Through, Department of Human Development, 1971.

Barrish, H., Saunders, M., Wolf, M. Good behavior game: Effects of individual contingencies for group consequences on disruptive behavior in a classroom. *Journal of Applied Behavior Analysis,* 1969, **2**, 119–124.

Broden, M., Hall, R. V., & Mitts, B. The effect of self-recording on the classroom behavior of two eighth-grade students. *Journal of Applied Behavior Analysis,* 1971, **4**, 191–199.

Bushell, D., Wrobel, P., & Michaelis, M. Applying "group" contingencies to the classroom study behavior of preschool children. *Journal of Applied Behavior Analysis,* 1968, **1**, 55–61.

Glynn, E. L. Classroom applications of self-determined reinforcement. *Journal of Applied Behavior Analysis,* 1970, **3**, 123–132.

Harris, F. R., Wolf, M., & Baer, D. Effects of adult social reinforcement on child behavior. *Young Children,* 1964, **20**, 8–17.

Lovitt, T., & Curtiss, K. Effects of manipulating an antecedent event on mathematics response rate. *Journal of Applied Behavior Analysis,* 1968, **1**, 329–333.

Madsen, C., Becker, W., & Thomas, D. Rules, praise, and ignorin: Elements of elementary classroom control. *Journal of Applied Behavior Analysis,* 1968, **1**, 139–150.

Mandelker, A., Brigham, T., & Bushell, D. The effects of token procedures on a teacher's social contacts with her students. *Journal of Applied Behavior Analysis,* 1970, **3**, 169–174.

McLaughlin, T., & Malaby, J. Development of procedures for classroom token economies. In E. A. Ramp & B. L. Hopkins (Eds.), *A new direction for education: Behavior analysis 1971.* Lawrence, Kansas: The University of Kansas, Support and Development Center for Follow Through, Department of Human Development, 1971. Pp. 29–40.

O'Leary, K. D., & Becker, W. Behavior modification of an adjustment class. *Exceptional Children,* 1967, **33**, 637–642.

Staats, A., Staats, C., Schutz, R., & Wolf, M. The conditioning of textual responses utilizing "extrinsic" reinforcers. *Journal of the Experimental Analysis of Behavior,* 1962, **5**, 33–40.

Wolf, M., Giles, D., & Hall, R. V. Experiments with token reinforcement in a remedial classroom. *Behaviour Research and Therapy,* 1968, **6**, 51–64.

An International Venture
in Behavior Modification

FRED S. KELLER[1]

There is a practice among the people of my country called *retirement*. It is carried out by workers in many organizations and many institutions. At Columbia University, for example, a professor must stop teaching when he reaches the age of 65 or, at the latest, 68. If he should be an officer of the administration, whose duties require greater powers of the mind, he *must* retire at 65, although he may go on to *teach* for 3 years more. These rules are based upon the wisdom of our leaders, who know exactly when the little grey cells within the brain begin to suffer a collapse.

With these hard facts of life and physiology to guide me, I began to think about my own retirement well before the time when it was scheduled to occur. I commenced to look around for a warmer, less expensive climate than that of New York City. I thought of Puerto Rico and Southern California; for awhile I even thought of Cuba, but the climate there became almost too warm.

Then, quite suddenly, I received an invitation to Brazil. It came from Myrthes Rodrigues do Prado, a student at the University of São Paulo. Myrthes had been a pupil of mine at Columbia several years before, but had been

[1]Present address: The Center for Personalized Instruction, Georgetown University, Washington, D.C.

143

compelled to leave her course because of a serious illness. She wrote me to ask if I would consider coming to São Paulo as a visiting professor.

I was sure that Myrthes, only a student, had little right to be extending invitations to professors, but I was flattered by her letter nevertheless. I wrote a pleasant answer, expressing interest in South America and a desire for further information. Then I dropped the matter, except for looking at a map to find out where Brazil would be, and speaking briefly with my colleague, Otto Klineberg, who had once been there.

That was in May of 1959. In December, I received another letter from my former pupil and, a few days later, a cablegram from Dr. Paulo Sawaya, the well-known physiologist, who was then Director of the Faculty of Philosophy, Sciences, and Letters at the University of São Paulo. He offered me a chair in experimental psychology. I decided that Myrthes, although just a little girl, must have a lot of power.

I replied to Dr. Sawaya's cable with another, again expressing interest, but requesting further information. He answered me with a letter that did not explain very much, but told me how happy he was to know that I would come. He suggested also that, in addition to my teaching, there were pressing psychological problems that I could easily solve within the University when I got there. If I had been a little less romantic or a little more perceptive, I might have read between the lines and stayed at home.

Many things took place within the year that followed. My manager, and center of my affection, had to be convinced that I was not insane; our house had to be rented; a leave of absence had to be arranged; and a loss of income had to be looked after by a Fulbright–Hayes award. We underwent inoculations and brought all-purpose clothing that could be washed in any jungle stream. I took a summer course in Portuguese at Columbia with three other students, taught by an engineer from Lisboa. Except for the Berlitz School, I could find no other place in New York City in which one could prepare to speak with 80 million "good neighbors" in Brazil. (I later learned that this one did not prepare me either.)

Finally, I was talked to by the State Department concerning "culture shock" and related matters, with examples drawn from Indonesian sources, except for one or two from Chile and Perú. Then, on a cold February evening in 1961, we took off from Idlewild Airport on the overnight flight to Rio, loaded down with erroneous ideas and 40 kilos of excess baggage. Five days later, after an official "orientation" (mostly on the beach of Copacabana), we arrived at São Paulo.

We were met by Dr. Sawaya, who had just been relieved of his duties as Director of the Faculty. He was accompanied by his successor, Dr. Mário Guimarães Ferri, and by Dr. Carolina Martuscelli Bori. Dona Carolina went with us that night to dinner and tried, without success, to clarify the local academic and political situation. It was obvious that I had a lot to learn within the year ahead.

Among the things that happened soon was a memorable encounter with Dr. Anita Cabral and a group of her assistants and co-workers in psychology at the University. It had not been *her* idea that I should come to São Paulo. In fact, she had a different plan entirely, but this I did not know. As soon as the formalities were over and we were seated at her conference table, she went directly to the point: "I hope," she said, "that you bring us something new—something that we do not already know."

Dona Anita was really not expressing a hope, nor was she being very kind to her embarrassed guest, but she was asking a very important question—a question that should be put to every teacher before he accepts an invitation to be a visiting professor in a foreign land: Is there a plausible academic reason for this journey? There are, perhaps, no better emissaries from one nation to another than its students and professors; but there must be something for the student to gain from his study that he could not get at home, and there must be something new, in terms of knowledge or of skill, that the professor carries with him if his appointment is to be worthwhile.

What I took to Brazil in 1961 were the seeds of reinforcement theory, and they fell on very fertile soil. My third- and fourth-year pupils at the University of São Paulo, both men and women, were especially alert to new ideas. Their number wasn't very large (10 or 15 at the most), but the quality of their understanding was as great as any teacher could desire.

In addition to the "experimental analysis of behavior," I brought a piece of apparatus to Brazil (at least it started out for there when I did) and a special kind of textbook in which many critical words were missing from each page but could be found upon the next one. The Skinner Box permitted us to carry on research in animal learning before the year had ended; and the Holland–Skinner programmed text was translated into Portuguese by Rodolpho Azzi and is still in use today.

Rodolpho was my first *assistente* and made the difference between success and failure in my work at São Paulo. His advice and counsel saved me from humiliation or disaster on more than one occasion. His experience in teaching and his keen awareness of my problems often helped to bridge the gap of understanding between me and my pupils. His patience and good humor were often put to test but never failed.

Besides Rodolpho, there was Dr. Martuscelli Bori, the psychologist who had greeted us upon arriving in São Paulo. Dona Carolina, in spite of her many other duties, found the time to attend my classes, to do the laboratory work connected with them, and to participate in several research efforts. Her support was critical in furthering the growth of reinforcement theory in Brazil, and, with Rodolpho Azzi, she later took an active part in the educational venture that I am going to describe here.

By the time that I was ready to go home, some progress had been made. In spite of interruptions produced by student strikes, the abdication of Jânio Quadros, and other events of lesser importance, a number of items could be listed. Our course had been successfully completed by almost all of our students; two collaborative studies had been prepared for publication (Azzi, Fix, Rocha e Silva, & Keller, 1964; Azzi, Rocha e Silva, Bori, Fix, & Keller, 1963); a primitive laboratory had been constructed for experiments in animal behavior; three students had applied for foreign study and were soon to be accepted; and I had succeeded in persuading John Gilmour Sherman, a former pupil and co-worker at Columbia, to come to São Paulo in 1962.

It would have been hard to find a better man than Gilmour Sherman for building up a laboratory and consolidating theory at the University of São Paulo. "Gil," as everyone called him, was effective from the start, and readily adjusted to the Brazilian *ambiente*. His classes were popular, his laboratory prospered, he worked well with all his colleagues, and his progress in speaking Portuguese was exceptionally good.

Near the end of his year at São Paulo, Sherman went with Dr. Martuscelli Bori and Rodolpho Azzi to Brasília. They were invited by Darcy Ribeiro, *Chefe do Gabinete Civil* under João Goulart, who was then recruiting teachers for the national university. Darcy was a former colleague at São Paulo, and wanted Dona Carolina to come to Brasília, with a staff of her own selection, to build a Department of Psychology in the new University. Darcy charmed the members of the group and excited them with the prospect of creating a splendid department, along whatever lines they chose to follow with respect to orientation, curriculum, and procedures of instruction. They were so enthusiastic and persuasive in the letters which they wrote to me that I agreed to join them. (I did not tell them that the time was approaching when my little grey cells would diminish in their function.)

As a first step in our project, my friends came to the United States. There they visited universities, hospitals, and other centers where psychology was taught, studied, or practiced in one way or another. They talked with teachers, researchers, and clinicians. They went to laboratories, libraries, and machine shops. They took notes on everything and tried to extract from every experience something of value to our program.

They bought or were given hundreds of books, and they ordered laboratory apparatus. They got many words of advice and counsel from psychologists who were later to become a corps of departmental consultants. And, finally, at the end of their travels, we all sat down around the fire in Englewood, New Jersey, at my home, to discuss our next objectives.

We began with the curriculum problem at Brasília and were soon involved in a consideration of the introductory course of study. The University was to open soon and we would have to be ready for those students of the first year who had picked psychology as their chosen field of science. While we were teaching them the fundamentals, we could prepare the courses that would follow.

We quickly agreed upon the content of this course, but not upon the way it should be taught. The more we considered our customary methods and the criticisms of them which my visitors had collected, the more unsuitable they seemed for South American export. We began to worry about matters that had not bothered us before, or matters that we had felt we could not change. We talked about the pros and cons of the lecture system; the validity of examinations; the significance of letter or number grades; the rigid frame of hours, months, or years into which our course materials were supposed to fit; and so on. And we continually tried to relate these matters to current applications of the analysis of behavior.

Darcy Ribeiro had encouraged my colleagues to be experimental, with respect to form as well as content of our teaching. Here was a chance to break away from old procedures. What about programmed instruction, for example? All of us knew about teaching machines and programmed textbooks. Rodolpho's translation of Holland and Skinner has been mentioned; Gil Sherman had bought a teaching machine while at Barnard College and written a program for it; and I had conducted a Columbia College seminar on this technique of instruction.

My friends had also been impressed by what they had heard and seen in Professor Skinner's Natural Science course at Harvard, and by the Behavioral Technology course that Charles Ferster had begun at the Institute for Behavioral Research in Maryland. Charles had prepared a sequence of experiments for the individual instruction of new staff members and visitors at the Institute. He would first expose his pupils to a fairly complicated study, letting each of them control the behavior of a pigeon by simply turning on and off a light within the bird's experimental chamber. After that, each student had to work his way alone through all the stages needed to achieve the same result as that which he had initially witnessed.

The result of our discussion was a plan which I described in my diary that night as a combination of Columbia, Harvard, and I.B.R. procedures that promised to become (I quote) "one of the most exciting and most radical ever given in a university setting." One month later (April 29th), I was more explicit:

> The Education program . . . represents a distillation of many things: the method
> of laboratory teaching at Columbia—in Psychology 1–2 [our first course] and

Psychology 127 [a sequence of experiments for individual graduate students]; the method used at I.B.R.; the use of programmed instruction where possible; the treatment of textbooks, lectures, conferences, etc., as *rewards* for passing through various stages of individual study and experimentation; the use of lectures as inspirational rather than truly instructional; the measurement of progress by compilations of things the student has successfully done, rather than by grades on examinations.

Soon after we made our tentative decision, my friends went back to São Paulo to fill in the details of our plan and otherwise prepare for the new Department. I agreed to join them when my obligations at Columbia were discharged. Then I went back to conventional teaching for one more term. I found it very difficult, however, to think about anything but Brasília and our future operations there.

By August of 1963, my commitment to the project was so great that I went on record at the Philadelphia meetings of the American Psychological Association with the description of a course that had never yet been given. Here are some of the things I said.

[This] is a course with lectures, demonstrations, discussions, laboratory hours, and homework. The lectures and demonstrations are infrequent and primarily inspirational. . . . Once the course has started, they are produced at suitable places along the way, but only for those students who have reached a point that guarantees an appreciation of their content. . . . Attendance at either lectures or demonstrations, however, is entirely optional, and no examination is based upon them. . . .

The laboratory work itself begins on the second or third day of the course, and is its most important feature. . . . The student's daily task begins when he has qualified for it—for example, when he has turned in a report on the preceding day's experiment, answered two or three questions on the last reading assignment, studied a description of his laboratory mission for the day, or done all of these things.

When a laboratory task has been completed . . . the student receives the assignment that will prepare him for the next. . . . It may include textbook study, plain or programmed; the reading of an article or technical report, carefully edited or supplemented to make it fully clear, and provided with a few key questions like those he may be asked at the beginning of his next laboratory session; and other readings may be given solely as . . . reward for work completed and to whet the appetite for more. . . .

The assistant's functions in such a course are very important. He . . . prepares and checks equipment, collects reports, passes out work materials and assignments, and records, in each student's individual logbook, each important step along the route. . . . He will also collect any student complaints, requests, comments, or suggestions. . . , which he passes on to the course director. . . .

The teachers, in a course like this, are not as conspicuous as they were under the old order. . . . They are the ones who design . . . each day's teaching program; and they are the ones who redesign this program in the light of student performance and assistant's reports. . . .

When all the course requirements have been met, the course is at an end. At this point, the student's logbook is examined by the course director, who records the achievement, places the book in the department files, and takes a few moments, perhaps, to offer his congratulations. No final examination is given, no course grade, no reward for speed of attainment, and no punishment for delay. Examining and teaching were inseparable parts of the same educational process; and something better than a letter or a number is available . . . a list of goals that were reached and the time it took to reach them. The student is ready for Course No. 2, a new logbook . . . a new assistant, a new body of fact and skills, and, probably, a new teacher [Keller, 1966, pp. 91–93].

Today, 9 years after this report was written, I am amazed at the similarity of this imaginary course to the one that was actually taught in Brasília and the really small number of basic changes in the format that have since been made. The daily *modus operandi* was altered slightly, the emphasis on laboratory work decreased, the student proctor was added to our staff, and we didn't get rid of letter grades entirely. But the self-pacing feature, the performance requirement for advancement, the down-grading of the lecture, and the general spirit of the course remains the same.

In my final term at Columbia, I sent up a trial balloon. With the aid of my graduate assistant, Lanny Fields, and five seniors in the College, I constructed a miniature program along the lines I have just described. Then, in the Christmas recess of 1963, this course was offered to three students—two high-school seniors and a college freshman—who agreed to act as subjects. Based on five experiments, the course was programmed in every detail, including equipment, procedures, and reading assignments. I talked to the class but once, on the first day of the course, and my assistant's interactions with the students were limited almost entirely to testing and handing out assignments. More than any other course I have taught, this one ran itself. And I would never give a course like it again!

My three young guinea pigs were positive, however, in their reactions to the course. They worked efficiently on their own, progressing at slightly different rates, and all of them were "graduated" within the vacation period. Their only complaint, which was not very loud and which I was too busy to hear, concerned the lack of opportunity for discussion. They wanted, and should have had, someone with whom to talk about their work.

One month later, on a Liberty Ship from World War I, bearing the Liberian flag, manned by Greeks, and carrying phosphate from Florida to Brazil, my wife and I set out on a 22-day voyage to join our colleagues for the next stage of our venture. She had definitely decided I was crazy, but did not feel she should desert me at a time when I needed her so much.

Our group had been working hard in São Paulo, assembling equipment, collecting books, and discussing our basic plan. They were making final preparations for the move to Brasília, where the space for our Department had been allocated and could soon be occupied. Then, suddenly, the nation underwent a governmental change. João Goulart was out of office and the country, and so was Darcy Ribeiro. The University was closed and we were left without a home for our Department. It appeared that our beautiful dream was shattered.

The Americans in our group prepared to leave the country, since they no longer held appointments and there was nothing else to do. We advanced the date of our employment at Arizona State University, where we were promised freedom to engage in teaching innovations. We still met together often, as if we had a future, but our meetings lacked in purpose and enthusiasm. We felt that we were simply killing time.

It takes weeks, however, to leave Brazil, in any kind of political weather; and, before the date of our departure, Dr. Zeferino Vaz, the new Rector at the University of Brasília, asked us to continue with our program. After some confusion, we agreed to do so. Early in May of 1964, our little group of *bandeirantes* advanced upon the capital city, ready to set up in business once again.

Nevertheless, our project had been delayed in its inauguration, and Sherman and I were far away in Arizona when the course which we had helped to conceive finally got off the launching pad. It was in early August when Rodolpho Azzi, with the support of his coordinator and a dedicated staff of young assistants, brought *personalized instruction* to the University of Brasília.

This course has never been described in detail, and I cannot do so here, but something must be said about it. It was a systematic course, an introduction to reinforcement theory. Each student progressed within it *at his own pace* through 42 units of work, including 12 experiments that came early in the course. In contrast with the current format in the United States and elsewhere there were no letter grades, no occasional lectures or discussions, no final examinations, and no student proctors. The experiments were evaluated by several assistants, most of them above the fourth-year level, and "reading checks" or unit tests were looked after by a departmental clerk, known to all as Senhor Daniel.

In our original plan, the course was to have three parts, each of which, in deference to tradition, was to require about one term for its completion. Only the first two parts were actually taught, however, before a University convulsion brought our whole curriculum to its end along with many others. Part I was twice presented in this period, with good results from both a student and a faculty point of view.

When asked about the course's most agreeable feature, the students usually said *self-pacing*, going at one's own speed—a "more responsible" way of working, as one of them described it. The least agreeable feature of the course appeared to be its failure to provide for discussion of the reading assignments with someone better qualified than Senhor Daniel.

Except for Rodolpho Azzi, who turned to another sphere of applied behavior analysis, the members of the Brasília staff moved on to other teaching positions in other institutions. What would have happened if they could have stayed together and the program had been continued we shall never know. Our original aim had been to let one course of study lead naturally into another, without delay, in accordance with the student's readiness and desire, until his training was complete. If this had been permitted to occur, these students might have been the first to show the way, by their example, of liberating higher education from the calendar and the clock. Instead, we had to take a slower, northern route, by way of Arizona, and we are only now arriving at this destination.

In the spring of 1965, at Arizona State University, two variations of the Brasília Plan were used in teaching introductory courses in the principles of behavior. In one of these, my own, 10 student aides, called *proctors*, took the place of Senhor Daniel in grading unit tests for a class of 94 students. In the other, taught by Gilmour Sherman, and involving fewer students, this function was performed by the instructor, with the help of a graduate assistant. Both courses were sufficiently successful to encourage further exploration.

Within a few semesters, we had reached a basic pattern of procedure—one that I have since described at many times and in many places (Keller, 1968). In all but one respect, it was simply a refinement and extension of the Brasília Plan, modified to meet the grim realities of the scene in an educationally underdeveloped country. At the risk of becoming an irritating echo, I shall enumerate once more the basic aspects of our system.

In the first place, as I noted before, the student is permitted to advance within a course of study at the rate which he himself prefers, within broad limits. He goes ahead, one step at a time, through successive units of the subject matter. The units are small in size, never larger than a typical week's assignment, and may be taken from a standard textbook or any other source that the instructor may wish to use. At intervals there are units of review, in order to consolidate the learning and to avoid unwanted fragmentation of the subject matter.

Secondly, there is a specified and high degree of mastery demanded in connection with each unit—something that can only be assured with student pacing. Near-perfection is the goal. Two-thirds of a readiness to move ahead is like two-thirds of an ability to swim.

Thirdly, the system permits repeated testing, with no loss of credit or of status in the case of failure, and with ample opportunity for the student to defend his answers.

Fourthly, in order to provide for this testing and individual evaluation, the system typically makes use of proctors—well-instructed and carefully directed students who have demonstrated that they understand the material in question.

These proctors came into the system because we had a shortage of graduate assistants; because we did not want a clerk (or a computer) to do our grading; and because we felt that such a task, especially when repeated many times, was a degrading one for a professor. They remained within the system for these reasons, and some others. We found that they helped to bridge the gap of understanding between the pupil and his teacher; that they provided opportunities for discussion of the course's content which we had lacked before; and that they furnished for each student a kind of personal–social contact that is often missing in present-day mass education. They eliminated the student's feelings of aloneness and neglect, and helped preserve his dignity and self-esteem.

Finally, the plan avoids as far as possible group instruction, or any other method in which there is no *quid pro quo*. This includes the usual lecture, the usual demonstration or other "visual aid," the usual discussion group, and the usual assignment of a paper to be written. Any so-called learning situation in which the objectives may be unspecified, the behavior absent, or the rewards noncontingent is not a learning situation worthy of the name, even if it should be one in which some learning may occur.

In these features of the Arizona version of our Brasília Plan, the student of behavior modification will discover most of the conditions of effective learning. He will recognize that we tried to guarantee, for student, proctor, and professor, a high frequency of generalized reinforcement of every kind within our reach, and a minimal degree of punishment and opportunity for extinction. In addition, we attempted to create an interlocking system, with each participant deriving his duties, as well as his rewards, from the activities of the others. We wanted a system of mutual reinforcement, mutual dependence, and mutual tuition.

The evidence today suggests that this is what we got. In all the tryouts of our plan, in Brazil or Arizona, the outcome was essentially the same. Students agreed, with rare exceptions, that it produced a greater understanding and remembrance of course materials, thus confirming test results. They reported a greater amount of work expenditure, a greater degree of enjoyment, and a greater feeling of achievement than that produced by other methods; and they said that it involved a greater recognition of the student as a person. Improvement in study habits was often attributed to the method, and the desire was expressed that other courses might be taught in a similar fashion. They were especially enthusiastic about working at their own speed and about the value of the proctor in the system.

The proctors obviously enjoyed their function, reporting pleasure from the progress of their students, from their own increase in understanding, and from the consideration they received from those above them in the system as well as those below. They developed a new perspective on the teaching process and a new appreciation of the learning potential in all of their students.

As for us, when we began our two courses at Arizona State, we worried about the willingness of students to go without lectures, to be frequently tested, to meet high standards of achievement, to accept the guidance and decisions of another student, to take care of themselves in general. (Students are typically less self-reliant in the United States than in Brazil.) I also feared that my proctors might be difficult to control.

These anxieties disappeared, however, as each course got under way. As managers and designers, with daily feedback on every aspect of our courses, we found ourselves working harder than before (at least in the beginning), but enjoying ourselves much more. We found new satisfactions and new challenges in our daily work. Less acquainted with our students as a group, we knew them better individually; less visible to them from day to day, we were intellectually more exposed; and in our personal contacts with them we found an unexpected appreciation of our labors and respect for our profession.

As soon as it was clear that students, proctors, and graduate assistants liked what we were doing, and that the university administration did not view us as subversives, I began to write and lecture on our plan, suggesting that we had the answer to democratic education. Gilmour Sherman was too young to take such chances and too busy with other academic obligations, so I became the spokesman for our group, at least in the United States.

The reaction of other teachers was, at first, depressing. I found that most of my colleagues were indifferent, condescending, or openly hostile. They applauded our efforts, on occasion, then instantly analyzed the method and decided it was not for them, for reasons that did not always seem profound. This was especially true of my closest colleagues, and still is (which may suggest a special knowledge that the others don't possess).

There were, however, a few exceptions—relatives, friends, or former pupils, who thought the scheme worth trying, and found, to their great satisfaction, that I had not lied about it. These teachers sometimes led others to adopt the same procedure, and they became the spearhead of a movement that now disturbs me in its magnitude and in the liberties taken with the basic format.

Examples of our plan in use now range throughout the academic spectrum and beyond. I have heard of courses in anthropology, astronomy, and art; in biology, business, and biophysics; in chemistry, electronics, education, and engineering (chemical, civil, electrical, mechanical, and nuclear); in geology, history, language, mathematics, medicine, music, and nurses' training; in physics, physiology, religion, sociology, and statistics, in addition to psychology, where it all began.

There are university departments in which the plan is used in every course; there is at least one college in which a student may earn his bachelor's degree without departing from our format; and I know of several applications outside the academic sphere. I have also heard of master's essays and a doctoral dissertation devoted to the history and current status of our venture. I expect at any time to hear that we have been denounced by some teachers college or some school of education—the ultimate sign of our success.

As a specific instance of what is going on, let me mention a meeting last November which Dr. Sherman and I attended. It was a 2-day conference on our plan at the Massachusetts Institute of Technology, arranged by its Education Research Center. The meeting was conducted by Dr. Ben A. Green, a physicist at the Center, and was attended by about 300 teachers from all over the United States and several foreign lands. They represented many fields of science and the humanities, especially the former. Most of them were not psychologists, but nearly all of them were teaching with our Brasília–Arizona method, or getting ready to do so.

Several features of this conference impressed me greatly. In spite of widely different backgrounds and long histories of insulation from each other, these teachers got along extremely well together. They displayed a common purpose—to improve their teaching; they had similar findings to report and experiences to be shared; and they showed an enthusiasm for our system that was (if you will pardon an expression) highly reinforcing to Sherman and to me. We felt like soldiers in a great crusade, and we wished that our Brazilian comrades could have been there.

Whether this particular system will survive is, of course, a question that I cannot answer here. But I feel safe in making one or two predictions. I believe the world is going to see an enormous change in its techniques of education within the coming years. This change will not result primarily from automation, televised instruction, information theory, sensitivity training, miracle drugs, or student participation in curricular decision making, whatever the value of any of these may be. Nor will it necessarily follow great expenditures of money.

It will come, instead, from "behavior analysis applied to education," as this symposium suggests, of which the Brasília Plan is only one example. It will eventually maximize the pleasure of scholarly endeavor and occupational training, for the old as well as for the young. In our educational institutions, it will involve less emphasis on rigid time requirements and more on quality of achievement; less use of group assembly and more attention to the individual; greater opportunity for success, but with nothing provided gratis; more privacy for the person and less invidious comparison with others; and a greater respect for human dignity than has ever been shown before in formal education.

I can also imagine a day when the length of any course of study will depend entirely upon its content and the student who undertakes it; when letter or number grades have disappeared or have been vested with new meaning; when no student is advanced in status unless he has deserved it; when everyone is free to "drop out" and return to study when he chooses; and when the use of well-controlled and well-instructed proctors will be a common feature in the practice of medicine, law, and other highly skilled vocations. But now my crystal ball grows cloudy.

I have tried to tell you the story of a venture in behavior modification—of the origins, the growth, and the final form of a system of instruction. I have sought to give you an idea of this system's present status, and I have guessed about the future. There is only one more comment to be made.

I have stressed the international aspect of our venture, mainly because it was developed in the United States and in Brazil, by citizens of each country. It did not involve, however, any summit meetings between John F. Kennedy and Jânio Quadros; Lyndon B. Johnson did not visit João Goulart to talk about it; and I am certain that Richard Milhous Nixon never brought the matter up with Humberto Castelo Branco or mentioned it in his conversation with President Médici. There has been no complicated interchange of diplomatic missions. No hotline was established for quick communication on the subject of our plan. There was just an unpretentious and cooperative interaction of four teachers, trained in the analysis of behavior, and dedicated to the proposition that something useful might be done about the educational problem. That may have been sufficient.

REFERENCES

Azzi, R., Fix, D. S. R., Rocha e Silva, M. I., & Keller, F. S. Exteroceptive control of response under delayed reinforcement. *Journal of the Experimental Analysis of Behavior,* 1964, **7,** 159–162.

Azzi, R., Rocha e Silva, M. I., Bori, C. M., Fix, D. S. R., & Keller, F. S. Suggested Portugese translations of expressions in operant conditioning. *Journal of the Experimental Analysis of Behavior,* 1963, **6,** 91–94.

Keller, F. S. A personal course in psychology. In R. Ulrich, T. Stachnik, & J. Mabry (Eds.), *The control of behavior.* Glenview, Illinois: Scott, Foresman, 1966.

Keller, F. S. "Good-bye teacher. . . ." *Journal of Applied Behavior Analysis,* 1968, **1,** 79–89. [This is the best-known of the papers dealing with the Brasília Plan in the United States.]

Ulrich, R., Stachnik, T., & Mabry, J. (Eds.), *The control of behavior.* Glenview, Illinois: Scott, Foresman, 1966.

A Permutation
on an Innovation[1]

J. GILMOUR SHERMAN

In the initial development of the Personalized System of Instruction (P.S.I.), several characteristics were built into the system quite deliberately in response to deficiencies, real or imagined, in the traditional teaching situation, plus what we knew at the time about learning theory. Many features of the system—self-pacing, mastery learning, specified objectives, small step sequenced material, etc.—exist in other recent and clearly related innovative methods. I know of no definitive statement of the characteristics that define the limits and province of P.S.I., or distinguish it clearly from these other methods and techniques. I personally feel some thinking and comments in this vein are needed, but I could be wrong and that is for another time. One characteristic, the proctors, *does* set us apart, and this is what I would like to discuss.

I have accused Fred Keller of using a functional illiterate as his first proctor in Brazil. Keller has said not guilty—it was our Brazilian colleague Rodolpho Azzi that made this selection. In any case, this proctor was to solve the

[1]Paper read at the American Psychological Association meetings, September 6, 1971. Published in J. G. Sherman (Ed.), *P.S.I.: 41 germinal papers*. Menlo Park, California: W. A. Benjamin, Inc., 1974.

problem of comparing the student's test with an answer key in a way we would now describe as "matching to sample." I may be wrong about Fred's experience, but at one time it *was* the plan to have the immediate feedback of test results handled by nonprofessional clerical help. However, the proctor function quickly became something more than nonprofessionals could provide.

At one time or another, several of us have taught P.S.I. courses, ourselves serving as test corrector, grader, proctor, tutor. In some ways this works very well, but the time it takes the professor to deal with these highly predictable, redundant, repetitious errors and questions precludes his dealing with the complex, personal, and unique questions that only he is equipped to handle. It is a waste of talent to ask the professor to handle what can be passed on to others, particularly when these tasks prevent him from bringing to his students the special insights, imaginative leaps, even artistry and magic that he alone is supposedly prepared to give.

In some P.S.I. courses the proctor role has been handled by graduate students. There is rather general agreement that these professionals-in-training sieze this opportunity to jump into the teacher role and quickly start to give lectures, even though the system has reduced the audience to one. In my own experience, I have overheard graduate students acting as proctors fabricate an answer, sometimes ingenious but wrong. The contingencies operating on these professionals-without-certification are such that we should not be surprised to find them responding under pressure to come up with an answer, especially when faced down by an undergraduate. The face-saving involved suggests that distorted tacts might occasionally be expected. The graduate student *is* under pressure to demonstrate his *own* mastery. In any case, I know of no one who has taught a P.S.I. course who recommends graduate students as the best occupants of the proctor position.

Most frequently proctors have been advanced undergraduates, generally chosen for their superior performance in the course during a previous term or year. Typically they have been paid for their services in either of two ways, money or course credit. Money seems to be a very satisfactory reinforcer, but is hard to come by with currently limited budgets. If money is available it does work well, there is nothing wrong with it, and the proctor problem is three-quarters solved. Teachers with unlimited budgets might well stop reading at this point.

When money is in short supply, course credit is frequently handy. I have nothing against it, and in fact I think we were the first to use that solution at Arizona State University, where a course called "seminar in course programming" was created for the purpose. Others have used the almost always present "independent study" course designation to award a couple of credits to upperclass majors to enlist their aid.

Again, I have nothing against this solution. Those who are using it successfully should probably be encouraged to continue. However, many colleagues about to initiate P.S.I. courses have said to me, "But I don't think my university, my dean, or my chairman will allow me to give credit for this activity." My answer has always been, "That's ridiculous, the proctors learn more than anybody." I still feel this way. This is the point where teachers using this reinforcer successfully might also stop reading.

But there is a message here. In a very early speech that Fred Keller gave to the assembled faculty at ASU, he said:

"The proctors have also been enthusiastic about the method and its educational value—*for themselves as well as their students.* They claim to have profited greatly from preparing for, and giving tests, talking with students about them and discussing the work to come with the instructor. The job appears to be especially attractive to those who plan to go on to graduate study and teaching, but its appeal is not limited to them alone." I might add that if Keller was right, this certainly seems worthy of course credit.

In a talk I gave to the American Educational Research Association in 1967, I said:

> The proctors are another happy story. They receive 2 points of academic credit for their work and *earn* it several times over. They come early, work late, learn even more than their students, and go on to take the top grades in the advanced courses (as yet traditionally taught). At weekly meetings they play an important part in program revision, suggesting a unit that is too large, a textbook passage that is unclear, or a test question that is ambiguous. The behavior of the students clearly reveals that the proctors provide a kind of reinforcement, however subtle and ill-defined, that has yet to be built into a programmed text. I think they are the key to whatever success we have had.

That was in 1967, but I was not yet listening to my own words. Dr. David Born, in his very excellent "Instructor Manual for Development of a Personalized Instruction Course,"[2] wrote: "The old saying that if you want to learn a subject you should teach it—applies to proctors just as it applies to faculty members." At another point in the same manual, Dr. Born said: ". . . in preparing for their teaching assignments, the proctor staff will learn at least as much about the course material as the students taking the course."

There may be other, perhaps better, examples of the theme we were all discussing. Still, we were missing the message. We did notice that a large percentage of our students applied to be proctors the following year,

[2]Available by writing: College Book Store, 200 University Street, Salt Lake City, Utah.

but we never went on to say there must be something about the position that is reinforcing. We did not listen to ourselves saying, ''The proctors learn more than anyone.''

In the spring of 1970 I was about to teach a new course in educational psychology. The money had run out, and there were no funds to pay proctors as I had done for a different course during the fall semester. My colleagues looked unfavorably on giving course credit. I thought they were wrong, but for other reasons I did not want to argue. The system was in ruins, and I would probably have gone back to lecturing if it had not been that I had forgotten how.

Out of desperation we decided to make proctors out of some of the students *taking* the course. Here is the way it works. My one assistant and I correct the first few tests for any given unit. The first 10 students to pass, on the first try, with a perfect score can become proctors and take on the function of grading, guiding, and interviewing classmates with a very extensive proctors' manual to guide them. They need not accept the job if they do not choose to. Students who miss the chance to become a proctor on Unit One can earn that position by being among the first 10 to pass Unit Two, essentially bumping some of the existing proctors—all of whom are working at high rates to retain their positions. Thus we have a constantly changing group of 10 proctors who are always those students furthest out in front. These 10 proctors work with their colleagues on all units up to and including the unit they have just passed. My assistant and I continue correcting the first 10 who are prepared to move even further ahead.

Clearly this procedure solves the money problem (and the course credit problem if anyone is squeamish about that). It also solves the proctor supply problem if someone is moving to a new institution or teaching a new course where already prepared upper-class candidates are not available. These advantages are substantial, and are essentially the problems the procedure was designed to solve. But it turns out that there are other more important advantages.

First there is always the problem of insuring that upper-class proctors who have taken the course a previous year actually review the material and are reacquainted with it in sufficient detail to guide the students whom they are now proctoring. Using *our* procedure, the proctors have, without question, recently read the material involved: They have recently passed a test on it.

Second, the system helps a bit with the procrastination problem. A substantial number of students work to gain the lead, so they do not fall behind. This may introduce some competition for the position (again, the position must be reinforcing), but that competition is not too severe. Those who fall a bit behind at the start have a chance near the end if they keep up.

As the leaders finish the course, take the final, and disappear to enjoy or make use of the free time their rapid progress has earned for them, the second string has its chance. A few of the early finishers stay on, reporting enjoyment in the job, but most do not return, making room for those who managed to proceed at a less rapid but still more than acceptable rate. During last spring's term about 40% of the students held the proctor position at some time during the semester. Some students earned the position, but declined it as taking too much time. The number precluded, then, is not large. Some preliminary data show that the general class progress is more rapid, and the number of students who fall dangerously behind is smaller with this procedure.

A third advantage is related to the precision of instruction. The proctors are clearly only a few units ahead of the student being examined, and they are not expected to be as wise as the more advanced student. With less reputation to protect, they are less liable to start giving lectures or inventing answers. They find it easier to say, "I don't know." This shows up as a greater number of referrals to the instructor. To those of us who have stood around feeling useless in a P.S.I. course, this is pleasing. To the extent that it keeps the instructor from getting bored and leaving the classroom, and increases his interactions with individual students, I would also count this as an advantage.

Perhaps a minor but important point for some of our most important students, the proctor position is especially appealing to the bright student. Those looking for the extra challenge and sometimes bored in programmed courses find their "thing" in the proctor role.

While economics, course credit, and proctor recruiting recommend it; while preparedness, precision, and lessened procrastination are secondary benefits; the most important result is what we have been saying all along—the proctors learn more than anyone. It makes more than a little sense to pass this advantage on to those *taking* the course. To indicate that this is the result, let me quickly include just a scrap of data from last fall's course, in which about one-third of the students worked as proctors. While some students who were *not* proctors received over 90 on the final, no proctor fell below 90. Seven of the 32 proctors scored 100 on the final, a score not attained by *any* student who went through the course without proctoring. Excluded from the highest rank were four students who went through the course with a speed equal to the leaders', always qualifying for a proctor position, but declining it as too time consuming. This seems to be a useful procedure for learning, and learning to the point of near perfection at that.

We can again refer to the old saying, "You don't learn something until you teach it." "Practice makes perfect" might have led us to predict a happy result from this permutation on an innovation. The data on overlearning, and massed versus spaced practice, might have led us to the same prediction from a more solid data base than an old adage. Alternatively one might say that since the proctors are exposed to nearly every conceivable error, the additional S-delta training leads to more precise discriminations. I am convinced that there is yet another reason, at least as important, why proctoring leads to such effective learning. It is related to the question of arbitrary versus natural reinforcers. This is best illustrated by the not infrequent comment of a student who finds himself unexpectedly in the lead, is asked to be a proctor, and responds by saying, "May I wait until tomorrow? I read the material and know that I could answer your test questions, but really feel I need to review it before being ready to explain it to the others." This student tells us something important.

The arbitrary reinforcers of grades, points, "pass" or some other instructor-administered reward, even praise, establish one kind of repertoire, sometimes minimal even at the "A" level. They maintain the minimal repertoire commensurate with the award. That repertoire can be achieved by a *kind* of study, in almost every way inferior to the behavior of the professional approaching new subject matter for professional or scholarly reasons. We all recognize in our own lives the difference between the perfunctory and patronizing slap on the back and the legitimate recognition of professional competence. Even with the student cry for participation and relevance there is little we can do, particularly at introductory levels, that makes the material in any way useful. Again the gold star is a fake. More important, when the repertoires established by arbitrary versus natural reinforcers are compared in the classroom, the gold star proves to be a defective reinforcer. While hopefully there *are* natural reasons to learn most of the material we teach beyond merely being able to teach it to others, nonetheless the proctor teaching function does reward learning by making the learning material *immediately* useful in a natural and professional sense. If a student has taken the trouble to learn what we have asked him to learn, it is little enough for us to treat him as professionally qualified with that material. When conferring that deserved, natural, and dignified respect for competence produces the very behavior we want to establish, applaud, and recognize, there appears to be in the proctor function a merit, the limits of which we have hardly begun to explore. What we ask for is competence, and this is followed by natural and appropriate recognition. The many papers on the topic, "reinforcers available in the classroom," have suggested so little that we should not throw this one away. The behavior this procedure generates seems to be precisely the behavior we are trying to establish.

The Essential Components of Effective Instruction and Why Most College Teaching Is Not

JACK L. MICHAEL

The field of behavior modification—and what is described here is a part of this field—derives its concepts and techniques from the animal laboratory. It would, perhaps, be beneficial to compare the animal training situation with college instruction. In many college courses what the student learns is to perform a particular response in the presence of a particular stimulus, and a different response in the presence of a different stimulus. For example, in learning to speak a foreign language, one learns to make the proper foreign-language response for a wide variety of different occasions. Similarly, in many science courses one learns a complex verbal repertoire that consists of making a particular type of verbal response in the presence of a particular verbal stimulus and a different response in the presence of a different stimulus—for example, naming different classes of animals or performing certain mathematical operations. In the terms of animal training, this type of college learning would be called multiple-stimulus, multiple-response discrimination learning. An example is teaching a monkey to operate a particular type of lever in the presence of one visual display, and to operate a different lever in the presence of another. The college student learning a foreign language, of course, must make many different responses appropriate to many different occasions, but the difference seems to be primarily one of degree. The type of animal training described above is something that operant conditioners do very well—perhaps better than they teach college courses.

What are the essential features of such an animal training situation? First, the trainer must have available a sequence of stimulus materials (or tasks, as they would be called in human education) that start with the animal's existing repertoire. Then, the trainer would gradually build in the components of the more complex repertoire that is the goal of the instructional system. It would be quite reasonable to refer to this as a programmed sequence of instructional tasks, or simply as a *program of instruction*. Futhermore, there is the implication of a mastery criterion for advancement through these stimulus materials, or tasks. That is, the monkey is not presented with a more difficult task until he has achieved some specified level of performance on the easier preceding ones.

The second component of the program is some form of differential consequation[1] for performing the instructional task rather than other activities. This is usually accomplished by (1) enclosing the animal in a chamber, thus isolating it from attractive or disturbing outside stimulus conditions; (2) depriving it of food to the point where food is a very strong reinforcer, and then giving this reinforcement for engaging in the educational task but for no other activity in the enclosure; and (3) sometimes delivering punishment in the form of painful stimuli or stimuli associated with periods during which no reinforcement is available (time out) to further weaken any tendency to engage in activities other than the desired ones. In short, we make it worth his while to participate in our educational task.

A third and final component of instruction is some form of differential consequation for correct as contrasted with incorrect or less correct behavior with regard to our educational task. This involves some clear-cut advantage (usually the food reinforcement mentioned above) for correct behavior, and some disadvantage (some form of punishment) for incorrect behavior.

It is unusual to separate these last two components when analyzing animal learning, since the same event—food reinforcement for correct responding—serves both to keep the animal "interested" in performing our educational task and to strengthen correct stimulus–response relationships. As we shall see, however, in much human instruction these two functions

---

[1]The term "consequate" means to provide an effective consequence—either a reinforcer or a punisher. "Differential consequation" could consist of reinforcing correct responses and ignoring incorrect ones, ignoring correct and punishing incorrect responses, or reinforcing correct and punishing incorrect responses.

are accomplished quite differently, and it is well at this point to keep them separate.

To summarize these three components then, it is essential that the trainer or educator have a program of instruction with a mastery criterion for advancement; that it be more to the advantage of the learner to participate in this educational activity than in other activities; and that it be to his further advantage to participate correctly rather than incorrectly.

Before considering college instruction in terms of these three components, it is necessary to deal with two rather obvious differences between most college learning and the animal situation described above. In the first place, when an animal is trained to make a particular type of response in the presence of one stimulus and a different response in the presence of another, it is easy to conceptualize the performance in terms of stimuli, responses, and their consequences; and it is also easy to identify these elements in the training situation. In much human learning, however, although it is usually possible to conceptualize the ultimate result in terms of stimuli and responses, and to identify some possible consequences responsible for the maintenance of the stimulus–response relationship *after* it has been established, the learning situation itself does not seem to consist of these elements in any obvious form. A student reads a section from a book, or listens to a lecture, and as a result the next time a particular stimulus is present there is an increased probability that he will make some relevant verbal response. While reading a text or listening to a lecture, the student is obviously being exposed to a rich source of verbal stimuli, but the relevant responses are not often *overt;* and even if we can make use of the concept of covert responses, how do the responses become functionally related to the relevant stimuli? When the monkey makes a correct response for a particular stimulus situation, the environment changes noticeably: A food pellet drops noisily into an easily reached container. Furthermore, the animal trainer who attempts to develop a discrimination performance without arranging for such a clear-cut consequence will have great difficulty obtaining an adequate performance. But consider the student reading his textbook: What are the consequences of correct behavior and, for that matter, what constitutes correct behavior when one is reading a textbook? The monkey acquires a repertoire by making rather obvious responses in the presence of environmental stimuli, whereupon correct and incorrect responses are immediately followed by different kinds of experimenter-arranged environmental changes. The college student, on the other hand, acquires his repertoire by being exposed to complex sequences of verbal stimuli, during which he may be making some verbal responses, but not at the overt level. Whatever he does, however, there are no instructor-arranged consequences; in fact, the surrounding environment remains quite constant.

It is sometimes erroneously believed that a professor's reactions to a student's examination performance—confirmation of correct answers, disconfirmation of incorrect answers—are the relevant consequences for correct or incorrect responding. On this basis some psychologists with a behavioral orientation argue that examinations should be returned quickly in order to avoid the deleterious effects of a delay in reinforcement. In most courses, however, the critical learning has occurred prior to the examination, or will certainly not take place during the examination. The exam grade serves primarily as a form of consequation for the behavior of studying, i.e., participating in the educational activity. It is the means whereby the grade for the course, a powerful form of consequation for many students, is brought into relation with the critical behavior of interacting with the source materials of the course.

Students undoubtedly do learn from examinations, but in general they sample such a small portion of the repertoire being acquired that if this learning constitutes very much of the total, the system is not functioning very well. Of course, if exams were very frequent and of reasonable extent, they would make contact with a sizeable portion of the repertoire; but if much of the learning took place during this contact it would imply that relatively little was occurring away from the exam, in which case the rationale for interacting with the source material outside of the exam situation would be questionable.

A second major difference between animal discrimination training and human learning at the college level concerns control of the stimulus materials. In animal training, the experimenter (or, more commonly, his electronic programming equipment) presents each unit or element of the stimulus material, monitors the animal's reaction to it, and on the basis of this reaction decides whether to reinforce, punish, go ahead to the next unit, go back to the preceding unit, etc. When a student studies a textbook, the stimulus presentation, response monitoring, and any decisions regarding advance, review, etc., as well as any form of reinforcement or punishment are all in the hands of the student himself. The lecture is a hybrid procedure in that the instructor controls the stimulus presentation but generally does not require or monitor responses, and although the student may obtain review by asking questions, he is more commonly expected to take notes and review these on his own. Also, differential consequation for correct responding (and again, what is correct responding?) is either absent or consists of some covert reaction by the student during the lecture or later when he studies his notes.

To summarize these differences for the most common form of college learning, i.e., studying a text: (1) the stimulus–response–consequence formula is difficult to apply, particularly with respect to the consequences; and (2) the learner himself is in control of the presentation of the stimulus materials, the decision to advance or review, etc., and, by his reactions to his own behavior, providing any relevant consequation.

Constituting as it does the main form of college learning, it is appropriate at this point to deal with this uniquely human way of acquiring a repertoire in some behavioral detail. But first, let us consider two very closely related types of learning where the behavioral processes are easier to discern: using flash cards and learning from a programmed text.

A form of flash card used quite commonly in college has an English word on one side and the equivalent term in some foreign language on the other. As a student works with the vocabulary cards, he presents himself with an English word and tries to state, let us say, the Spanish equivalent. He then turns the card over and reads, perhaps aloud, the correct Spanish word. This activity results in at least two rather clear-cut operant processes and a collection of as yet relatively unanalyzed respondent-like processes. First, there is an obvious form of operant consequation: When he makes the Spanish vocal response and then looks at the other side of the card, what he sees functions as a reinforcer or punisher for the response, depending upon whether he was correct or incorrect. Second, what he sees as he turns the card over also functions as a form of discriminative stimulus (assuming the normal earlier experience with such study materials) for the next step in the sequence of activities; if he was correct he will go on to the next card, but if he was incorrect he will reexamine the English word, lay the card aside for future study, or in some other way react to this indication that his repertoire is not yet adequate. Third, during the use of the flash cards there are a number of stimulus–stimulus pairings that probably result in a type of respondent conditioning. It is not smooth-muscle or glandular responses that are of primary significance here, however, but rather the less understood private events described in terms of imagery, or Skinner's (1953, pp. 266–270) "conditioned seeing" and "conditioned hearing." For example, the English word as a visual stimulus may under similar future circumstances "elicit" a form of visual imagery related to the sound of the student's own voice as he says the Spanish word. Since the use of such flash cards involves fairly frequent pairings in the opposite order as well, the Spanish word may come to elicit imagery related to the objects or events that control the use of the English word, a useful result for future "understanding" of the Spanish word. And there are many other variations of this kind of relationship. These respondent-like processes, because of the privacy of many of the critical events, have not been systematically studied within the behavioral movement, although Skinner discusses them in detail in *Science and Human Behavior* and makes frequent reference to them in *Verbal Behavior* (1957). A fourth and even less understood "conditioning" process also plays a role in this type of learning. There is some reason to believe that when a neutral stimulus is paired with a stimulus that already controls some operant behavior, the neutral stimulus will acquire some aspects of this control. Thus, some of the operant effects that the English word has on the learner as a listener may be transferred to the Spanish word. It is also quite likely that some of the stimulus conditions that control the English word in the learner as a speaker will now also control the Spanish word as a result of the pairing. The respondent processes and the mixed operant–respondent effects described above undoubtedly contribute to the developing repertoire, but to what extent is not known at the present time.

In the use of a programmed textbook, the two operant functions accomplished by the answer to the frame—consequation of the preceding response and stimulus control of the next activity—are very similar to the same functions accomplished by the "answer" on the back of the flash card. The respondent[2] processes are somewhat more complex, however, because in the programmed text the stimulus pairing is embedded in the syntactical stimuli of our language. A behavioral analysis of the role of these syntactical stimuli in directing and facilitating repertoire acquisition is only just beginning to be made (Skinner, 1957, pp. 357–367; Staats, 1968, pp. 511–520), but there is no question that this role is a critical one. The respondent pairing effects are probably quite weak under conditions of stimulus pairing; they may become very effective, however, when properly embedded in linguistic stimuli for which the learner has an appropriate history.

Now, in the use of an ordinary or "unprogrammed" textbook, since there are no "questions" or frames to which the reader is supposed to respond, there are no answers to serve as consequation for correct behavior or as discriminative stimuli for appropriate use of text materials. The respondent effects are even more intricately involved in linguistic syntactic stimuli than in the programmed textbook, and there is little more that can be said about them at this point. Before attempting to discover processes in the use of an ordinary text that are analogous to the operant consequation and discriminative functions of the "answers" on flash cards and in programmed materials, we must determine what constitutes "correct behavior" when one is reading an ordinary text. Skinner's (1957, pp. 268–280) analysis relates directly to this point.[3] He shows how a text serves as a supplementary stimulus for corresponding verbal behavior in the reader. That is, the reader is making verbal responses (usually not overt) under the control of the textual

---

[2]For the purposes of this paper, I shall refer to both the third and fourth effects described above as "respondent," although the analogy to the respondent conditioning of glandular and smooth muscle responses is somewhat tenuous in both cases.

[3]This analysis of "correctness" in responding to an ordinary text, based as it is on Skinner's *Verbal Behavior*, will not be completely understandable unless the reader is more than casually familiar with Skinner's treatment of multiple control in verbal behavior.

stimulus, but ordinarily the same responses are controlled by other variables as well as the textual stimulus; this can usually be demonstrated by blocking off a part of the text and showing that the reader can and does fill in some of the missing material. It is useful to conceptualize a continuum in terms of the necessity of the textual stimulus: At one extreme the textual stimulus is the only controlling variable—the reader can pronounce the words, but does not "understand" what he is reading. At the other, the textual stimulus is unnecessary—the reader can and does say the same thing without the help of the text (not in the sense of memorized material, but in that the various verbal relationships are also a part of the reader's repertoire). At one extreme there is much we do not understand, and at the other we understand all the issues so thoroughly that we are not learning anything. Textbooks generally fall somewhere in the middle of this continuum. The student could have made many of the responses without the aid of the text—the author explains his topic by relating it to topics with which he believes the readers are already familiar. The critical and novel relationships were not in the reader's repertoire prior to his exposure to the text, but if the author has built his case well the student finds himself "joining in" with the author as he reads these sections; that is, he finds himself making the critical verbal responses at least partially for the same reasons that controlled the author's behavior. The student "understands" to the extent that his reading responses are controlled by other factors than the textual stimuli and to the extent that these other factors are the important ones relevant to the author's point. To the extent that he understands in this sense, he is "correct"—just as the user of the programmed text is correct when his answer to the frame "question" matches that supplied by the writer of the program. The student *does not* understand if the only controlling variables are the printed textual stimuli, or he *misunderstands* if his reading responses are partially controlled by variables other than the textual stimuli but not the variables that were responsible for the author's verbal behavior: In this case he is incorrect. If the reader is an effective scholar, this "correctness" and "incorrectness" will serve the same two functions that it does in the programmed text—reinforcement or punishment for the controlling relationship responsible for the "understanding" and a discriminative function for the next activity, for example, rereading the passage, looking up a critical term in the glossary, etc.

A similar analysis applies to the lecture, where the listener is behaving echoically. The lecturer is supplying a supplementary stimulus for the listener's own verbal behavior, and to the extent that the listener finds himself making the same verbal responses and for the same reasons he is behaving "correctly"—he should be appropriately reinforced and should take appropriate subsequent action. Unlike the reader, the listener has the opportunity to stop the speaker and ask for supplementary explanation, justification, etc., but he must do this at some cost in terms of effort and possible disapproval from the speaker and/or the other listeners.

In a good deal of college learning, then, the learner is much more in control of the situation than the animal is in a typical operant conditioning experiment. Furthermore, the most common college learning situation—acquiring a repertoire by studying a textbook—involves a very subtle type of differential consequation for correct responding, and may depend to some considerable extent upon respondent-like acquisition processes.

What is the implication of these differences for the previous analysis of the essential components of effective discrimination learning? Irrespective of the way in which the material is presented, or of the learning process responsible for repertoire acquisition, it is still important that the stimulus material be sequenced so that the necessary prerequisites for later aspects are contained in the preceding units; and, of course, this has the same implications for a mastery criterion for advancement. Differential consequation for participation is still essential, irrespective of the source of the repertoire or the processes responsible for its acquisition, since if this requirement is not met the learner will spend his time on activities other than the learning task. Only the third essential component of animal training is brought into doubt by the differences between college learning and the animal training situation. Since some of the learning may take place without the necessity of consequation, differential consequation for correctness may not be essential. If it *is* essential, then our educational practices are very defective in their neglect of specific training for effective use of textbooks. The consequation and discriminative processes described above are quite subtle and probably not very functional for large numbers of college students. However, most students do seem to acquire repertoires from text materials, if they work at it sufficiently, so perhaps we can neglect this third component, pending the development of more effective programming of the essential skills, and consider the extent to which ordinary college instruction deals with the first two. Looked at somewhat differently, we cannot be too sure at this time exactly how a student learns from a textbook, but we can be quite sure that he will not learn from one unless he reads it, and his learning will be rendered more difficult if the textbook is ineffectively arranged or incomplete, or contains much irrelevant material.

With respect to programming, most introductory textbooks are rather well sequenced in the sense that the prerequisite skills and knowledge for the later portion of the text can be developed from interacting with the earlier parts of the same text. More advanced textbooks that have been especially prepared for instructional purposes are also well sequenced, or "programmed," in this broader sense of the term. However, a course instructor may use well-programmed materials in such a way as to circumvent the sequencing goals of the author. (College instructors, after all, receive no training in instructional technology except that which inadvertently results from their having been instructed themselves in a similar setting and with a similar subject matter. Any gross inability in this respect almost never interferes with obtaining the Ph.D. degree in the various subject matters, and, in fact, any significant expenditure of time on the topic of instruction would probably be viewed suspiciously by those supervising the Ph.D. training.) The instructor may not wish to spend the time required to go through a text in the proper sequence, and may skip large sections so that he can assign other material. Or he may assign the sections in a different order from that intended by the author.

Quite commonly, however, assignments may consist of written material that was not prepared for instructional purposes (journal articles, for instance) in which there was no attempt to build in prerequisite repertoires for later sections. Even more commonly, an instructor may rely on his lectures to generate a sizable portion of the repertoire being developed, and the programming of these may be completely inadequate.

However, even if the material being used *is* well programmed, there is no guarantee that it will be used properly, since the actual use of the written assignment is controlled by the student. Probably the most common difficulty in this respect is the student's use of an ordinary textbook. If, as he studies, his own behavior and the factors responsible for it do not provide an adequate discriminative stimulus for subsequent behavior—advance, review, look something up in the glossary, etc.—the programming effectiveness of the stimulus material will be lost, irrespective of whether the learning process is operant, respondent, or some mixture.

The most serious defect in programming, however, is not related to the source material at all, but rather to the complete lack of a mastery criterion for advancement within a course. There are mastery criteria for between-course advancement in some cases, as when one must pass an entrance examination or a prerequisite course before being permitted to enroll in a particular course. Within a course, however, failure to master the material taught during the first portion seldom if ever prevents the student from encountering the later portions of the same course. The result is a good deal of what can be referred to as *cumulative failure:* A student is unable to develop a particular repertoire simply because he has not developed the prerequisite repertoire. Such cumulative failure is quite familiar to most instructors, who would probably not permit it if they were conducting some form of individual tutorial instruction. With groups of students, however, it is tolerated as the inevitable result of student heterogeneity with respect to background knowledge, ability, and motivation, and because of the limited manpower available (for example, one instructor and one graduate assistant for a class of 100 students) to carry out the instructional activity. And of course, once the mastery criterion is dropped, the programming requirement of effective instruction is missing no matter how well the materials themselves are programmed.

On the other hand, it is possible to overemphasize the necessity of a within-course mastery criterion for advancement. Many courses cover a number of unrelated topics, failure to master any one of which will not interfere with the acquisition of behavior regarding a different topic. Introductory psychology courses are often of this kind, where one studies scientific method for a week or so, then the nervous system, then learning, intelligence, etc. Cumulative failure can occur within a topic, but once a new topic is under consideration one's past failings can be forgotten. Also, even if the subject matter being taught is more tightly organized than introductory psychology usually is, the text and the lecturer may build in a good deal of review as the course advances (at the expense of new material, of course) so that one has a ''second chance'' to acquire prerequisite material. Still, it is probably true that a good deal of college inadequacy *is* attributable to the type of cumulative failure described above.

Since the actual prerequisites beyond the introductory ones for any course are often somewhat vague in the minds of the faculty in charge of instruction, any instructional difficulties due to defects in programming can be erroneously attributed to laziness, ignorance, or both on the part of the students having the difficulties, especially since there are usually a few students who acquire an adequate repertoire under almost any conditions.

Now let us consider the second essential component of an effective discrimination training situation: differential consequation for participating in the task. Unless it is more reinforcing or less punishing to look at the stimulus lights and to operate the levers, etc., of the discrimination task than to do other things (for example, to sit in the corner and scratch), the monkey being trained will do these other things. The student living in our society has a great many more reinforcing options to compete with the educational task than the monkey confined to the experimental chamber. Why should he spend his time learning psychology, for instance, rather than engaging in social activities with his peers, watching television, going to plays and movies or, for that matter, studying other school topics? In terms of stated educational policies, the time commitment is quite heavy. Many universities advise incoming freshmen that to pass their courses they should expect to spend at least 2 hours studying outside of class for every lecture hour they spend in class. Thus, if a student took the typical 15-credit-hour load (these figures are based on the semester system) that consisted of five different courses, each worth 3 credit hours and each meeting for 3 lecture hours per week, he should be spending about 45 hours a week in actual schoolwork. Presumably, to obtain a better grade than "pass" would require even more time.

What are the consequences that are supposed to maintain this considerable amount of study activity? To make the situation more concrete, consider the student trying to decide whether to study his psychology textbook during the early hours of some particular evening, or to spend the time doing something else, such as socialize with his friends, go out with a member of the opposite sex, watch television, etc. We can safely assume that the activities which compete with studying are closely linked with reinforcing and punishing consequences, and although these may not be strong, they are usually immediate. The student being urged to participate in some form of social activity often receives immediate social disapproval if he refuses, and immediate approval if he agrees, plus whatever other reinforcers are related to that activity once it begins.

To compete with the consequences of doing other things, there are two possible immediate consequences of studying. One arises from contact with the study materials themselves. For various reasons, usually related to previous training of some sort, such materials may be called interesting by the student, and may function as sources of reinforcement irrespective of their relation to any other reinforcers. Perhaps we all have a "natural curiosity" about any topic that we know little about. Text writers attempt to enhance this type of reinforcement by relating their subject, when possible, to other current topics that they believe are likely to be interesting to their readers; by varying their style of presentation; by including pictures even when the subject matter is not made clearer by such illustrative material; and in a number of other ways. This form of reinforcement, although immediate, is apparently not very strong for many of the subjects that must be mastered by the student and, for some students, seems to be quite weak for all college subjects. College teachers often complain about the weakness of this factor, formulating their complaint in terms of the intellectual and motivational deficits of the contemporary student. However, we should not expect too much from "intrinsic interest" in the subject being learned as a source of reinforcement. Although many of us are naturally curious about a wide variety of topics, our curiosity is usually satisfied with a less intense exposure than most instructors consider adequate for college credit. The nonscience major, for example, is usually somewhat interested in finding out about the various sciences, but this interest will not generally maintain the 6 to 8 hours of careful study—outlining, memorizing, etc.—each week for 15 weeks that is necessary to acquire the repertoire that the chemistry instructor may consider minimal for 3 hours of college course credit. That kind of "intrinsic interest" is occasionally encountered in college. There are always a few individuals for whom nothing competes in fascination with a chemistry textbook. This usually comes about, however, as a result of the student having already acquired a highly specialized repertoire in this topic, and our elementary and secondary educational system does not generally encourage the development of such specialized repertoires. Even when such a "specialist" appears on the college scene, he is only permitted to take about a third of his college work in the areas related to his special interest.

The interest inherent in the study materials, even if strong, often loses the competition with other forms of reinforcement simply because of its unlimited temporal availability as contrasted with these other forms. The social invitation, for example, often represents an opportunity that is available for only a brief period. The study materials, on the other hand, will be available indefinitely. Of course, a student is often studying for an exam and the opportunity to prepare will not be available indefinitely, but studying to pass a exam (which will be considered later) is clearly not equivalent to what most people mean by "intrinsic interest" in the subject matter.

A second type of consequence that can be made immediately contingent upon studying or not studying consists of the social reaction of some other person in the student's environment such as a parent, spouse, roommate, or anyone who is present and has an interest in the student's welfare. It would appear, however, that in the United States, this type of consequence does not occur often, or it is not very effective when it does occur. This type of consequence would be more effective in a society that placed a greater emphasis on mutual social responsibility, as appears to be the case in China, for example.

Although reinforcement inherent in the study materials and the social reaction of someone else in the student's environment are the only obvious immediate consequences of studying, there are a number of more remote effects that are often cited. Studying results in the development of repertoires necessary for future vocational and avocational activities. Being able to carry out these future activities is certainly an important consequence, and is almost always mentioned when a student is asked why he is pursuing a particular college curriculum. A more specific aspect of this same general type of consequence consists in the public acknowledgment of the repertoire by the college in the form of course grades and degrees. It is not always clear how necessary the knowledge of some particular course material is for a future activity, but it is usually quite clear that unless the course is passed it will have to be taken over again or some other course taken in its place. Because of this stricter contingency, course credit is probably more important as a consequence for most students than the long-range value of the repertoires being acquired. The student makes contact with this contingency when his repertoire is examined for the purposes of assigning the course grade, and the power of this variable can be seen during the periods immediately preceding important examinations.

There are a number of other consequences that may be relevant to studying. Some repertoires have relatively immediate value, as when a student learns something about political science that helps him understand and behave appropriately toward some current political or social problem. Many college courses, however, have no immediate application and serve primarily to prepare one to take more advanced courses in the same or related areas.

Another type of consequence is the social approval that peers and instructors may deliver for the display of knowledge and skill. When this approval is based on exam scores, it simply supplements the course credit as a form of consequence, but a student may receive a considerable amount of approval for academic behavior that occurs in private conversations with instructors and with other students.

None of the effects mentioned above—future use of the repertoire, course credit, current use, social approval—occur at the time that studying is taking place, and for this reason they cannot function as direct consequences for studying. However, some of the student's own verbal behavior regarding these consequences can occur as he studies and in this way can mediate the effects of the more remote events. Not much is known about this type of self-management, but it obviously plays an important role in many forms of human behavior.

Irrespective of the effectiveness of verbal self-management skills regarding such consequences, all of them have two weaknesses. One results from the vagueness of the relationship between the details of the studying behavior and the remote consequence. It is not usually clear to what extent failure to master a particularly difficult passage in an assigned reading will affect any of these remote consequences. In addition, these and similar events, which are temporally far removed from studying behavior, have the same weakness as the intrinsic interest value of study materials: With respect to any particular moment of decision as to whether one should study or do something else, the remote consequences have an almost unlimited temporal availability. It is easy to believe that one can accept the social invitation, which is only available for a brief period, and study later. These two weaknesses, while they may not completely counteract most students' self-management skills, certainly strain them.

Considering the general ineffectiveness of the consequences of studying, it is not surprising that few students, instructors, or administrators take the expected time commitment, "2 hours outside of class for every hour in class," very seriously. Instructors generally yield to this defective motivational situation by defining, as an adequate repertoire, one that can be acquired by attending most of the lectures and studying 5 or 6 hours immediately prior to each major exam, but not between these times at all. This lowering of standards further reduces the effectiveness of course credit and grades as consequences.

The lack of a mastery criterion for advancement, discussed earlier, also results in a further weakening of some of the consequences described above. Text and lecture material presented late in a course may depend upon a repertoire that should have been but never was developed earlier in the same course. There is probably not much intrinsic interest value in study materials that one can only partially understand, and such an obviously inadequate repertoire is certainly not relevant to future vocational or avocational activities.

In summary, then, the materials that college students study are often inadequate to start with; and since there is no within-course mastery criterion for advancement, they may become increasingly inadequate as a course proceeds. Thus the first essential feature of an effective discrimination training situation—a good program of instruction—is usually not a part of most college education. For many students, the consequences of studying are not very effective competitors of the consequences contingent upon other activities available in the academic setting; thus, the second component, differential consequation for performance of the instructional task, is also under poor control in college education. Because of some rather marked differences between human and animal learning situations, a behavioral analysis of the third component, differential consequation for correctness, is quite complex. The relevance of this factor to college learning is not clear, but if the operant aspects of reading a text and listening to lectures turn out to be of major significance, then here too the college contingencies are quite defective.

The situation is by no means hopeless, however. Improvements can be and are being made at many points, as is obvious from some of the other papers in this volume. It is hoped that the present type of analysis can provide the rationale for changes that have already been made, and perhaps suggest additional improvements.

REFERENCES

Skinner, B. F. *Science and human behavior.* New York: Macmillan, 1953.
Skinner, B. F. *Verbal behavior.* New York: Appleton, 1957.
Staats, A. W. *Learning, language, and cognition: theory, research, and method for the study of human behavior and its development.* New York: Holt, 1968.

Behavior Modification and the Role of the University in Effecting Social Change

ROGER E. ULRICH

Universities in the United States have grown out of a European tradition that stressed exclusiveness and almost monastic separation from the surrounding community. Today, exclusiveness has been forfeited to mass education, and sequestration has been diminished by numerous financial and administrative ties with the government. For the most part, however, the behavior expected of students and faculty harks back to the days of the quadrangle and the gate. Faculty are expected, first, to pass on to students their particular segment of culturally accumulated knowledge. In some institutions, faculty are also expected to make their own discoveries, which are then communicated principally to colleagues. The traditional role of the student is passive almost to the point of catatonia. Some universities, especially in their catalogues, picture an intellectual exchange between student and professor. However, the student's job, basically, is to imitate or approximate the verbal behavior or research technique of his professors. With exceptions, such as soliciting government grants and student teaching, the university often requires very little behavior from faculty or students that relates to people or institutions outside the university. Throughout, the emphasis is on the discovery and transmission of knowledge, almost to the total exclusion of its utilization.

In the past few years, the anachronistic goals and practices of universities have increasingly been questioned. Students feel that they are capable of more than sponging up the wisdom of the ages. They do not want to be locked away from American society and its problems. Some faculty are also becoming restive, especially when they see in their areas of specialization some hope for improving the lives of their fellow human beings. Finally, the citizens, parents and governmental agencies who supply the financial support of universities are asking what they receive for their money. If institutions outside the university find more effective answers to the problems of poverty, ignorance, and violence, one can only expect them to take priority over universities in funding. For the sake of their own survival and prosperity, universities should deliberately add to their present activities programs for solving social problems and for positive cultural change.

The need and opportunity for applying academic knowledge outside the university should be especially apparent to behavioral psychologists. Psychology, through the analysis of behavior, has reached a firm understanding and control of behavior. Behavioral psychologists can arrange environments so that the organisms will learn things once believed beyond their capacity, so that the organisms will be more productive and, to an extent, so that the organisms will be happy. They also know how to arrange environments so that organisms will behave inappropriately, or freeze up and not behave at all. They know how to cause aggression and the behavioral equivalent of fear. Knowing the effect the environment has on behavior, they look at the environments human beings have arranged for themselves: the schools, homes, factories, hospitals, prisons, offices, and universities in which people function. They see appropriate behavior punished. They see inappropriate behavior reinforced. They see an overall neglect of positive reinforcement as a controller of behavior and a subsequent reliance on aversive stimuli. Considering the design of most cultural institutions, it is little wonder that many people are ignorant, unhappy, aggressive, and unproductive.

Many behavioral psychologists feel that they are in the unique position of being able both to diagnose many social ills and to suggest some remedies. Some behavioral psychologists have in fact introduced their techniques into schools, hospitals, homes, therapy situations, and many other settings (e.g., Ullmann & Krasner, 1965; Ulrich, Stachnik, & Mabry, 1966, 1970). The techniques of behavior modification both have withstood the tests of practicality and have offered new hope to the teacher, mental health worker, or parent whose traditional techniques have failed. Current attempts at intervention indicate that more ambitious attempts will meet similar success. Behavioral psychologists have an expertise badly needed by the community.

The application of the techniques of behavior analysis to human institutions provides an excellent model for the involvement of university departments of psychology in constructive social change.

The present paper uses the Department of Psychology at Western Michigan University as a case study in some of the possible applications of behavioral psychology to social institutions. Western is not unique; wherever psychologists interested in behavior modification have gathered, programs in the community have proliferated. At Western, a variety of approaches have been taken. First, since institutional redesign should begin at home the department has attempted to follow the principles of behavior in its own program. In addition, the program has been designed to give students the behaviors they will need to effect change themselves. Second, students and faculty have become involved in existing institutions in the community. Involvement in these institutions has explored ways both of remedying difficulties and, within the limitations imposed on those institutions, of redesigning programs. Finally, some members of the department have established a new institution (in this case, a school) comprehensively designed in accordance with the principles of behavior. All of these activities have been carried on in addition to large-scale teaching and research responsibilities.

EFFECTING CHANGE IN THE UNIVERSITY

In 1965, Western Michigan University had a Department of Psychology typical of many universities. Each professor was a specimen of a different approach to behavior. The primary responsibility of the faculty was teaching. Little research was conducted, little was published, and virtually no extra-university funds were coming into the department. The teaching methodology was traditional. Students attended lectures, wrote papers, and took exams. Professors lectured, evaluated student performance, and turned in grades. Beginning in 1965, the author came to Western Michigan University as head of the department[1] and a number of new faculty were hired. All of them were committed to the experimental analysis of behavior. They wanted a department with a strong program of basic research. Many of them also wanted opportunities to apply basic research in nonlaboratory settings. The new members also shared a similar view of the causes of behavior, including the factors that cause students to learn.

Initial changes in the department's program grew, in part, out of the faculty's need for help in fulfilling their ambitions. Programs of basic and

[1]Much of the change pertaining to the period described in this report was initiated during Dr. Ulrich's tenure as Head of the Psychology Department at Western Michigan University, from 1965 to 1968 (editor's note).

applied research need skilled personnel. An obvious source of personnel is students. As the faculty looked at its pool of potential research associates and technicians—and potential Ph.D. psychologists—it found them engaged in reading, listening, taking exams, and writing papers. They were not learning most of the skills essential to successful functioning as professional psychologists. The terminal behaviors of a psychologist are teaching, planning and conducting research, raising money, reporting research, and overseeing the application of research. Yet what the students were actually taught was to read, listen, and write—all in a classroom setting.

The Apprenticeship Program

Although courses and classrooms were not eliminated, an apprenticeship program was added to the usual curriculum (Ulrich & Kent, 1970). Under the apprenticeship program, students could earn credit or money by engaging in approximations of the behaviors they would need as professional psychologists. Some of these are approximations of the traditional academic duties of psychologists. For example, second-semester freshmen teach discussion sections of first-semester freshmen. More advanced students teach in more advanced courses. Beginning students can assist in research by weighing and caring for animals, recording data, or carrying out the day-to-day running of experiments. As students become more involved in research, they participate in designing experiments and in designing and constructing equipment. Advanced undergraduates submit proposals to the department for their own research. When their research is completed, they report the results at a professional meeting and submit them to a professional journal. Similarly, graduate students attend meetings, teach courses, and conduct research. In addition, some graduate students supervise the work of other students and help submit proposals for support to foundations and governmental agencies.

Students also participate in the application of behavioral psychology to community institutions. These programs will be discussed later in greater detail. Briefly, students can participate by teaching in schools or working in hospitals where behavior modification is practiced. They can design and carry out their own research projects within these settings. Advanced students also help design and implement comprehensive programs for changing institutions in the community or for establishing new institutions.

Apprenticeship has not been limited to university students. High school and even grade school students have participated in their own and in department research. Some of these were interested students from the community; others were participants in special institutes designed to supplement high school and grade school curricula (Kent, 1965; Farris, Kent, & Henderson, 1970). Pre-university students who participate in basic and applied research are especially likely to enroll in universities and usually plan to major in psychology or education. In the case of students from so-called disadvantaged backgrounds, the apprenticeship program and the increased likelihood of attending college are particularly critical. In general, students who enter the university with a history of apprenticeship seem better skilled and more likely to succeed.

The apprenticeship program has made the relationship between faculty and students a symbiotic one. The students contribute essential assistance to the programs of the department, and the faculty provide the conditions under which the students develop behaviors they will need later in their professional lives. Some notion of the success of the relationship can be obtained from Fig. 1. Figures 1(a) and 1(b) show the rise that occurred during implementation of apprenticeship in extra-university financial support and faculty authorships. Figure 1(c) shows a similar rise in student authorships. Incidentally, since new sources of income have become available to the department, in part through student effort, an increase in student-earned income has also occurred.

BEHAVIORAL INSTRUCTION

Most university courses are designed more as intelligence tests than as instructional situations. Exams are infrequent, objectives foggy, approximations neglected. Behaviorally designed alternatives to the usual academic format have been described in detail elsewhere (Keller, 1966, 1968, 1970; Lloyd & Knutzen, 1969; Lloyd, 1971; Malott & Svinicki, 1968). Briefly, they involve clearly stated behavioral objectives, specification of approximations to these objectives, frequent quizzes, immediate feedback on performance, repetition of quizzes until they are passed, in some cases self-pacing and programmed instruction, and use of lectures as reinforcers. Behavioral courses are designed, not to test whether or not the student can learn, but to create the conditions under which he surely will learn. Dick Malott and Donald Whaley were the moving force behind instituting such a program in the introductory psychology course at Western. Over 2,000 students take the course every year. At present the course is taught by Malott and about 50 student assistants (Malott and Svinicki, 1968). The course is designed by Malott. The quizzes, discussion sections, and laboratory sections are all administered by the student assistants. Pop culture is used to make the material as reinforcing as possible. Examples are a comic book (Malott, 1971) that features Captain Contingency Management (Con Man) and Behavior Man and songs such as the Determinism Suite (Malott, Ulrich, Fullmer, & Gideon, 1968). Virtually every student that completes the course receives a grade of "A" or "B."

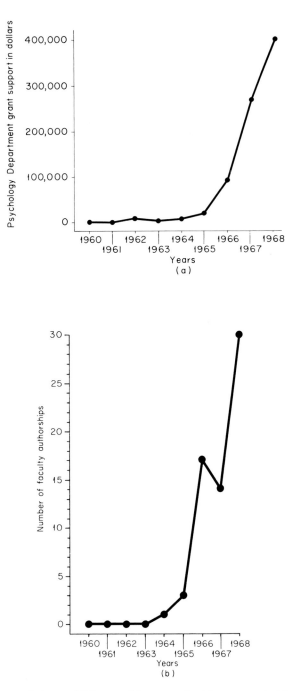

Fig. 1. *Increase, during establishment of the apprenticeship program, in (a) extra-university financial support; (b) faculty authorships; and (c) student authorships (see opposite page).*

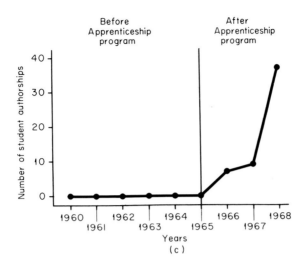

(c)

Behavioral design is also used in undergraduate and graduate psychology courses presently taught by Jack Michael (Michael, 1969), David Lyon, Louise Kent, Neil Kent, Howard Farris, and Paul Mountjoy. Besides teaching more effectively and extending the professor's effectiveness, behaviorally designed courses provide many opportunities for student apprentices to participate in the teaching process.

Since behavioral instruction was begun in the psychology department, interest throughout the university in behavioral education has increased. As a result, an experimental college called the Student Centered Education Project (SCEP) has been established to offer behavioral instruction in non-psychology courses (Malott, Hartlep, Keenan, & Michael, to be published). SCEP has its own student residences and sections of courses such as logic, philosophy, management, arts, and physical sciences. The fact that some students opt for behavioral instruction suggests that it can be a reinforcing, as well as educational, experience.

EFFECTING CHANGE IN COMMUNITY INSTITUTIONS[2]

By bringing the behavioral objectives of the psychology program in line with those behaviors needed by psychologists, and by bringing the teaching methodology used in courses in line with what is known about learning,

[2]Many of the programs described in the following paragraphs are featured in the film, "One Step at a Time: An Introduction to Behavior Modification," distributed by Communications / Research / Machines, Inc., Del Mar, California.

the members of the psychology department at Western Michigan University reshaped their own institution. Concurrent with the revamping of the department, the members began to establish ties with institutions in the surrounding community.

One of the first institutions contacted was the Kalamazoo State Hospital (for the mentally ill). The director and staff members of the Michigan State Department of Mental Health helped overcome the initial reluctance of some personnel at the hospital. Drs. Billie Hopkins and Wade Hitzing were instrumental in establishing programs at the hospital. A token economy was established on a ward of chronically psychotic patients. Eventually the patients themselves administered the system, serving as pay masters, data collectors, and behavioral engineers (Kale, Zlutnick, & Hopkins, 1968). One patient is currently being trained to act as a therapist for other patients. There have been difficulties and setbacks in working in the state hospital environment (Hopkins, 1970). Nevertheless, because of the program, patients have had the opportunity to attend school (Hopkins, 1970), improve their social behavior (Hopkins, 1968; Kale, Kaye, Whelan, & Hopkins, 1968), learn new skills (Kaye, Mackie, & Hitzing, 1970a, b), and relinquish some psychotic symptoms (Hitzing, Waters, & MacCormick, 1969).

Many of the behavior modification programs at the state hospital have been and are being carried out by students. A 3-week course trains students to translate what they have learned in the classroom in terms of what they see on the ward, to control their own behavior toward patients, and to be conscious of the ethical questions involved in treating institutionalized people. The students move from the course to supervised work with patients, and finally to relatively independent research and treatment.

A similar program, under the direction of Donald Whaley, Louise Kent, and Neil Kent, was established at Fort Custer, a state home for retarded children. Again, students and faculty work with individual residents, teaching basic self-care and intellectual skills and eliminating self-destructive behavior (Whaley & Tough, 1970).

Numerous ties have been established between the department and the Kalamazoo public schools. Neil Kent instituted a Parent Consulting Clinic that taught parents techniques of modifying the behavior of adolescents. Since the most basic problem of many adolescents seemed to be an inability to read, Kent now directs a reading clinic operated in conjunction with the Kalamazoo high schools and Vocational Rehabilitation. The program gives 1-hour remedial reading classes 5 days a week to 25 high school students. Tokens are given for work successfully completed. The tokens can later be exchanged for items bought at a local store or for opportunities to go on field trips.

The department has been fortunate to have as an ally the Kalamazoo Valley Intermediate School District (KVISD). In 1966, KVISD hired Rob Hawkins and the author as consultants. Initially, we and students from the university consulted with classroom teachers on behavior problems (Ulrich, Wolfe, & Bluhm, 1970). Hawkins went on to establish the School Adjustment Program, the first special education program in Kalamazoo County for so-called emotionally disturbed children. The method used in most schools that attempt to deal with problem children is to call in a consulting psychologist who simply diagnoses the problem, suggests "therapy," and hopes for the best. Hawkins has set up a system that solicits from teachers behavioral definitions of the problems and desired terminal behaviors (Hawkins, 1971). The classroom or special education teacher is instructed in techniques for making the necessary behavioral changes. Teachers are encouraged to take an empirical approach to their problems, and a journal (SALT) has been started to help teachers exchange ideas on classroom technique. Hawkins' program has been successful in developing techniques for changing the behavior of children (Schwarz & Hawkins, 1970; Hayes & Hawkins, 1970), in helping parents and teachers cope with specific behavior problems (Hawkins, 1967; Tough, Hawkins, McArthur, & Van Ravenswaay, to be published; Sluyter and Hawkins, 1969; Hawkins, Sluyter, & Smith, 1972), and in returning many children to the regular classroom (McArthur & Hawkins, to be published).

The need for programs such as Hawkins' is obvious to anyone who has encountered a grossly disturbed child. However, as work in the schools continued, the need became apparent for programs that both would prevent such problems from arising and would accelerate the development of all children. Remediation, no matter how effective, has certain inherent difficulties. Obviously, time and money are diverted from more constructive pursuits. Furthermore, reliance on remediation, in effect, reinforces problems. A child may be more or less ignored until he shows behavioral disturbance. Then he is showered with attention from his teacher, the principal, his parents, the school psychologist, and the special educator. One child I encountered found her remedial reading teacher so reinforcing that I recommended the student be required to improve her classroom reading performance *before* she could take a remedial lesson.

The initial attempt to establish a schoolwide, preventive program took place at the Indian Lake Elementary School in Vicksburg, Michigan. At Indian Lake, an in-service training program was instituted to familiarize teachers and administrators with behavior modification and to allay their doubts (Ulrich, et al., 1970b). At other schools in the district, in-service training programs were also offered, taught by David Lyon, Wade Hitzing, and Howard Farris. At Indian Lake, a reinforcement room was created that contained a slot-car set and other attractive toys. An all-school token system was instituted. In the classroom, the teachers could give tokens as reinforcers. for desired behaviors. With their tokens, the children could buy time in the reinforcement room, a chance to help the janitor sweep the halls, use of the P.A. system in the gym, extra free time, or a ride home in a teacher's sports car. The tokens became powerful tools for the preventive strengthening of desired behaviors (Ulrich, Wolfe, and Surratt, 1969).

Problems arose, of course. Parents phoned the principal and complained that their children were being bribed. Other parents had heard rumors that children were being placed in boxes and shocked. Parent training classes were then instituted both to calm and to inform parents. Parents were taught to set behavioral objectives for their children, to keep records of their children's behavior, and to reinforce desirable behavior. Eventually parents were able to conduct their own studies at home and to present them at class meetings (Ulrich et al., 1970b).

At Indian Lake, no schoolwide attempt was made to control precisely each teacher's classroom behavior, and no systematic measures of the children's academic achievement were available. However, the effects of the program were seen in a marked decrease in teachers' referrals of problem children to the school social worker, the child guidance clinic, and the family services center. The program at Indian Lake was instituted in 1966. After only 2 years of operation, referrals had dropped to a level near zero. Apparently most behavior problems formerly referred to specialists could now be handled by the teachers themselves. More important, the figures suggest that, by improved classroom techniques, teachers may have prevented many problems from arising.

The success at Indian Lake helped further expand the efforts in the Kalamazoo public schools. At the Lincoln Elementary School, an in-service program for teachers was conducted by W. Scott Wood. Teachers in the program conducted their own "research" in their classrooms. They identified, recorded, and controlled behaviors such as talking and leaving one's seat, temper tantrums, and inattention (Wood, 1970).

Still another program was conducted at the Hurd School, a special school for children unable to cope with the usual public-school environment. A token system was instituted at Hurd. Tokens were most often used to buy lunches and use of a pool table installed (by courageous administrators) at the school. After the token economy was in effect, school attendance increased from 63 to 80%, and studying time at school from 67 to 93%. Use of special reading materials increased from zero to a high rate (Ulrich, Wolfe, & Cole, 1970).

University students have been a conspicuous and essential part of the programs in the public schools (Ulrich et al., 1970b). Students most often work with teachers in their classrooms (e.g., Hawkins, McArthur, Rinaldi, Gray, & Shaftenaar, 1967). Sometimes the students remediate the deficit of an individual child or eliminate a problem behavior (Ulrich et al., 1970b; Schmidt & Ulrich, 1969; Surratt, Ulrich, & Hawkins, 1969). Occasionally students consult with teachers on techniques of classroom discipline or instruction. Such experience has been described as a laboratory section in educational psychology (Stachnik & Ulrich, 1969). The students have an opportunity to use the methodology they hear described in the classroom. They become aware of the strengths of the methodology and the problems it can entail. In addition, the students themselves become skilled in using techniques of behavioral education. Some more advanced students have assumed much of the responsibility for designing and implementing school-wide programs. These students are now thoroughly familiar with the possibilities and problems of using behavior modification in the public schools. Some of the students who once served as apprentices in the public schools now serve as consultants.

The programs in existing community institutions were successful in improving the operation of those institutions and in making the lives of many individual patients, residents, and students happier and more productive. However, as we worked within these settings, our ideas seemed to become more grandiose. The more psychotics, retardates, and emotionally disturbed children we encountered, the more our thinking focused on extending the type of preventive program created at Indian Lake. We became more and more convinced that a well-designed educational program would be the best medium for the prevention of mental illness, retardation, delinquency, and crime. Although community educators had proved enlightened and cooperative, they necessarily worked under constraints. We became more and more inclined to cut loose and design our own system.

ESTABLISHING A NEW INSTITUTION

While working in the public schools, some faculty and students had been conducting a small-scale program in preschool education (Ulrich et al., 1970b). Frequent positive reinforcement was used to teach basic skills to children ranging in age from several months to 4 years (Ulrich & Hunt, 1968). The accelerated intellectual and social development of the children in the pilot program strengthened our belief that we could design an effective educational environment. For 1 year, we operated a preschool program in two small rooms in my home and later at Western Michigan University. Most of the children in the program were taken from the waiting list of the traditionally oriented Campus School. Some children also came from academically disadvantaged backgrounds. Scores on the *Metropolitan Reading Readiness Test* suggested that the program had indeed accelerated the intellectual development of the children (Ulrich *et al.,* 1970c; Wood, Ulrich, & Fullmer, 1969). Nevertheless, the space used at the university was rescinded after the one year of operation.

At that time, the program was placed under the legal umbrella of the Behavior Development Corporation (BDC), which then served as the licensing agent for private school ventures. Gradually, and with a great deal of difficulty (Wolfe, Ulrich, & Ulrich, 1970), the BDC obtained licenses to operate a nursery school, a grade school, and finally an infant nursery. Establishing the infant nursery was especially problematic, since such an operation was entirely new to the licensing agency, in this case the Michigan Department of Social Services. Many social workers are convinced that infant day care will seriously disrupt the child's physical, cognitive, and affective development. However, we felt that a truly comprehensive preventative program should begin as near to birth as possible. It seemed to us that if a child were systematically reinforced for desirable behaviors from a very early point in his life, behavior problems would be kept to a minimum. The child should develop few behaviors that have to be extinguished or punished. By the age of 2, many children already have problems. We simply wanted to provide an environment in which such problems would be circumvented.

University students took an active part in every aspect of establishing the school. They helped locate, rent, remodel, and finally purchase space. They helped procure equipment and educational materials. They helped cope with the endless licensing procedures. Many of these activities might be regarded as trivial. However, just such trivia often stand between ideas and action. If more professors knew how to deal with agencies, realtors, wholesalers, and fire commissioners, more of the knowledge of academia would actually be applied in the community. The students who did much of the work in establishing the school now have many of the skills that must form the bridge between inspiration and implementation.

The school, called the Learning Village, has been in operation for over 3 years. It presently enrolls children from age 2 months to 11 years. Approximately half of the children receive some sort of financial assistance; the other half pay tuition.

The program of the Learning Village has been described in detail elsewhere (Ulrich, Louisell, & Wolfe, 1971). Basically, techniques of positive reinforcement are used to shape and accelerate intellectual, social, and motor develop-

TABLE 1
Performance of the Learning Village Kindergarten Students on the Reading and Arithmetic Sections of the Wide Range Achievement Test

Child	Years in Program	Age Years–Months	Reading Grade level Grade.Month	Reading Percentile in age group	Arithmetic Grade level Grade.Month	Arithmetic Percentile in age group
K1	1	4–11	2.5	99	1.8	98
K2	1	5–0	1.4	90	1.4	90
K3[a]	1	5–1	1.4	90	1.2	82
K4	1	5–3	2.5	99	2.1	99
K5	1	5–5	1.7	97	1.8	98
K6[a]	1	5–5	1.4	90	1.0	70
K7[a]	1	5–10	2.5	99	2.2	99
K8[a]	1	7–1	3.8	95	1.9	39
K9	2	5–7	2.6	99	2.4	99
K10	2	5–10	4.2	99	1.9	96
K11[a]	2	5–11	1.6	90	1.4	82
K12[a]	2	6–1	3.0	99	Kg.9	34
K13[a]	2	6–1	2.3	96	1.0	39
K14	2	6–2	3.1	99	2.1	92
K15	2	6–2	3.9	99	2.4	97
K16	2	6–4	4.2	99	2.8	99
K17	2	6–6	1.7	53	1.0	21
K18[a]	2	6–7	3.6	99	1.9	63
Mean		5–9	2.6	89	1.7	77
Median		5–10	2.5	99	1.8	69

[a] Received financial assistance

ment. Assessment of the program is just beginning. However, Table 1 gives some indication of the program's ability to accelerate academic performance. In Table 1 is shown the performance of the kindergarten children on the reading and arithmetic sections of the *Wide Range Achievement Test*. The children have spent 1 or 2 years in the program. On reading tests, almost all of the children are performing at several grade levels above that normal for their age. In some cases, the gap is enormous. Virtually all the scores are at least in the 90th percentile. In math, the performance is less spectacular, but half the scores are above the 90th percentile. The children were not preselected for intelligence. Approximately half come from home environments that supposedly fail to promote intellectual development. The scores of "disadvantaged" children are indistinguishable from the "advantaged" ones. The one child whose scores were far below the others comes from an upper-middle-class home.

An evaluation program is presently underway that will track the students' progress using tests that range from the *Bayley Scale of Infant Development* to standard achievement tests. As children spend more years in the program and as testing becomes more extensive, the results of the program should become even more obvious.

Students participate in every aspect of the operation of the Village, and many of the teaching staff are students. Students also design curricula, prepare materials, and participate in evaluation programs. In addition, they help in the practical business of raising money, complying with regulations, buying materials, and hiring personnel. Students who teach at the Village have an exceptional chance to see the positive side of behavior modification. Many of these students have already worked in remedial programs at Fort Custer, the state mental hospital, or the public schools. At the Village, they can see the acceleration of development that results from the preventive use of positive reinforcement. In the long range, such an experience will probably be more important to the effective use of behavioral psychology than experience in remedial programs.

The Learning Village has provided a base for establishing new ties between the university and the community. Many community people work at the Village. Forty percent of the Village students have parents who work there. Many of these people would ordinarily not interact with university-connected people and would not be exposed to behavior modification. Recently the Behavior Development Corporation contracted with the Department of Social Services to train teaching and nonteaching parents in the techniques of behavior modification. Another program trains high school students, especially those from disadvantaged backgrounds, to teach at the Village (Arnett, Clark, Spates, & Ulrich, 1969). These students spend half of their day in public high school and half working at the Village.

The Learning Village and the other projects conducted in conjunction with Western Michigan University have demonstrated the power of behavior modification and have helped reshape community institutions. The potential applications of the techniques derived from behavioral psychology seem nearly limitless. Every aspect of society presents problems that behavior modification can remedy or prevent. At the same time, the process of intervening in the community can revitalize the university. Professors are reminded of what the world is really like. Students are released from isolation and passivity and are given the opportunity to develop skills and make a direct contribution to the welfare of others.

Caution is in order, however. Pollution and depletion of natural resources are some of the unforeseen side-effects of the application of technology to the physical environment. The application of behavioral technology may similarly produce unforeseen problems in our social environment. We must do our best to avoid such problems. We must also be aware of the great potential for the abuse of both the name and substance of behavior modification. Old-fashioned coercion may masquerade as a treatment program. Behavioral techniques may be used toward ends, such as the suppression of dissent, that university people should deplore. When we become involved in the community, we risk the side-tracking or misuse of our involvement. The tools we design for solace may be forged into weapons of oppression. Nevertheless, for the sake of our universities and our society, we must become involved.

ACKNOWLEDGMENTS

The program described is, of course, the result of the efforts of departmental staff members, students, and other individuals both within and without Western Michigan University. Hopefully, the names of most of these people have found their way into the text or references of this paper. Support for these programs has come from many agencies, including the Office of Naval Research, the National Institute of Mental Health, the Kalamazoo Valley Intermediate School District, the Michigan Department of Mental Health, the Michigan Department of Social Services, and the Western Michigan University Research Fund. Special thanks go to Bob Pierce, Tom DeLoach, and Kay Mueller for editing and proofreading the manuscript.

REFERENCES

Arnett, M., Clark, D., Spates, R., & Ulrich, R. An in-service training program for high school students. Paper read at American Psychological Association, Washington, D.C., 1969.

Determinism Suite, an audio tape by The Behaviorists. Kalamazoo, Michigan: Behaviordelia, 1969.

Farris, H. E., Kent, N. D., & Henderson, D. E. Teaching behavioral science in the elementary and junior high school. In R. E. Ulrich, T. Stachnik, & J. Mabry (Eds.), *Control of human behavior.* Vol. II: *From cure to prevention.* Glenview, Illinois: Scott, Foresman, 1970. Pp. 309–315.

Hawkins, R. P. The public school classroom as a behavioral laboratory. Paper read at American Psychological Association, Washington, D.C., 1967.

Hawkins, R. P. The School Adjustment Program: Individualized intervention for children with behavior disorders. Paper read at Second Annual Kansas Symposium on Behavior Analysis in Education, Lawrence, Kansas, May, 1971.

Hawkins, R. P., McArthur, M., Rinaldi, P. C., Gray, D., & Shaftenaar, L. Results of operant conditioning techniques in modifying the behavior of emotionally disturbed children. Paper read at 45th Annual International Council for Exceptional Children conference, St. Louis, Missouri, 1967.

Hawkins, R. P., Sluyter, D. J., & Smith, C. D. Modification of achievement by a simple technique involving parents and teacher. In M. B. Harris (Ed.), Classroom uses of behavior modification. Columbus, Ohio: Charles E. Merrill, 1972.

Hayes, J. E. & Hawkins, R. P. An analysis of instruction duration as a consequence for correct and incorrect answers. Paper read at American Psychological Association, Miami Beach, Florida, 1970.

Hitzing, E. W., Waters, R. J., & MacCormick, J. P. Application of video tape procedures in the modification of stereotyped behavior. Michigan Mental Health Research Bulletin, 1969, 3, 15.

Hopkins, B. L. Effects of candy and social reinforcement, instructions, and reinforcement schedule leaning on the modification and maintenance of smiling. Journal of Applied Behavior Analysis, 1968, 1, 121–129.

Hopkins, B. L. The first twenty years are the hardest. In R. E. Ulrich, T. Stachnik, & J. Mabry (Eds.), Control of human behavior. Vol. II: From cure to prevention. Glenview, Illinois: Scott, Foresman, 1970. Pp. 358–365.

Kale, R. J., Kaye, J. H., Whelan, P. A., & Hopkins, B. L. The effect of reinforcement and the modification, maintenance and generalization of social responses in mental patients. Journal of Applied Behavior Analysis, 1968, 1, 307–314.

Kale, R. J., Zlutnick, S., & Hopkins, B. L. Patient contributions to a therapeutic environment. Michigan Mental Health Research Bulletin, 1968, 2, 33–38; and in R. E. Ulrich, T. Stachnik, & J. Mabry (Eds.), Control of human behavior. Vol. II. From cure to prevention. Glenview, Illinois: Scott, Foresman, 1970. Pp. 96–99.

Kaye, J. H., Mackie, V., & Hitzing, E.W., Applications of reinforcement principles to occupational therapy. Michigan Mental Health Research Bulletin, 1970, 4, 26. (a)

Kaye, J. H., Mackie, V., & Hitzing, E. W. Innovation in occupational therapy. American Journal Occupational Therapy, 1970, 24, 413–417. (b)

Keller, F. S. A personal course in psychology. In R. E. Ulrich, T. Stachnik, & J. Mabry (Eds.), Control of human behavior. Vol. 1: Expanding the behavioral laboratory. Glenview, Illinois: Scott, Foresman, 1966. Pp. 91–93.

Keller, F. S. "Good-bye, Teacher. . ." Journal of Applied Behavior Analysis, 1968, 1, 79–89; and in R. E. Ulrich, T. Stachnik, and J. Mabry (Eds.), Control of human behavior. Vol. II: From cure to prevention. Glenview, Illinois: Scott, Foresman, 1970. Pp. 298–309.

Keller, F. S. A programmed system of instruction. Behavior Modification Monographs, 1970, 1 (3).

Kent, N. D. Aspirations, successes, and failures in teaching the experimental analysis of behavior. American Psychologist, 1965, 20, 542.

Lloyd, K. E. Contingency management in university courses. Educational Technology, 1971, 11 (4), 18–23.

Lloyd, K. E. & Knutzen, N. J. A self-paced programmed undergraduate course in the experimental analysis of behavior. Journal of Applied Behavior Analysis, 1969, 2, 125–133.

Malott, R. W. Contingency management in education and other equally exciting places, or I've got blisters on my soul and other equally exciting places. Kalamazoo, Michigan: Behaviordelia, 1971.

Malott, R. W., Hartlep, P. A., Kennan, M., & Michael, J. Groundwork for an experimental college. *Educational technology*, to be published.

Malott, R. & Svinicki, J. Contingency management in an introductory psychology course for 1000 students. Paper read at American Psychological Association, San Francisco, California, 1968.

Malott, R., Ulrich, C., Fullmer, W., & Gideon, B. Examples of the use of pop culture in education: A multi-media presentation. Paper read at American Psychological Association, San Francisco, California, 1968.

McArthur, M. & Hawkins, R. P. The modification of several classroom behaviors of an emotionally disturbed child in a regular classroom. *Journal of Applied Behavior Analysis*, to be published.

Michael, J. Management of behavioral consequences in education. *Revista Interamericana de Psicologia*, 1969, **3**, 204–259.

SALT (School Applications of Learning Theory). R. P. Hawkins (Ed.), Kalamazoo Valley Intermediate School District, Box 2025, Kalamazoo, Michigan, 49003.

Schmidt, G. & Ulrich, R. E. Effects of group contingent events upon classroom noise. *Journal of Applied Behavior Analysis*, 1969, **2**, 171–179.

Schwarz, M. L. & Hawkins, R. P. Application of delayed conditioning procedures to the behavior problems of an elementary school child. In R. E. Ulrich, T. Stachnik, & J. Mabry (Ed.), *Control of human behavior*. Vol. II: *From cure to prevention*. Glenview, Illinois: Scott, Foresman, 1970. Pp. 271–283.

Sluyter, D. & Hawkins, R. Delayed consequation of classroom behavior by parents. *Michigan Mental Health Research Bulletin*, 1969, **3**, 28–30.

Stachnik, T. J. & Ulrich, R. E. A laboratory section for educational psychology. *Psychological Record*, 1969, **19**, 129–132.

Surratt, P.R., Ulrich, R.E., & Hawkins, R.P. An elementary student as a behavioral engineer. *Journal of Applied Behavior Analysis*, 1969, **2**, 85–92; and in R. E. Ulrich, T. Stachnik, & J. Mabry (Eds.), *Control of human behavior*. Vol. II: *From cure to prevention*. Glenview, Illinois: Scott, Foresman, 1970. Pp. 263–271.

Tough, J. H., Hawkins, R. P., McArthur, M. M., & Van Ravenswaay, S. Modification of enuretic behavior by punishment: A new use for an old device. *Behavior Therapy*, to be published.

Ullmann, L. P. & Krasner, L. (Eds.) *Case studies in behavior modification*. New York: Holt, 1965.

Ulrich, R. E. & Hunt, L. The operant shaping of verbal imitation in a 6-month-old infant. Paper read at Midwestern Psychological Association, Chicago, Illinois, 1968.

Ulrich, R. E. & Kent, N. D. Suggested tactics for the training of psychologists. In R. E. Ulrich, T. Stachnik, & J. Mabry (Eds.), *Control of human behavior*. Vol. II: *From cure to prevention*. Glenview, Illinois: Scott, Foresman, 1970. Pp. 288–298.

Ulrich, R. E., Louisell, S. E., & Wolfe, M. The Learning Village: A behavioral approach to early education. *Educational Technology*, 1971, **11** (2), 32–45.

Ulrich, R.E., Stachnik, T., & Mabry, J. (Eds.), *Control of human behavior*. Vol. I: *Expanding the behavioral laboratory*. Glenview, Illinois: Scott, Foresman, 1966.

Ulrich, R.E., Stachnik, T., & Mabry, J. (Eds.), *Control of human behavior*. Vol. II: *From cure to prevention*. Glenview, Illinois: Scott, Foresman, 1970. (a)

Ulrich, R. E., Wolfe, M. M., & Bluhm, M. Operant conditioning in the public schools. *Behavior Modification Monographs*, 1970, **1** (1). (b)

Ulrich, R. E., Wolfe, M. M., & Cole, R. Early education: A preventive mental health program. *Michigan Mental Health Research Bulletin*, 1970, **4**, (1). (c)

Ulrich, R. E., Wolfe, M., & Surratt, P. New methods for treatment delivery. *Michigan Mental Health Research Bulletin,* 1969, **3**, 41–44.

Whaley, D. L. & Tough, J. Treatment of a self-injuring mongoloid with shock-induced suppression and avoidance. In R. E. Ulrich, T. Stachnik, & J. Mabry (Eds.), *Control of human behavior.* Vol. II: *From cure to prevention.* Glenview, Illinois: Scott, Foresman, 1970. Pp. 154–155.

Wolfe, M., Ulrich, R., & Ulrich, C. Administrative hurdles blocking preventive mental health programs for children. *Michigan Mental Health Research Bulletin,* 1970, **4** (2), 44–48.

Wood, W. S. The Lincoln Elementary School projects: Some results of an in-service training course in behavioral psychology. *Behavior Modification Monographs,* 1970, **1** (2).

Wood, W. S., Ulrich, C., & Fullmer, M. Early education: An experimental nursery school for four-year-olds. Paper read at Michigan Academy of Arts, Letters and Sciences, Ann Arbor, Michigan, 1969.

Are Behavioral Principles for Revolutionaries?[1]

JAMES G. HOLLAND

We are justly proud of the accomplishments that have emerged from the operant conditioning laboratory. The uses of behavior modification in therapy, in prisoner rehabilitation, and in education in the form of programmed instruction and classroom management are feats that promise to make the lives of everyone better as these techniques become increasingly prevalent in our society. In contingency management, we have already moved from working with individuals in the correction of "symptoms" to the management of small groups in classrooms or on hospital wards, and we see promise of moving on to larger groups or to whole societies. While we feel the flush of success, there are growing objections from those who view our proud accomplishments with alarm. These are the people who, in the terms of Skinner's *Beyond Freedom and Dignity,* are the writers of the literature

[1]Much of the time in preparation of this paper was supported by the Learning Research and Development Center supported as a learning research and development center by funds from the United States Office of Education, Department of Health, Education, and Welfare. The opinions expressed do not necessarily reflect the position or policy of the Office of Education and no official endorsement should be inferred.

of freedom and the literature of dignity. I believe that behind their concerns there are problems that merit every bit of the alarm they express. It is unfortunate, and even dangerous, however, that they draw the issue along invalid lines. They argue the case for free will and speak against the proposition that all behavior follows certain fundamental laws which make possible the manipulation of behavior. Or at least they argue that if behavior were left alone by the managers, there would be basic personal freedom. On the other hand, we counter with our evidence of the lawfulness of behavior and our success in the clinic, the school, and in prison rehabilitation. Given this lawfulness, we advocate deliberate design in the control of human affairs, rather than leaving human affairs at the mercy of accidental contingencies.

The two parties to this dialogue, the writers of the literature of freedom and dignity and the designers of behavior modification systems, must properly define the issues. In the design of culture and in the use of behavior management in the society we see today, what are the possibilities and the probabilities of the ultimate use of our work? Into what will our present society evolve as the present decision makers increasingly make use of our talents? Can we expect to see a further deepening of the problems in our society discussed in the literature on freedom and dignity? In fact, does not the contingency management in the form we most often see today automatically establish some of the worst features of our society as a by-product? On the other hand, are there alternative societal values and structures, however different, however revolutionary, that may require us to transform ourselves to move toward them? Given a completely different set of goals for society, what role might be played by contingency management in the formation and maintenance of such a society?

I will suggest that: (1) there is a real and critical basis for resistance by critics who oppose behavior analysts in the design of social control systems. The danger is all the greater because the techniques of behavior modification do work, notwithstanding the critics' claims that they do not work or work only for limited ends. (2) In a radically different society, there is not only a great role for the design of deliberate behavior change, but in fact the successful transition from the present society to a revolutionary society requires such planned change. (3) The form that behavior modification takes in revolutionary societies, while reflecting the same underlying laws of behavior, will be quite different in the nature of reinforcers and in the way contingencies are set and assessed.

To develop these points I must necessarily characterize our present system and outline a potential alternative system so that we may explore the implications of behavior modification in each of them. It is easy for a traditional laboratory-trained psychologist to become embarrassed at taking even a brief sojourn into political science, but, after all, the potential use of behavior modification techniques for cultural design makes such a sojourn inevitable. Modern American society, the Western European tradition from which we spring, and our global sphere of influence on subservient nations euphemistically labelled ''the free world'' are governed by and for a small elitist class. Social psychologist William G. Domhoff has assembled impressive data demonstrating this point. In his books, *Who Rules America?* and *The Higher Circles,* he provides clear operational definitions for membership in the upper class and demonstrates that this upper class has its basis in the American corporations, constituting a governing class that controls the corporations through its disproportionate ownership of corporate stock, heavy representation on corporate boards, and as executive officers in the corporations. Moreover, the same individuals are heavily represented on the boards of foundations, universities, and leading corporations in communications; they control the United States government by determining which persons can receive the nominations of either major party and obtain the indispensable campaign funds required in working toward that office. Moreover, the upper class members are in return placed in direct control of the major departments and critical agencies of the government, by representations on the Cabinet, in the Departments of State, Commerce, and Labor, and in their membership in the inner circle around most presidents. Beneath this top corporate elite, there is a hierarchy of jobs and roles for the people. In the corporations, this is described by the usual corporate chart showing the board at the top, officers under the board, top managers under the officers, department heads and so forth, down to the lowest worker. Everyone's position in the hierarchy is defined; there is a top and a bottom; everyone can identify his place according to his degree of worth within the system. In the army, this is represented by the familiar officer structure from general down to private. In schools, there are principals, vice-principals, teachers, and paraprofessionals, and at the bottom, of course, there are students.

An analysis of the natural reinforcement contingencies that exist within the system is an interesting exercise which, I would suggest, is a very worthwhile and profitable one for modern behavior modifiers. The reinforcement systems in this society are based primarily on acquisition of personal material gain and personal privilege and status. The reinforcement systems tend to encourage competition: getting more than one's neighbors, gaining recognition and status above one's peers, gaining raises to the next level in the hierarchy of the elite. It should be added, though, that society is fairly rigidly stratified, more so than is commonly believed. Often, the upward movement is more of an illusion, with much channeling of the population by means of rather tight social controls. Nevertheless, the poor work hard to ''make it" by getting a janitor's job or a job as a helper to some middle-class professional. Although there are countertrends within the culture that account for the existence of the literature of freedom and dignity, nevertheless the dominant elements in the reinforcement system are selfishness and competitiveness for goods and privileges. The student struggles for the competitive grade in school—to attain the top grade average and admission to graduate school or a good corporate position, etc. In each instance, the contingency is set by the next higher rung in the elite, and one moves up by pleasing this elite. But recall that at the top is a largely hereditary ruling class that sets the general goals for all of the social institutions.

We might next ask where the professional psychologist fits into this system. He usually operates with grant support, and is employed in a university or another institution. Both the granting agency and the employing institutions are controlled by the upper class and are in the service of the general goals of society. Hence we find that ultimately, most work stands either in its initial form directly in support of the power elite and the system, or indirectly in the sense that after the initial procedures have been developed, the methods are ready for use by those with sufficient money and resources to use them. The psychologist is then no longer needed. With a little training, technicians can be taught to arrange the necessary reinforcers or aversive stimuli to carry out the procedures of behavior modification. Training workshops are common for teachers, parents, psychiatric nurses, and prison personnel, among others, to prepare them for using behavior modification. Therefore, responsibility for its use often will not rest with a small identifiable professional group who might be guided by an ethical code and could more easily be held accountable by society.

The relationship between the psychologist and the recipient of behavior modification will often not be the traditional one of professional to client. The person, or group of persons, whose behavior is being modified may not only lack direct contact with the psychologist, but his behavior may be controlled for the benefit of some other person or group. It seems clear that in our present social system, the people who will determine whose behavior is to be changed and toward what end will be those in established positions of power. The science will be at the service of those who command the means to use it.

That this is the direction to be expected in the applications of behavior control procedures is illustrated by the U.S. Army's use of the contingency management system designed by psychologists for basic training. Lieutenant Colonel Datel and Lieutenant Colonel Legters (1970) developed a token economy reinforcement system covering all aspects of basic military training from barracks inspection, standing formation, and rifle range training to various objective test performances. Officers and noncoms punched designated areas on the trainee's card when criteria for reinforcement were met. The points accumulated were exchangeable for privileges such as attending a movie or getting a weekend pass. Moreover, the highest third received a promotion and raise in pay at the completion of the 8 weeks of training.

This is a clear instance of the use of behavior modification in the service of power. Behavior modification techniques in basic training were used to create a better army. Many may like the fact that positive reinforcement has here replaced the traditional aversive control, and it certainly must seem more humane to the trainee. But it was not done for the purpose of humanity, it was done to make a better army—one that could better carry out its mission of protecting and extending the American empire. Colonels Datel and Legters learned well the lessons of experimental behavior analysis, noting that aversive control generates countercontrol, and that a more effective army could result from the introduction of positive reinforcement. The second point to make is that the form of the contingency management they used, and typical of many token economies, has as a by-product the concept of an elitist structure. It is the trained cadre who hand out the points: the drill sergeant, the platoon sergeant, and the officers. A secondary message of the system is that there are those who are better, who are higher in the elite, and who rightfully have greater power and privilege. [A similar side effect has been discussed by Illich (1971) in his description of how the schools sell the concept of schooling and convince the population that proper learning comes only from within a school context.] Here and in other instances, we see that the form of the contingency management system itself takes on the characteristics of the elitist structure it serves. But the important point here is the relationship between the person the system is operating upon and the person or institution it serves. The reinforcement system was not designed for the soldiers, it was designed for those who run the army. The army is the client, but the individual soldier is the one who receives the treatment. And the ultimate worth of the system must depend on the evaluation of the army's mission, not on its effect on the soldier.

From the military, we see many other examples of our science in the service of the power structure. Psychologists under contract with the army responded to a situation identified in the data from past wars which showed less than 25% of the men in actual combat conditions fired their weapons (Marshall, 1966). The psychologists added procedures to basic training to increase the soldier's willingness to fire more frequently and effectively. These procedures raised the percentage in the Vietnam war to 55%, thus showing a decrease in young Americans' reluctance to kill. The true client of the professional product was the army, while the recipient of the procedure was the enlisted man. The fact that these techniques serve those in power and not those directly receiving their impact can be unequivocally illustrated by the use of behavior modification in foreign pacification programs. The resources for using our techniques exist here on a gigantic scale compared to the occasional worthy use in mental hospitals at home.

A survey (Gordon & Helmer, 1964) among experts in weapons systems conducted by the Rand Corporation projected as a major weapons system the behavioral control of mass populations, and most of these experts expect it to be a reality by 1980, i.e., good old American knowhow beating by 4 years the English masters of 1984. Are we unwittingly and unwillingly contributing to this development? Already, crude versions of contingency management are playing a role in our pacification programs. Howard Walters (1968), in a chapter on military psychology, described a case study in a so-called "Token Civic Action Program," which included the use of candy to reinforce village children and the use of a lottery (i.e., a sort of "community variable–ratio schedule") to reinforce retention of propaganda leaflets. A number of other contrived efforts to use trivial positive reinforcement are included in the so-called "pacification" of a village. Fortunately, the procedures are primitive and relatively ineffective. But as the war lords learn from us, will the people of Vietnam and elsewhere fare so well? One can hardly argue that the recipients of behavior modification are being served by these manipulations.

A yet more odious and obvious example is found in a research proposal prepared by the American Institutes for Research (1967), which requested and received more than a million dollars. The Institute proposed that social scientists work on problems of counterinsurgency in the country of Thailand. The following quote from its proposal will indicate a little of the insight they have into possible behavior management:

> . . .the effect of a given stimulus element on a given individual at a given moment in time is shaped by the experiences of that individual in responding to that stimulus in the past [American Institutes for Research, 1967, p. 6].

Moreover,

> . . .conditions that change established stimulus–response patterns—either by changing the individual's history of experiences with that stimulus element or by changing the contemporaneous circumstances on which the effectiveness of that stimulus element depends . . .we shall call "disposing conditions" [American Institutes for Research, 1967, p. 8].

For example,

> The offer of food in exchange for certain services affords a convenient example. If this has in the past been a strong stimulus, it can probably be weakened by increasing local agricultural production. *If it has been a weak or neutral stimulus, it can probably be strengthened by burning the crops* [American Institutes for Research, 1967, p. 7].

Take heart. We are not to limit these insights in behavior engineering to foreign lands. They continue:

> The potential applicability of the findings in the United States will also receive special attention. In many of our key domestic programs, especially those directed at disadvantaged subcultures, the methodological problems are similar to those described in this proposal; and the application of the Thai findings at home constitutes a potentially most significant project contribution [American Institutes for Research, 1967, p. 34].

For whose benefit are they planning to manipulate the reinforcing value of food? For the army and the American Imperialists? And whose behavior is being modified?

To come back closer to home, one of the stories circulating among operant conditioners is about a visit paid by the right-wing politician, Ronald Reagan, Governor of California, to a hospital ward at Patton State Hospital in California. Reagan watched with interest the token reinforcement system used to control the ward behavior of psychotic patients. Reagan, who has a long history of fighting what he considers "welfare handouts," was impressed by what he saw at Patton State and commented that this was the kind of giving that he was in sympathy with because "it was given for doing something." The story is usually told with some glee at the fact that the liberal psychologist seems to have deceived Reagan. But I think Reagan may be the more perceptive one in this case. The token economy in this instance and in many other instances follows an elitist system, and, at least as a secondary effect, seems to legitimize that form. Moreover, while I know those conducting such token economies on hospital wards and in prisons, etc. will take issue with me, the decisions as to what behaviors should be reinforced very often seem to depend upon the creation of the kind of ward behavior pleasing to hospital personnel—to "Big Nurse" for those fans of Kesey's novel, One Flew Over the Cuckoo's Nest. I will admit here some of my own ambiguity and uncertainty. Well-made beds, well-groomed patients, patients sweeping the floor and keeping neat may be valuable behaviors to the patients themselves, but it is clear that they reflect most definitely what Big Nurse desires. It is questionable whether nurses who walk around handing out tokens do much to establish personal self-esteem in the patient.

A clearer instance is a case of a psychologist who used reinforcement procedures in what he called "survival training" for young kindergarten children who were to enter conventional schools. The phrase "survival training" suggests to the reader a psychologist helping the client struggle in an oppressive system. But, reading on, one finds that the so-called survival training consisted of teaching the children to line up and sit quietly and to avoid engaging in talking or other behavior that the teacher might consider disruptive. In other words, it consists of the student's doing what the school establishment demands. I assume that all this is to be gained through positive reinforcement rather than through aversive techniques, but it seems more like capitulation than survival.

For the behavioral scientist who has set aside the old rationalization of scientific neutrality, what, if he is involved in the struggle for justice, can he do? At the very least we should give priority to developments that have the possibility of being useful to people generally. Often it is not even theoretically possible for technology to be used by those lacking wealth and power. But more than this is needed. Some have proceeded with the kind of analysis given above and have closed their laboratories. But there is yet another possibility. We can attempt to convey our technological findings to the people and to develop applications that are more likely to be useful to them than to the elite. It is most important in this regard for the behavioral scientist to analyze the operation of behavioral control in our society and communicate this analysis to others so that they may better equip themselves for countercontrol. Using these data, he could also analyze the potential effects of different forms of countercontrol. Moreover, he could develop technology intrinsically suited for use in the struggle.

To illustrate the first possibility of analyzing and interpreting societal instances of behavioral control, Skinner's new book, *Beyond Freedom and Dignity,* would be an extremely valuable tool. It is a shame that those persons most involved in the struggle for justice view Skinner and operant conditioners as the enemy, thereby forfeiting a powerful tool to analyze the control exerted within the system they oppose. To illustrate the use by the government of an elaborate and effective contingency management system, we may examine the draft.

The Selective Service System is designed not simply to fill the ranks of the military, but to channel manpower much more generally. A Selective Service document on channeling describes this as the primary role of the draft, as it was in 1965 when the Selective Service distributed its Orientation Kit containing a document on *Channeling.* It describes the use of occupational deferments to keep a flow of manpower into jobs considered to be in the "national interest." So potential poets became engineers. The occupational deferment also forced many to turn to teaching or into quietly accepting lower pay than they might otherwise have insisted on because their principal aim was to avoid the draft. The Selective Service document also notes that an annual review of occupational deferments keeps the potential draftee at his job in the "national interest." In other words, an annual contingency check.

Likewise, sons of middle class parents were channeled into college by student deferments less available to the poor, who could not afford college. They were made to keep their grades above passing, to avoid an extended vacation, and there was minor pressure to avoid anti-war demonstrations.

All of these risked the loss of the prized deferment. Contingency checks on flunking and nonenrollment (as a semester trip to Europe) were automatically provided by most universities. At the universities, the entering freshmen found contingencies pointed up to encourage them to enroll in ROTC. The oldest (that is, the 26-year-olds) were drafted first, because otherwise they would too soon be lost from the contingency management system. Similarly, medical examinations were given late to avoid the too early assignment of a medical deferment and permitting another to escape the contingency management. Why was this form of manpower control used instead of direct assignment of people to jobs? You might think direct assignment too repugnant to a society enjoying the delusion of democracy, but the reason given by the Selective Service is that their channeling system provided the same results more efficiently. The ROTC program is itself a whole scenario of contingencies prepared in common by the military and the university, with a major objective being to make our new freshmen into career officers.

The difficulty in any contingency management system involving many people is determining when contingencies have been met. This has very much limited the possibility of governmental or other authorities extensively controlling the activities of the population. Modern technology, however, shows considerable promise in overcoming this difficulty. The development of modern surveillance techniques, the rapid extension of the capacity of computers, and the creation of large data banks considerably extend the possibilities. A psychologist, Schwitzgebel (1969), described preliminary work on a special belt that allows two-way voice communication both to monitor a subject's voice and simple physiological data, and to give feedback to the subject. The belt will work outside of a room in a small locale, although with some difficulties. Attempts to remove the belt can also be determined. He has suggested that the belt might be useful in monitoring people with such medical problems as diabetes or epilepsy, and that it could also be used to monitor the movements and activities of parolees. It has recently been estimated that it would be technically feasible to monitor several hundred individuals in a single city wearing such belts. Other recent developments in the technology of secret surveillance are already used extensively by agencies of the federal and local government and by numerous private companies. Westin (1970) has summarized the state of the art of the invasion of privacy by describing a host of gadgets including cameras, radios, and video recorders. Coin-sized radio transmitters easily planted in briefcases, pockets, cars, and elsewhere track an individual's movements. Very small radio transmitters can transmit conversations over short distances. The radio pill can be substituted in bottles of antihistamines and, when swallowed, enable a person to be tracked throughout the day. TV camera monitoring has become commonplace in apartment elevators, lobbies, subway cars, prison cell blocks, stores, and even on street corners. Moreover, there are techniques for hiding TV cameras in rooms, including the use of fiberoptics to transmit images around corners. Techniques perfected by the military enable surveillance even in darkness. Surveillance of speech over long distances requires antennas, and there are ingenious devices for hiding antennas in the seams of clothing and in the thread that stitches a coat. Receivers can be concealed in belts and belt buckles. Microphones and transmitters come disguised as a variety of common objects, including water coolers, desk sets, clocks, and ashtrays. Also a variety of techniques have been perfected for bugging rooms that the agent cannot enter.

Additional developments of a rapidly growing technology, which increase the possibility of determining reinforcement or punishment contingencies, are data banks. The U.S. Government is already putting together information from a large number of government agencies pooling the information they have on every citizen. This information is on taxes, social security, census, the draft, applications for federal jobs, etc. Other computerized information exists in other segments of society and, theoretically, with the rapid development of computer technology, could be drawn upon easily and further combined in some future consolidation of computerized information. These include credit information, information gathered by insurance agents, computerized medical and educational records, and computerized library records. Moreover, it is projected by many that we will move to a "cashless" society in which the credit card is used in all purchases and pay is automatically credited to accounts. This projection already includes rapid access to the computer at the time of purchase. An individual could be tracked across the country as he traveled, rented cars, checked into motels, and made purchases of all types. The future potential for large-scale contingency management in these systems seems impressive indeed, although not for the immediate future. Behavioral scientists need not be the agents of such implementation, but rather can serve to inform the public of the dangers and facilitate their efforts at countercontrol. The second area to which the behavioral scientist may turn his talents would be towards creating a technology of countercontrol actually suitable for the struggle. There are a few examples to illustrate this. Abbie Hoffman, in *Steal this Book* and William Powell in *The Anarchist's Cookbook* describe a range of possible uses of technology, not all behavioral, by today's activists and revolutionaries. Powell is especially good on simple bugging procedures, radio jamming, and sabotage. Hoffman's greater range includes how to set up legal and illegal radio and TV broadcasting stations. Neither Hoffman nor Powell is sophisticated in behavioral technology, and many of their suggestions are very poor ones.

There is a quite recent example, however, of what seems to be a carefully thought out contingency system. The author of the system, if the F.B.I. is to be believed, is a psychologist named Ronald Kaufman, who has a Ph.D. from Stanford University where, according to Newsweek, he worked with pigeons (Radicals, 1972). Kaufman designed an interesting device based on a calendar clock, which shows not only the time but the day of the week and the month. The cycle of days and numbers recurs after 217 days; hence, by converting into switches the day of the week and the date portions of the electric timer, Kaufman was able to create a long-delay timing device for setting off a bomb. He placed a number of demonstration bombs in safe deposit boxes in several different banks in cities across the country. He then informed the authorities where each of the bombs was located, thereby demonstrating his capacity to arrange for long delayed explosions. Bombs, he promises, will be placed in a variety of locations in the future, including foundations of newly constructed buildings, bridges, and highways. He suggests that he will then hold property as ransom for people, demanding the release of political prisoners, for example, in exchange for information on the precise locations of bombs placed in strategic spots. Thus he has set up a well-defined, deliberately designed contingency system. It will be interesting to see if his procedure works. The technique he is using is, of course, an aversive one that has the potential of generating undesirable countermeasures, such as an increase in the F.B.I.'s budget, and accelerating repressive tendencies. Nevertheless, it is a deliberately contrived contingency management system directed against those in power. This is as rare as it is ingenious. Surely we could look forward to seeing the ingenuity of modern contingency management developing yet better countercontrol measures when emphasis is shifted from contingency management in service of power to contingency management in service of people.

What is the possible role of operant conditioning in a new revolutionary society? When a revolutionary force seizes power, the revolution is not complete; it has barely begun. Let us suppose that the goal of the revolutionary society is one in which every citizen is truly equal in his status and in his access to material needs (with no possibility of one group amassing wealth at the expense of others). Hence, there is no exploitation. There is to be stress on group wisdom, and individual accomplishment is valued as it contributes to group accomplishment, not individual gain. Here the old reinforcement systems of competition, accumulation of wealth, and climbing in the elite system of power are to be replaced by altruism. The society would have such values as pride in work. The labor of workers and peasants would be prized. Cooperation rather than competition would characterize society. Signs of separate managerial class or a separate intellectual or academic class would go unreinforced. Most socialist revolutions have aspired to such a culture, but many (perhaps most) have failed to attain this ideal—after initial sizable reform in breaking up and redistributing large estates, often new elites arise and people continue with many of the values of the old culture.

To succeed, the reinforcement systems must change. Revolution requires remaking of man. Reich (1970) has suggested that the new counterculture in the United States constitutes such a revolutionary change without the necessity of seizing power by force. Castro and Mao and other revolutionary leaders have described their revolutions, presently in progress, as one of changing man. China's cultural revolution was an apparently successful attempt to rid society of continued or new forms of elitism. Intellectuals and managers were re-educated and now work a part of their time in manual labor; students entering the university are not from an entrenched middle or upper class, nor are they even given entrance exams. They are chosen by their fellow workers in participating meetings in which discussion presumably centers around question of who might best use the education in serving society.

If the success of revolution depends on changing the nature of man or his values, then changing the nature of each individual's reinforcement system surely must be an important role for the science of behavioral modification. However, there remains the serious problem of identifying how the science can be used. Too much of present behavior modification is wedded to prerevolutionary values and forms. How must work in classroom management and other instances of behavior modification change so that the work would be potentially useful in the changing of man toward a new revolutionary value system? This is a difficult question, which psychologists interested in serving a different value system must ask. No definitive answer can be offered in this paper, even though it seems apparent that a valuable basis for such work will be found in the experimental analysis of behavior. Skinner's *Beyond Freedom and Dignity* provides a valuable analysis of behavior change procedures in a cultural setting, and as such should be a useful guide in moving toward a revolutionary society.

While I have suggested that much behavior modification work is counterrevolutionary, there are a few examples that may have merit as the type of system that could fit into a new society. One example is found in Skinner's *Walden II,* in which he describes an egalitarian society with managers having no special status and doing regular work as well. He describes a work credit system with quite interesting properties as a societal token reinforcement. The total work pool is constantly reassessed and "work credits" divided up among the jobs. The principle of assigning credits is in the reverse order of the empirically determined desirability of the job. That is, a highly undesirable job would earn the most credits, and someone choosing it might need to work only an hour a day, while someone choosing the most enjoyable work might work four hours a day. There is a premium on improved techniques and no need for "make-work," because the more efficiently tasks are done, the lower the total work pool and the better it is for everyone. Although this is a fictional society, the work credit system is being tried currently in an experimental community called Twin Oaks near Lyons, Virginia.

A second example of a system with compatible revolutionary values is found in Keller's (1968) system for conducting a college psychology course. With the reading, lab work, or other source materials, there are questions and exercises prepared for the student. Test answers on the study material are reviewed and discussed with other students (proctors) who have previously completed the units with success. Although some lectures and demonstrations may be given by the instructor, they are relatively infrequent and are not required. The critical conduct of the course, completing one's own units and/or monitoring one's peers, has moved into the hands of the students. The elitism of conventional classrooms is reduced.

A third example emerges from a deliberate effort to use reinforcement principles in the struggle for social justice. Miller and Miller (1969) developed a token economy (using "freedom money") to reinforce welfare recipients for activities in organizing and working for welfare rights. Although they initially arranged reinforcement for such things as attendance at meetings as the activities got under way, the group took over the task of determining the criteria for reinforcement and in dispensing reinforcement.

A fourth and last example is a more far-reaching change, less compatible with traditional behavior modification, and, as a consequence, more difficult to cast in the old system. Rozynko, Swift, Swift, and Boggs (1971) developed a therapeutic setting for alcoholic patients at Mendocino State Hospital in California. The "patients" became "students" who, through the study of behavioral psychology, developed the view that their problems could be coped with by altering the determining conditions and by working on the different problems that had caused their drinking. Individually, they developed their own desensitizing procedures with the help and criticism of their peers—other "students." The conditions were created to increase their self-esteem and deal with the types of social situations that have, in the past, been problems for them. In short, a reinforcing community of peers was established that changed the values, attitudes, and social behavior of its members, using the principles of behavior as a basis. The work is all the more critical because they refrained from direct tangible reinforcement of a specific symptom and instead built a social reinforcement system designed to change the "student's" whole concept of himself and the nature of his reinforcement systems.

If a science of behavior is to serve a new egalitarian society, we have to make extensive changes in the way we work. First, we must stop doing work that has the highest likelihood of serving wealth and power. Second, we should adapt our work more to the direct needs of the people who struggle to free themselves from control and exploitation by the power elite. This includes both analyzing the forms of control used in society and developing a means of countercontrol usable by individuals with very limited resources. And third, we should explore forms of behavior modification compatible with an egalitarian, nonmaterialistic, and nonelitist value system that could at least be constructive in developing the means for the necessary revolutionary change in man.

REFERENCES

American Institutes for Research. *Counter-Insurgency in Thailand.* A research and development proposal submitted to the Advanced Research Projects Agency. Pittsburgh, Pennsylvania, 1967.

Datel, W. E. & Legters, L. J. The psychology of the Army recruit. Paper presented at the meetings of the American Medical Association, Chicago, Illinois, June, 1970.

Domhoff, G. W. *Who rules America?* Englewood Cliffs, New Jersey: Prentice-Hall, 1967.

Domhoff, G. W. *The higher circles.* New York: Random House, 1970.

Gordon, T. & Helmer, O. *Report on a long-range forecasting study.* Santa Monica, California: Rand Corporation, 1964.

Hoffman, A. *Steal this book.* New York: Grove Press, 1971.

Illich, I. *Deschooling society.* New York: Harper, 1971.

Keller, F. S. Goodbye teacher. . . . *Journal of Applied Behavior Analysis,* 1968, **1**, 78–89.

Kesey, K. *One flew over the cuckoo's nest.* New York: Viking, 1962.

Marshall, S. L. A. *Men against fire.* (Rev. ed.) New York: William Morrow, 1966.

Miller, K. & Miller, O. Maintaining attendance of welfare recipients in self-help programs by supplementary reinforcement. Paper presented at the meetings of the American Psychological Association, Washington, D.C., September, 1969.

Orwell, G. *1984.* New York: Harcourt, 1949.

Powell, W. *The anarchist's cookbook.* New York: Lyle Stuart, 1971.

Radicals: The bomb suspect. *Newsweek,* 1972, **79**(4), 17.

Reich, C. A. *The greening of America.* New York: Random House, 1970.

Rozynko, V., Swift, K., Swift, J., & Boggs, L. J. Controlled environments for social change. Unpublished. Mendocino, California: Mendocino State Hospital Operant Behavior Modification Project, 1971.

Schwitzgebel, R. L. A remote instrumentation system for behavior modification: A preliminary report. In R. Rubin & C. M. Franks (Eds.), *Advances in behavior therapy, 1968.* New York: Academic Press, 1969. Pp. 1–9.

Selective Service. *Channeling.* Washington, D.C.: U.S. Government Printing Office, July, 1965.

Skinner, B. F. *Walden II.* New York: Macmillan, 1948.

Skinner, B. F. *Beyond freedom and dignity.* New York: Knopf, 1971.

Walters, H. C. *Military psychology: Its use in modern war and indirect conflict.* Dubuque, Iowa: Wm. C. Brown, 1968.

Westin, A. F. *Privacy and freedom.* New York: Atheneum, 1970.

Index

A

Abacus, as programmed event, 48, 49, 53, 54, 55, 56
Academic behaviors
  differential consequation and, 172-176
  frequency of occurrence, 123
  problems of, 75-77
  socioeconomic status and, 129-130, 190
Accuracy, token systems and, 128
Adolescents, modification of behavior of, 184
Alcoholics, therapy for, 207
Apprenticeship, for students of psychology, 180-181
Army, use of behavior modification in train-in for, 198-199
Arranged events, 27-28, 29
  choice of, 61-62
  experimental data, 30-44
Attention, effect on classroom behaviors, 128

B

Behavior
  experimental analysis of, 107-108
  incompatible, 76
  lawfulness of, 196
Behavioral objectives, 68, 72, 132
Behavioral psychology, applications of, 178-179
Behavioral scales, 108
  construction of, 108-112
Behavior analysis
  elements of, 131-133
  experimental data, 134-141
  usefulness of, 128-129
Behavior Development Corporation (BDC), 188
Behavior modification
  basic principles, 75-77
  as weapon, 200
Behavior problems, program for coping with 185

C

California Achievement Test (CAT), 71
Checkpoints, for programming decisions, 58
Classroom behavior
  functional analysis of, 112-115
  problems in management of, 75-77
College instruction
  animal training compared with, 164-170
  programmed, 147-154, 170-171
Competition
  defined, 2
  experimental data, 3-11
Conditioned hearing, 167
Conditioned seeing, 167
Conditioning
  operant, program of instruction for, 164
  respondent, in human learning, 167-168
Consequation, 164
  for college students, 166, 167, 172-176
  necessity for, 170
Cooperation
  defined, 2
  experimental data, 3-11
Correctness, in verbal behavior, 168-169
Countercontrol, 204-205
Cuisinare rods, as programmed event, 48, 52-53
Curriculum
  for behavior analysis, 131-132
  sequencing, 128

D

Data banks, use in control, 204
Data processing, value of, 133-134
Differential consequation, *see* Consequation
Discrimination learning, 163
Discriminative function, in imitation, 23
Distar, 68

E

Elitism, 197-208
Engelman–Becker Program, 68, 69

Environment, control relations of, 112-115,
     123-124
  experimental data, 115-123
Ethics, 196-208
Evaluation
  of individualized programs, 70-72
  of relevant behaviors, 108-112
Examinations, learning and, 166
Extinction, 76

F

Failure, cumulative, 171-172
Flash cards, learning from, 167-168
Flash sampling system, 109
Follow Through, 129-134

G

Game procedure, 128
Gates, MacGinitie Reading Test, in evalua-
     tion of behavior analysis, 138
Generalization, programmed events and,
     55-59
Ginn reading series, 68

I

Imitation
  experimental data, 13-24
  generalized, 12
  sources of control, 24
Individualization, in supportive tutoring,
     66-72
Individually Prescribed Instruction, 67, 70
Instruction
  college-level, 170-172, 181-183
  effect of, 56
  failure to learn and, 65
  imitation and, 12
  small-group, 131

L

Language
  behavior analysis and, 138-139
  learning, 163-164, 167-168
Leadership, in cooperation and competition,
     2
Learning, human, animal learning compared
     with, 164-170

Learning disabilities
  prevention of, 67
  remedial programs in, 64
Learning Village, 188
  evaluation of, 189-190

M

McGraw-Hill Programmed Readers, 68, 69
Manpower control, Selective Service System
     and, 202-203
Mastery criteria, 171-172, 176
Mental hospital, behavior modification pro-
     grams in, 184, 201
Metropolitan Reading Readiness Test, in eval-
     uation of programs, 136-137, 188
Motivation, arranged events and, 29

O

Observation graphing, 77-80
Operant conditioning, program of instruc-
     tion for, 164

P

Percentage charts, usefulness of, 59, 60
Personality traits, 2
Personalized System of Instruction, 157
  proctors for, 157-162
Physical spaces, control exerted by, 113-114
Preschool program, 187-190
Prevention
  of behavior problems, 185-186, 188
  of learning problems, 67
Proctors, in Personalized System of Instruc-
     tion, 151-152, 157-162
Programmed instruction
  college-level, 147-154, 170-171
  for language, 168
  programmed events in, 27-29
     choice of, 61-62
     experimental data, 44-59
  in reading, 68-71
Project Follow Through, 129-134
Punishment, 76

R

Rate charts, usefulness of, 59-60
Reading, individualization of materials in,
     67-71

Reinforcement, 74 *see also* Consequation; Token system
  of academic or classroom behaviors, 75-76
  in competition, 2
  in cooperation, 2
  in imitation, 24
  in societal system, 197-198
Reinforcement schedule, in cooperation and competition, 2
Reinforcers
  effective, 66
  environmental factors as, 112-115
Reliability
  of behavioral scales, 111
  interobserver, 5, 9-10, 19
Remediation, prevention and, 185
Respondent conditioning, in human learning, 167-168
Responding, covert, 165
Response rate, token systems and, 128
Retardation
  academic, individualization and, 66-72
  behavior modification in treatment of, 184
Revolution, 205-207
Risk, interpersonal, in cooperation and competition, 2

S

Schools, behavior modification programs in, 184-191
Selective Service System, contingency management by, 202-203
Self recording, 128
Sensitivity, of behavioral scales, 111
Setting event, 112
Social motives, 2
Socioeconomic status
  academic performance and, 129-130, 190
  behavior analysis and, 134-141
Special education, 64
  behavior-modification project in, 65-73
Specific scale, 110-111
  calibration of, 111-112
Stimuli
  discriminative, 167
  in cooperation and competition, 2
  environmental factors as, 112-115
  imitation and, 23
  syntactical, 168

Stimulus control, in college learning, 166
Student Centered Education Project (SCEP), 183
Students, control exerted by behavior of, 114-115
Study, differential consequation for, 172-176
Subtraction,
  arranged events and, 30-44
  programmed events and, 44-59
Sullivan Programmed Readers, 67, 68
Surveillance, contingency management and, 203-204
Survival training, 201-202

T

Teacher
  attention of, 128
  control exerted by behavior of, 114
  effect of token system on behavior of, 123
Teacher aides, 131
Teacher prompts, 128
Tests, *see also* specific tests
  utility for evaluation, 141-142
Textbook, unprogrammed, 168-169, 170-171
Token system, 128, 184, 186
  in behavior analysis classroom, 132-133
  in mental hospital, 184, 201
  for military training, 198-199
  teacher behavior and, 123

U

Unspecific scale, 109-110

V

Validity, of behavioral scales, 111
Verbal behavior
  correctness in, 168-169
  encouraging, 1
  frequency of, 5-6, 11, 123-124

W

Wide Range Achievement Test, in evaluation of programs, 134-135, 137, 139, 189